The Summer of a Thousand Cheeses

by

Russell J Hall

Peg Rooney Hall

For Wendy
So happy to meet you
at ACS in Seattle. Have fun
in Italy!
Peg Hall
August 2010

Lighthall Books

Gainesville, Florida

The Summer of a Thousand Cheeses

by
Russell J Hall
and
Peg Rooney Hall

Published by **Lighthall Books**

P.O. Box 357305

Gainesville, Florida 32635-7305

http://www. lighthallbooks.com

Orders: gem@lighthallbooks.com

Quantity discounts may be available to educational and civic sector organizations.

ISBN: 978-0-9764263-7-0

Library of Congress Control Number: 2010904118

Books by Russell J Hall

Nonfiction:

Gem of the Adirondacks
Star Lake
Patuxent, Policy, and the Public Interest

Fiction:

Salt Marsh Slider
Orebed Lake
Oswegatchie Green

By Peg Rooney Hall

Nonfiction:

The Dean's Role in Fundraising

Acknowledgements

We gratefully acknowledge the cheesemakers, cheese retailers, cheese enthusiasts, and the other cheese, food, and historical experts who shared with us their parts of the story of the new American cheeses. We also acknowledge with great appreciation the professional expertise of our editors and our manuscript readers. Some helped us particularly with cheese-related facts and narrative and others with writing style and accuracy. We thank the photographers and others who shared their images and graphics. For any miscues, errors, and glitches remaining in the text, we take full credit ourselves and bid you as readers to hold no one but us responsible.

We thank in particular Bev Browning, Gainesville, FL; Cabot Creamery, Montpelier, VT; Ron and Debbie Craig, Holly Grove Farm, Mount Olive, NC; Ron Davis, McCadam Cheese, Chateaugay, NY; Dan Eddy and Robbie Sipes, Gainesville, FL; Sheila Flanagan and Lorraine Lambiase, Nettle Meadow Farm, Warrensburg, NY; Great Lakes Cheese, Hiram, OH; David Green and Dawn Taylor-Green, Winter Park Dairy, Winter Park, FL; Lauren Groff, Gainesville, FL; Barbara Jenness and Jim Hott, Dogwood Farm, Byron Center, MI; Jean Grimm, Star Lake, NY; Caroline Harless and Dane Huebner, Flat Creek Lodge, Swainsboro, GA; Shirley and Don Hitchman, County Meadows, Canton, NY; Sherri Krams, Saratoga, FL; Thomas Mafrici, Cicero, NY; Bunky Mastin, Gallery of Wine and Cheese, Gainesville, FL; Melody Milewski, Erie Canal Village, Rome, NY; Michael Perlmeter, Molto Formaggio, Dallas, TX; Dimitri Petropolis, Community Driven Institute, Tucson, AZ; Joe Pietrangelo and Greg Yurish, Glades Ridge Dairy, Lake Butler, FL; Liza and David Porter, Longview Farm, Argyle, NY; Anna Prizzia, Office of Sustainability, University of Florida, Gainesville, FL; Carol Quinn, Wayne, NJ; Mary and Randall Ray, Erick's Cheese and Wine, Banner Elk, NC; Roger Rixom, Apollo Beach, FL; Rich Rogers, Scardello Artisan Cheese, Dallas, TX; Roth Käse USA, Monroe, WI; St. Lawrence County Historical Society, Canton, NY; Lindsey Schechter, Houston Dairy Maids, Houston, TX; Ron Schmidt, Gainesville, FL; Lisa Seger, Blue Heron Farm, Field Store Community, TX; Heath Silberfeld, Gainesville, FL; Karen and Richard Silverston, Dallas, TX; Dianna Tonnessen, Gainesville, FL; Eric Tremblay, Gainesville, FL; Lynne Stokes, Dallas, TX; Larry Uffelman, Mansfield, PA; Vermont Butter and Cheese, Websterville, VT; Karen Weinberg, 3-Corner Field Farm, Shushan, NY. We are grateful to Sylvie Lortal of the Comité Interprofessionnel du Gruyère de Comté for permission to use the image of the aroma wheel on page 127.

A few months after our interview with the Craigs, Ron died at the early age of 57. He has been inducted into the Agriculture Hall of Fame for Wayne County and is greatly missed by all in cheese and farming.

Dedication

We dedicate this project and book to our daughters, Pam Hall and Meg Hall. Their earnest childhood attention to gardening, harvesting, preserving, and eating propelled our love for real food. Their adult love of cooking and of fresh, local foods helped lead us to our adventure with the new American cheeses.

Table of Contents

Adirondack Mountains

Crescent of cheese factories

The **Adirondack Crescent.** The larger image above is a photograph of a four by four foot map hanging in the New York Sate Museum of Cheese. It shows the location of cheese factories in the state in 1899. In the original, green dots represent cheese factories, blue open circles indicate butter factories, and red plus signs indicate combined butter and cheese factories. Obviously much detail is lost in this reduced black-and-white reproduction. A heavy concentration of cheese factories, more than 600 of them, forms the Adirondack Crescent— the dark cluster of dots extending south of the St. Lawrence River, east of Lake Ontario, and continuing eastward through the center of the state. A smaller cluster of cheese factories can be seen in southwestern New York. The dots extending southward from central New York toward the Pennsylvania border are mainly butter factories. The world's first cheese factory, in Oneida County, NY was located in the cluster of dots just south of the Adirondacks. In Part One we relate our discovery of what we call the Adirondack Crescent and explain its significance to us and to the history of American cheesemaking.

Introduction

as told by Russ and Peg

Standing in line on a sunny, cool June morning in the tiny Canadian village of Warwick with a cow, a sheep, and a goat looking down on us from posters overhead, we wondered if others might be as amazed as we were. Who would expect an exhibit of cheeses to draw such huge crowds? The local paper said this remote and rural town of 5,000 people expected 25,000 visitors over the weekend. We were early and waiting behind dozens of even earlier arrivers for the 10 o'clock opening of the *Festival des Fromages de Warwick*. Others were quickly filling in the entrance road behind us. Children, parents, young couples, "mature" people like us, and even teenagers were chatting with others waiting near them. All around us, lining the path to the ticket booths, were posters from previous years' festivals, competing for attention with this year's poster. People were debating, in French and English, the merits of the current poster versus previous ones.

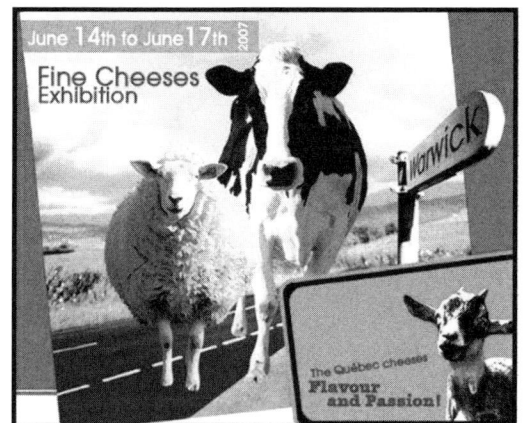

A cow, a sheep, and a goat looked down on us from the 2007 poster as we waited in line to buy our entrance tickets and sampling coupons for the festival.

Who were all these people, and what had brought them here? And what were we doing all the way from Florida, queued up on a Saturday morning in rural Quebec? In fact, we didn't know what we would find once we got inside the complex of pavilions and tents ahead of us. We were sure of one thing, however: the festival was a bigger deal than we had expected.

We had come north as part of our research on the growing interest in the new American cheese. Uncovering its story and telling it to you were part of a new beginning for us, a series of wholly new activities to research a succession of topics, give presentations on our discoveries, and ultimately write books capturing the most engaging things we

The line formed early for the Festival des Fromages de Warwick. It attracted more than 25,000 cheese enthusiasts to this town of 5,000 people.

found. We had come to Warwick for a peek at this new cheese world to see what a "festival of cheese" looks like.

We'll have more to say later about the festival. For now we will just report that once inside the pavilion we were to get our first hints of experiences ahead of us in the months and years to come. Inside the pavilion we would find cheeses, unique and intriguing varieties — more kinds than our imaginations had prepared us for. Outside the throngs of eager visitors waiting were jostling, ready to fully take in the delights they expected in the pavilion. And there would be cheesemakers — often whole smiling families of them. Proudly standing behind counters with tasteful displays of their cheeses and often flanked by blue, red, and white ribbons and photographs of snowy farm scenes, they would eagerly engage any and all of us who wanted to know more. The cheeses, the enthusiasm of the customers and the friendliness of the cheesemakers all would exceed our expectations. We would find something else there too, and later encounter it over and over again.

This would be the invisible bond among all three — customers, cheeses, and cheesemakers. We would find ourselves linked in that bond too, because buying a bit of cheese would give us a real sense that we were also buying a bit of a remote rural landscape, an image of a young girl posing with a prize-winning calf, and a small part of the lives of the family who lovingly tended their animals and turned their milk into our cheese. To a greater or lesser extent, this sense that the new American cheese is more than the sum of its parts was to follow us almost everywhere in our quest of discovery.

We had also come north to visit the Adirondacks. So what, you might ask, does New York State's Adirondack region have to do with our cheese interest? To start, it has much to do with us, and this book is not just about the new American cheese but also about our discovery of it. Russ grew up in Star Lake, a hamlet in the Adirondack Park, which by the way is the largest park in the country. Peg grew up in nearby Rochester, and visited the Adirondacks every summer. We knew that the counties surrounding the Adirondacks had long been dairy and cheese country. And, as it turned out, the Adirondack region was not a bad place to start if we were to understand the changes affecting American cheesemaking. Even before we came to realize this, we felt that studying trends in that region and visiting cheesemakers there would help us understand what was happening in the broader world of the new American cheese.

Our lives were changing. We had enjoyed rich and rewarding experiences in the world of work. But our time for being part of the workforce was done. We were at the long-awaited and occasionally dreaded stage when we would no longer leave home every workday to save the nation's wildlife and educate the future electorate. And, although admittedly we were now retirees, we were uncomfortable with an image of retirement as an endless or aimless vacation. We needed new careers; and doing research, speaking, and writing seemed to fit the bill. Russ is a biologist and Peg an educator. Russ was a professor, research scientist, and government science manager and Peg a public school teacher, university administrator, and professor. In long talks over several years we had created a set of criteria for how we wanted freedom from employment to work for us.

Sheep in a field. *Our belief that most cheeses are made from cow milk was in for revision when we began discovering the new American cheeses. Although in terms of pounds of cheese produced, cow milk cheeses still dominate, the variety of cheeses now available includes many made from sheep, goat, and other milks.*

First, we should take on new activities mostly unrelated to, and in no way continuations of, our earlier careers. Instead, we should build on the skills and knowledge we had developed along the way—that is to say, neither of us wanted to become a consultant and continue doing what we'd been doing nor to go to law school, or become a concert pianist, or breed horses. The new activities should let us follow up sequentially on potentially unrelated topics. They should involve subjects that people care about, but that also are based on our own interests and preferences at the moment. We would be working on things that didn't tire or bore us—not that our work assignments ever did. They should require us to learn, and maybe also to travel and meet people.

We also thought we might like to work together, adding new insights by viewing the same things from our different perspectives. At least we wanted to try it, thinking that some kinds of risky behavior are good for you when you reach a certain age. The new American cheese would be the first topic we tackled together.

Although we collaborated on all the writing, it did not feel right, nor was the writing always clear if we used "we" all the time. So each of us became the primary speaker for various sections.

Not being experts on the topic, we were going to write neither a book about the history or technical aspects of cheese nor a primer describing, comparing, and contrasting cheese varieties, nor a manual on how to make cheese. There are excellent books on those subjects by real experts. (A list is at the end of this book.)

We wanted to unearth the story behind the apparent burgeoning of interest in the cheeses of the United States and Canada -- the new American cheeses. Thus our book is the story of our discoveries. Each part tells of a different aspect and contributes in a different way to our tale of discovery. In Part One we get our first glimpses of the phenomenon that is the new American cheese. These lead us to reflect on the roots of our interest in cheese, which feeds into a growing curiosity and seems to culminate with our discovery of the Adirondack Crescent. In Part Two, we come face to face with one part of the world of cheese with a visit to a recently closed cheese factory. This encounter encourages us to learn what basics we can from books and to bring our newfound knowledge to life by trying to make cheese at home. Part Three traces our attempts to find out what happened to cheese in America. This sends us to history books and leads to discoveries about the current status of factory cheesemaking and the unsettled state of dairy farming in America. In Part Four we meet the new American cheese in all its glory and encounter farms, animals, and the fascinating mix of people who are the new cheesemakers. Part Five has us venturing forth to learn about the relationships among cheesemakers, cheese sellers, and the growing number of us who

Entrance to the exhibition hall at the Warwick cheese festival.

are the objects and beneficiaries of all they do. In Part Six we circle back, first introducing you to examples of cheeses you might want to try and then reflecting on what we have learned. An epilogue provides a poignant example of the delicate balance on which hang the fates of the old and the new American cheeses. Topics of interest that supplement and expand on the narrative are presented as a series of "Short Takes."

Come with us as we ferret out the origins of our cheese enthusiasm, discovering its long lost roots under our Christmas trees, in our vegetable gardens, and in sharing adulthood with our natural-food loving daughters. Let Russ's microbiologically inclined brain explain for you what cheese is, why and how there can be so many varieties, and how various types of cheeses get to be so different from each other. Watch him making cheese at home using shortening cans, tuna fish, and bricks while Peg is off tasting Czech cheeses. Discover cheese festivals with a thousand varieties of cheese to sample. Share our visits to cheese rooms in factories and on farms. Meet cheesemakers, cheese retailers, and cheese enthusiasts with us. Smell and taste the cheese, and know there are people making it for the beauty of the craft and love of the animals.

What is the new American cheese?

The new American cheese is NOT the old "American Cheese."

For years the term "American Cheese" has been applied to forms of processed cheese that are basically blends of aged cheddar and unaged cheeses, with various added constituents to give them smooth textures and excellent shelf life. We often encounter them on hamburgers, in cheese spreads, and in convenience foods. While the old "American Cheese" may be a paragon of sameness and predictability, the new American cheeses provide unending surprises and unexpected delights.

The new American cheese includes:

Artisan or Artisanal Cheese

The word "artisan" or "artisanal" implies that a cheese is produced primarily by hand, in small batches, with particular attention paid to the tradition of the cheesemaker's art, and thus using as little mechanization as possible in the production of the cheese. Artisan, or artisanal, cheeses may be made from all types of milk and may include various flavorings. (American Cheese Society)

Farmstead Cheese

In order for a cheese to be classified as "farmstead," the cheese must be made with milk from the farmer's own herd, or flock, on the farm where the animals are raised. Milk used in the production of farmstead cheeses may not be obtained from any outside source. Farmstead cheeses may be made from all types of milk and may include various flavorings. (American Cheese Society)

Part One: From Childhood Cheddar to the New American Cheese

as told by Peg

Defunct cheese. *Label of a brand of cheese no longer made in New York State.* Image courtesy of the New York State Museum of Cheese.

Just when we were approaching the retirement cliff with mixed anticipation and fear, the cheese world blossomed before our eyes. Tracking down the story of the myriad of new American cheeses held promise for both intellectual and gastronomic adventure.

When we would mention to friends the idea of learning about new cheeses, a few responded with a puzzled "Cheese? What do you mean you're doing research on cheese?" But we mostly got enthusiastic comments such as "Really? What are you doing? I've always loved cheese." And "Isn't it amazing how many more types there seem to be these days?" People would weigh in with stories of a new cheese they had found recently or of someone they had heard about who had taken up life as a goat farmer and cheesemaker.

We began exploring cheeses in our local stores and looking for cheese everywhere we happened to find ourselves visiting. We discovered cheese festivals and conferences of cheese lovers. Learning about cheese was leading us in directions we had never previously gone. Many of the cheeses we found were totally new to us, making us wonder if we simply had missed them in the past or if they did not exist until recently.

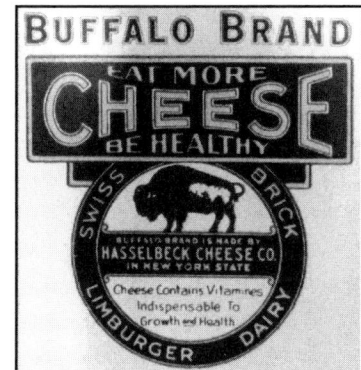

We thought about our own cheese history and wondered whether it was typical or exceptional. The cheeses we knew in childhood seemed to remain unchanged and then, decades later, abundant new varieties of cheeses seemed suddenly to emerge. During those decades when cheese seemed to remain static, our attitudes toward food had not. We had come to favor more natural and locally produced foods over the processed foods we had grown up with. Thus, as we relate in Part One, the surprise for us was to find that out of our view the same forces and trends affecting our food attitudes were shaping those of a cadre of cheesemakers. Their paths and ours have now converged and we find ourselves in this whole world of new cheeses.

Finding New Cheeses

A huge whiteboard hangs above the cheese corner in the wine store we visit every few weeks. It lists all the offerings and their prices, sorted by country of origin. Perhaps a hundred or more cheeses are on the board at any given time.

At first, we wanted to browse. The trouble was that all the cheeses were in a cooler in big uncut wheels or chunks, not on display. At this type of cheese counter, there is no way to look over the cheeses and make a guess at what you might want to taste. By the pound, the prices were shockingly high, but that was not as big a hurdle as the fact that we did not have a clue where to start picking out something. The cheese clerk offered to cut samples for us to taste; nevertheless we fled empty handed on our first few forays because choosing what to taste was decidedly intimidating. We needed some guidance to deal with such close-to-home abundance.

We bought and read Steven Jenkins's *Cheese Primer* and Laura Werlin's *The New American Cheese*. They were interesting and helpful in a general sense, but we found all their data to be a bit overwhelming. We recalled reading Italo Calvino's *Mr. Palomar*. In a cheese shop for the first time, Palomar encounters so many kinds of cheese on display that he thinks he is in a museum. Dazzled, perplexed, and humiliated, he orders only a common, well-known, and mundane kind.

Despite our sense of overload, the abundance displayed in these books reassured us that the cheese world really was expanding and it wasn't just that we had been unconscious for a few decades. Armed with a bit more knowledge about types of cheeses, we tried again. This time we went to a recently opened fresh food market where we could browse. We bought things like Yancey's Fancy Natural X-Sharp Cheddar, Point Reyes Original Blue raw cow

An unimaginable variety of cheeses. *One of many tables of cheeses at the Festival of Cheese, American Cheese Society 2007 Annual Conference in Burlington, Vermont.*

milk cheese, and Westfield Farm's Capri Classic Blue goat cheese.

Back at the wine store soon afterward, we tried three-year aged Gouda from Holland and fell in love with it. We bought French Comté and Spanish Manchego. Both were new and delightful experiences. We are lucky enough to have three shops where we live that cut cheese to order. We ventured downtown to visit another one, where we tasted and bought two cheeses made by Cypress Grove—Humboldt Fog, a goat cheese, and Lamb Chopper, a sheep cheese. Yum. We began exploring other cheeses and found the mild creaminess of white-rinded Bries, the pungent, stinky mildness of orange-rinded Munsters, and some exotic leaf-wrapped cheeses.

We began keeping a journal with the label from each new cheese and an accompanying description of how it impressed us. Our descriptions now seem a bit uninformed, after a couple more years of tasting cheeses. But they show where we were at the time:

Manchego, by Casa del Campo in Spain:

> "Delightful, a wonderful subtle flavor."

Point Reyes Original Blue, by Farmstead Cheese Company:

> "Pungent, piquant. Very good with crackers – a bit strong without. Best blue I have tasted."

Classic Reserve Extra-Aged Vermont Cheddar, 2 year old!, by Grafton Village Cheese Company:

> "Sharp and creamy, but not as sharp as some of the New York State cheddars of memory."

About this time, we learned of the American Cheese Society (ACS). This discovery further expanded our confidence that a real change was occurring in cheesemaking in the United States and Canada. And, finding the ACS pulled our attention back to America, away from Holland, France, and Spain. We certainly didn't stop eating European cheeses, especially aged Gouda. But between getting involved with the ACS and our soon-to-be-discovered Adirondack Crescent, we knew American cheese was the story we wanted to tell.

The ACS surprised us. We found it to be the epitome of a "big tent" organization and not the close-knit group of cheese experts we had expected. According to its website, it began in the 1980s as a "national grassroots organization for cheese appreciation and home and farm cheesemaking." I wonder how many meetings it took for members to craft that tightly packed self-description. They called themselves "national" and "grassroots" at a time when the cheese nation was divided into big industrial factories cranking out processed cheese food and little farmsteads where a few people, mostly women, turned their goats' milk into hand-made cheeses. Leaders of the ACS stated their appreciation for all cheeses and then made special mention of home and farm cheesemaking.

The primary founders of ACS were Frank Kosikowski, a Cornell University professor, his students, and several colleagues. They all were stalwarts of the mainstream dairy science profession. Yet, despite their connections with factory-based cheesemakers apparently on a mad rush to industrialization, they seemingly wanted to preserve and rejuvenate traditions that advancing science and technology were about to leave behind. The heritage of their complex involvement with both factory and farm cheesemaking has created a culture within the ACS of honoring and supporting all American cheese while promoting handmade and artisanal traditions.

When we first found it, the ACS boasted about 750 members. They sorted themselves into categories, such as cheesemakers, writers or authors, distributors, retailers, and enthusiasts. We joined as enthusiasts. Apparently we were not the only ones discovering ACS at the time. Having taken 20 years to accumulate that modest number of members, the organization had over 1,400 five years later at the time of its 25th anniversary celebration in 2008.

We learned from our experience with the ACS that parts of the cheese business in America are extraordinarily vibrant and are on a rapid growth trajectory. Numbers of cheesemakers, consumption of cheeses of all kinds, public interest, and the choices available to consumers are all increasing dramatically. During its two-century history, cheesemaking in America proceeded from a cottage industry to a clearly industrial enterprise. Now it appears to be reverting at least in part to its pre-industrial origins—having come from the farms to factories, it now seems to be moving back again to farms.

As part of its annual conference, the ACS sponsors a competition and judging of American cheeses. We read that almost a thousand different cheeses competed at the conferences. Who would have guessed there were that many different cheeses to enter into a judging? And, most of the competing cheeses seemed to be made by small, independent cheesemakers. We were astounded to learn there were so many. No wonder some of our friends knew of people who were taking up goat farming—the business seemed to be booming.

This apparent resurgence of independent cheesemakers posed questions to us. We wondered if the new American cheese industry relates to – or possibly issues from – the one that operated the factories abundant in the Adirondack region of our youth. So many factories seem to have closed or been consolidated in recent years, and yet new cheesemakers were appearing on the scene.

Is the new American cheese a reaction against industrial cheesemaking? Are science and technology discredited in the cheese industry and destined for the dustbin? Are American cheesemakers rejecting technology and mimicking the European cheesemakers, who seemed to us to have resisted industrialization and maintained more handmade ways? What had become of the industrial cheesemakers? Were they thriving also? Or would the growth of artisanal cheesemaking perhaps doom the industrial cheesemakers? How were they reacting to the artisanal cheese boom? Could it be cheesemakers laid off by their industrial employers are finding ways to continue the craft through application of new business models?

We thought we already had come across some clues pointing toward the answers to our questions. We had long been keenly interested in food and had certainly noted changes in people's attitudes about food. We hypothesized that perhaps an increasing maturity and sophistication of the American palate since the 1960s had contributed to a rediscovery of the virtues of handmade cheese. We thought part of the new enthusiasm might be rooted in the fact that cheese can be a "natural" product. Artisanal cheese's credentials as natural and wholesome might appeal to people who like to be knowledgeable about food and to be informed food consumers.

We sensed we were part of this growing phenomenon and the first step in our investigations would be to trace the roots of our own fascination with cheese.

Cheese shop in Léon, Spain. *Because we were on foot and carrying all our belongings, we could sample only a few of the available local cheeses.*

Short Take: Cheeses in Europe

We were newly confirmed enthusiasts and expected memorable cheese experiences on trips to Europe in 2008 and 2009. Our primary reason for those visits was to walk parts of the 1,000-year-old Way of St. James, but we also hoped to get to sample some great new cheeses. We did have some memorable cheese experiences over several weeks each in France and Spain, but they did not completely live up to our expectations. We naïvely expected all the great cheeses we had heard about or sampled at home to be readily available almost everywhere in Europe.

We found cheese shops in most cities, and these generally seemed to specialize in regionally made kinds. We were eager to try everything they offered, but we were traveling on foot, carrying our belongings on our backs, and spending no more than one day in any place. We couldn't purchase any more than we were willing to carry, and we couldn't carry our purchases so long that they would turn into foul-tasting puddles. Typically we would buy one or two smallish cheeses or wedges and snack on them for one, two, or even three days along the trail or later in our lodgings. This pattern often tested the limits of soft cheeses, which were sticky or soupy by the time we finished them.

Supermarkets and convenience stores usually carried only factory-made cheeses, and we enjoyed these while realizing that we were sampling nothing particularly artisanal.

Despite the foregoing, we were able to sample some great cheeses. Highlights were the Roncal we found in shops and the fresh pungent Cabecous of southern France we got at farmers markets, the hard sheep milk cheeses of the Pyrenees, and the soft cow milk Tetillas of northwestern Spain.

We encountered a few artisanal and farmstead cheesemakers on our hikes in both France and

Spain, but they seemed no more abundant than in some parts of the United States. We later learned from reading McGee that at the time of his writing (1984) less than 20% of the cheese produced in France could be certified as being made by traditional methods.

We visited none of the really famous cheese destinations, and had to conclude, perhaps prematurely, that the cheese landscape in much of Europe suffers from the same ills as that in North America; unless one makes a special effort to obtain a particular cheese, daily offerings are likely to be one kind of local specialty or to be made in factories and undistinguished.

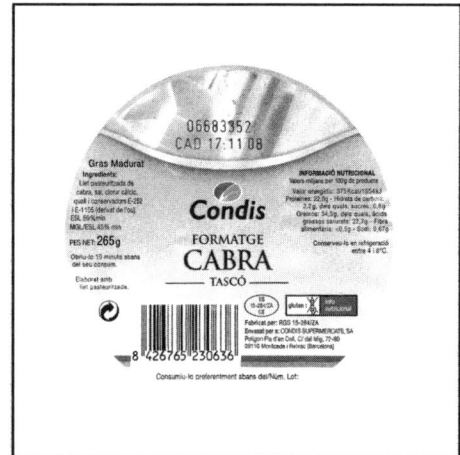

Supermarket cheese. Many of the cheeses we were able to obtain in Europe were factory made, like this goat cheese, which was produced for a Barcelona supermarket.

European artisans. Signs for artisanal cheesemakers in northern Spain (above) and southern France (below).

A cheese from the French Basque Country.

A farmstead fromagerie in southwestern France. We passed this one in 2008.

Trouble in France?

A February 2010 newspaper article carried by the Associated Press told of the declining number of small independent cheesemakers in France. The article cited the loss of dozens of cheesemakers since the Second World War, including some producing cherished varieties. The article implicated supermarket chains, pasteurization, and the increasing dominance of a small number of high-volume brands. The trend seemed the opposite of what we have seen happening in North America. However, perhaps the report was not as surprising as it at first seemed. High-volume factory-made cheeses are here to stay in America, they have a secure place in our cuisine, and they will doubtless continue to command the lion's share of our cheese consumption. Maybe the French are discovering the virtues of these everyday cheeses, while we are newly discovering the virtues of distinctive handmade cheeses.

Velveeta for Everyday, Cheddar at Christmas

Without a doubt, the new cheeses themselves drew us to this exploration. We wanted to taste them all and tell their story. At first it seemed as if we had never known cheese before. But soon ghosts from our past arose and pointed to old experiences. We began to see that childhood cheese had primed us for the new cheeses. We suspected that the same might be true for many others of the new cheese enthusiasts.

Cheese was not a childhood food for me the way it was for Russ. But we both remember our childhood cheeses.

Cheese curds and cheddar were favorites in Russ's family. His grandmother worked in a cheese factory early in the twentieth century. Decades later, every Thanksgiving dinner came the retelling of "the cheese curd story." When his father and uncle were little boys with no one else to care for them, their mother took them to work with her at the factory. They fell in love with cheese curds and would secretly eat them until they got sick…again, and again, and again. Being sick never made them sorry they did it and never made them stop eating cheese curds.

In fact, Russ's father never did lose his taste for cheese curds. When he was a New York State trooper he worked near a cheese factory where he could get fresh cheese curds, which often showed up on the kitchen table at home. He learned to love all cheese, and every year a wheel of sharp cheddar would be a special treat under the family Christmas tree. So Russ and his sister knew the joy of cheese curds and good cheddar from an early age. Russ introduced me to cheese curds on my first visit to Star Lake, when we were in college. I took to them from first bite.

Family photos. Peg's family (above) was likely to have cheese on the table at holiday times, whereas Russ and his sister (left) were able to enjoy cheese as a year-round treat.

Rooney's House of Pickles.
This photo is probably from the
1920s. Owned and operated by
Peg's grandfather, we count it
as a part of our heritage that has
subtly influenced our thinking
about food.

Cheese curds are actually an early step in the cheesemaking process. But the cheesemaker can stop at this step, process them ever so slightly, and sell the curds instead of using them to make a more sophisticated cheese. I cheer for the cheesemakers who choose to make them the end product. At their best they are a very fresh piece of cheese, random in size, often about as big as a giant peanut in its shell, and sometimes as much as half an inch in girth and an inch to two inches in length. Their texture is smooth, springy, and chewy but never tough or gummy. They taste like milk, sour-cheesey milk, with salt in it. They are a little bit yellow, since they are usually made of cow milk, which when whole is often quite yellow. Characteristically, they squeak against your teeth, the way fresh spinach can. Although they are now sold over the Internet, they really ought to be eaten at the cheese factory or within a day or two of being made. I think of them as a classic "local" food. You need to live near a cheesemaker to get them at their peak. They are my Star Lake treat. Every time I visit I look for them right away. With cheese curds to lead the way, Russ liked real cheese before I did.

My father, like Russ's, was a cheese lover. I remember my dad's taste for sharp cheddar cheese, especially with a martini. I think he would have loved cheese curds and if there had been a cheese factory nearby, I feel sure he would have discovered them. But there wasn't and so cheese came to our house from the grocery store. It didn't show up on the table very often since my mother was less of an enthusiast, and of course in the 1950s dads seldom did the grocery shopping. Cheddar was, however, my dad's treat for us kids on special occasions and was served at all the adult parties at our house. And we always had cheese at Christmas— sharp white cheddar, of course.

"Real" cheese, for both Russ and me when we were young, was white, and it was only for special occasions. There was also everyday cheese, which usually was yellow. We have heard that some people grow up thinking all cheese is yellow. That put us in mind of a friend. When we took her bird-watching for the first time, she trained the binoculars on a hedgerow in an old orchard and said, "Amazing! I never knew birds are so many different colors. I've always thought of them as either big brown birds or little brown birds!" Perhaps if we had only known Velveeta, Cheese Whiz, and Kraft Macaroni and Cheese, we would have thought all cheeses are yellow.

Russ remembers Velveeta on grilled cheese sandwiches, his favorite lunch food. I was into sweeter sandwiches, like peanut butter and banana. But I too have fond memories of the creamy Velveeta texture and its bland, faintly smoky, almost sweet taste —especially when it was the crown on a dinnertime cheeseburger. Both our childhood refrigerators also housed other everyday cheeses, including the salty, pale cheese in cylindrical cardboard boxes that we religiously sprinkled on our spaghetti sauces.

Occasionally some Swiss cheese would show up along with pickles. A fancy Rooney picnic would include sandwiches with cold cuts and a piece of Swiss cheese. I thought it was a treat, but Russ thought it was pretty tasteless. Even though it was white, he thought it was "fake" cheese because he and his sister once had discovered incompletely punched out holes in a package of it. Being the closest thing in Star Lake to kid cheese experts, they decided it had been doctored superficially and fraudulently to resemble the real thing.

In the late 1950s, the pizza craze made its way to our corners of northern New York and we both met another everyday cheese, mozzarella. I first saw pizza in the weirdly lit, hot, and revolving warming oven

On patrol for cheese. *This mounted patrolman is Russ's uncle, Charles Hall, as he appeared in 1928. Both Charles and Russ's father visited and sampled the wares of many cheese factories as they patrolled the northern reaches of the Adirondack Crescent. Their travels became easier soon after this photo was taken when the New York State Troopers reluctantly began to accept the virtues of motorized transport.*

at Neisner's five-and-dime in downtown Rochester where I often stopped for a snack with friends between busses on our commute home from high school.

It took us a day or two of looking at the pizza before we decided to try a wedge. I remember my first impression was that it felt like cardboard, and the second impression was that the cardboard texture was worth it to get the salty, sweet taste of the mozzarella cheese topping. Maybe that was when my palate started maturing from all sweet to sweet and salty. In any case, mozzarella expanded the world of cheese for me.

A decade later another everyday cheese appeared again in a food craze that took the country by storm. Led by McDonald's, we fell in love with hamburgers glued together by a yellow processed cheese product not too much different from Velveeta. We never considered it to be a "real" cheese.

Blue cheese existed in our childhoods but only as a bottled salad dressing. Russ remembers advice his family received from neighbors who were surely the most worldly and sophisticated people in Star Lake. "We prefer Gorgonzola," the matriarch said. "It is milder and more flavorful than blue cheese. You should try it." Russ did not get to try it right away; it was nowhere to be found in Star Lake. He cannot imagine where the neighbors managed to buy it.

Then there was Limburger. My dad talked about having a Limburger cheese sandwich at a lunch shop, but I feel certain it never showed up at our house. Russ, on the other hand, actually saw adults eating it with saltines and mustard. They washed it down with beer. Unlike the taken-for-granted Velveeta, pizza, and cheeseburgers, whenever Limburger appeared Russ could be sure that adults were celebrating. Despite the festivity, the Limburger was never a hit with the kids. How could people eat something that smelled like that! Creamy and mild like Velveeta, true, but yuck...it had much too subtle a flavor to overcome the burden of its aroma.

If asked to draw a picture of cheese when we were in high school, either of us might have produced a yellow wedge, as might most Americans. Each of us looked forward to Christmas cheddar with our families, and each of us had a few other cheese encounters while growing up that nurtured our developing ability to appreciate sophisticated cheese tastes. But a large gulf separated the "real" cheddars and "fake" processed cheeses of childhood from the untraditional and handmade cheeses that we were finding in our current world of the new American cheeses.

Short Take: Grandmother

and the Cheese Factory

One summer day while visiting in Star Lake, we drove to the Town of Cicero, New York to meet with its historian, Thomas Mafrici. Having contacted him earlier we knew he had information about the cheese factory made famous at the Halls' Thanksgiving Day dinners.

Mafrici's office is in an old schoolhouse he restored to serve as combination historian's headquarters and home for his day job as an attorney. At a long school-library table in front of a blackboard and chalk tray with actual white chalk and good-old black felt erasers, we pored over folders crammed with clippings, manuscripts, and artifacts he pulled from the collection for us. We left with scanned images of cheesemaking in Cicero, including some from the turn of the century. He found for us a photograph of the Addison Loomis factory, the very one in which Grandmother Hall, with sons in tow, had once worked.

Grandmother the cheesemaker. *Russ's grandmother and her two sons (circa 1912): his father is on the left, and his uncle on the right.*

Addison Loomis cheese factory in Cicero, New York*. Date unknown.* Image courtesy of the Town of Cicero Historian.

Raising Daughters in a Vegetable Garden

With the exceptions of holidays, for two decades or more as we established our adult lives and our children grew, cheese continued to follow the pattern from our childhoods...cheddar for parties and processed cheeses for everyday. It did not play an important role in our lives or at our table. We didn't raise our daughters on cheese curds. Like me, they had to wait until they were grown up and visiting the Adirondacks before experiencing their wonders. And cheddar for them, as for us, made childhood appearances primarily as a special treat. Their grandfathers and great uncle kept up the tradition of ensuring that a wheel of sharp, white New York cheddar was always under the Christmas tree.

Mother and daughter in the vegetable garden, 1974.

Looking back, we remember discovering all kinds of new foods and new ways of cooking in the 1970s and 1980s, but new cheeses were not among them. Stores where we lived did not feature European cheeses or tempt us to go exploring in the wider cheese world. The cheeses available were our familiar and not very exciting childhood choices.

It seems as if during those decades we essentially abandoned cheese, or perhaps in its sameness it had all but abandoned us and most of our fellow citizens. Cheese was out of our sight and never became a part of our emerging food consciousness We used it as a cooking ingredient and for an occasional snack, but it never became an adventure for us. Like the pasta and milk we put into our macaroni and cheese or the tomato sauce and pepperoni topping our pizzas, it was always more or less the same.

However—speaking of pasta—our family and many of the other young families we knew during those years were eagerly embracing other new ways of eat-

Home Gardening. *Russ toiling among cabbages, pole beans, and sweet corn in our garden on Pickle Hill in northern Pennsylvania.*

ing and cooking. Whole wheat pasta became part of our lives. We grew aware of healthier foods and lifestyles. As we look back now, it seems to us that when handmade, farmstead American cheeses appeared in our world in the 1990s our earlier forays into growing our own food and shopping for natural foods had primed us and many people like us to welcome it.

We spent a lot of time in our daughters' first several years growing into "foodies." We were proud to be part of the cohort that went out of its way to buy natural and organic foods, confident of their nutritional and social superiority to processed food. Our food interests, nurtured by our grandparents' and parents' proto-foodiness, took on a whole new dimension when our daughters were young.

Recently we found some old photos of our 1970s vegetable garden, and it dawned on us that in part it may be organic gardening guru Robert Rodale's fault that we are writing this book. At least the photos helped us see the trend that started with our turning to natural and unprocessed foods as young parents and led to our appreciating artisanal cheeses when they appeared decades later. For several years, with our daughters by our sides, we grew many vegetables in our one-acre homestead on Pickle Hill in northern Pennsylvania.

We learned to can our garden's tomatoes and to make ketchup from them. We bought bushels of pears and peaches for canning, picked apples in our neighbors' old orchard, canning applesauce for them and us. We even dried beans and shelled them…not a very good use of time, but the garden muse drove us hard. We bought cookbooks and figured out what to do with things like Jerusalem artichokes.

Before Pickle Hill, when we lived in an apartment, we happened upon David Reuben's *Save Your Life Diet*, Frances Moore Lappé's *Diet for a Small Planet* and Mollie Katzen's *The Moosewood Cookbook*. We began shopping at a natural food co-op for our whole grain pastas and bread, unbleached flour, and eggs from free-range chickens. We used honey instead of refined sugar.

We were probably insane, but when it came time to move away and leave our mini-farm, we had crops in the field that we could not bear to abandon. The night before we left we stayed up several exhausting extra hours shelling a 30-gallon trashcan full of fresh peas we had picked so we could bring our produce with us.

We moved to Maryland, had a typical suburban yard with little garden space, and everyone in school or working full-time. We began to slide back into more conventional and less health-conscious eating. But we still shopped at a food co-op, made our own bread on the weekends, and fixed ourselves wholesome brown bag lunches. One Christmas many years later, while we were sipping some particularly revealing red wine and eating from a large wheel of aged cheddar that Russ's uncle had sent from New York, our grown daughters told us they used to open those lunch bags on their walk to school and toss the bean sprouts to the birds so as not to be accused of eating "worm sandwiches." They also remembered having cheese sandwiches for lunch in the College Park, Maryland food co-op's snack bar where we sat at very low tables on pillows instead of chairs and were serenaded by a pony-tailed man playing a guitar.

Russ's sister Phyllis. *She is posing with the family's stand of sweet corn, about 1954. A passion for vegetable gardening has been in his family for at least four generations.*

Unknown to us, while we were tilling the stony soil in Pennsylvania, shopping for whole wheat flour in Maryland, and trying to educate ourselves generally about natural and organic foods, in faraway places like California pioneering cheesemakers were taking the emerging appreciation for natural, healthful foods in a new direction. Their influence was to grow slowly, and it would be 25 years before the fruits of their enterprise became known to us. During those years we were unwittingly on converging paths—we learning to appreciate good nutritious food made close to home and they creating new American cheeses that fit our ideals of good, nutritious food, made close to home. When the new American cheeses did arrive, we were ready for them.

Craig's Forgotten Coast Cheese. *Here it is shown for sale in the former Parrot Tales Pizza, Cedar Key, Florida.*

On a long weekend in a part of western Florida with a grown up daughter turned vegetarian and restaurant owner, we happened upon a new kind of cheese. The omnipresent Florida seafood restaurants presented few options for vegetarian dining. Amazingly, in a little grocery store in tiny Port St. Joe, we found a delicious hand-smoked cheese produced by a local family. Within a few months our daughter was selling Craig's Forgotten Coast Cheese and other specialty cheeses in her restaurant and becoming quite an enthusiast for other cheeses that were new to all of us. With her in the lead, we found ourselves eating more cheese, new kinds of cheese, and more natural rather than factory-made cheese. These new cheeses were suddenly everywhere, and they were neither the special occasion cheeses nor the everyday cheeses of childhood.

We became members of Slow Food USA as the result of a fortuitous birthday gift from our daughters. In the newsletters and e-mails that followed, we noted echoes of our Pickle Hill days of home gardening and Maryland days of natural food shopping. "Good, clean, fair" — the Slow Food tagline — resonated with us. Artisanal cheese seemed to us to be a perfect fit: good for you, fresh from the farm's cheese house, and fair to the cheesemakers, both the humans and the animals. We began to see a clear connection between our enthusiasm for new artisanal cheeses and our years of gardening, canning, breadmaking, and co-op shopping. Decades of evolving food consciousness had set us up to be led by our daughters back to the celebration food of our parents: real cheese.

Fresh vegetables. *Prepared vegetables are ready for packing at a lactic fermentation workshop near our home in north Florida.*

We now see the changes to our food attitudes that happened in those years as part of why many years later we are so intrigued with all these new American cheeses. With the clarity of hindsight, we can now see our food interests flowing in a direct line from childhood, through the time we spent reading *Organic Gardening and Farming* magazine in the 1970s and implementing its messages in our huge vegetable garden, right up to our discovery of the new American cheese and our decision to learn more about it.

Finding the Adirondack Crescent

Our enthusiasm for cheese wrapped around us from two generational directions, and then by chance, we found the Adirondack Crescent. (Don't feel bad if the Crescent is unfamiliar to you; we believe we invented it—more or less.)

We had reconnected with the Adirondacks for reasons completely unrelated to cheese. Enticed by a friend to return to Star Lake one summer for Russ's high school reunion, the little hamlet with its now-dead iron ore mine and its forever wild glacial lake continued to draw us back year after year. Although Russ's parents and most of his classmates' parents were gone, we 60-year-old kids, and sometimes our 40-year-old kids and their littler kids, gathered there to soak up the summer cool, the call of the loons on the lake, the camaraderie built on a shared past, and the off-the-grid peace the place offered us.

One particularly lovely Adirondack day we decided to take a ride in the countryside. Our route took us near to Heuvelton, a town with fewer than a thousand residents and three cheese factories. The smallest also operatad a store selling cheeses made in the factory, so we went to see it and bought some cheese curds and several chunks of cheddar. We did not get to see the production of the cheese, but we actually met the cheesemaker when he came into the shop with some fresh cheese curds. Being at the little factory piqued our curiosity about the cheesemaking process.

Doing some Internet research on cheese factories, we came across an article by Danny Hakim in the *New York Times*. It mentioned the New York State Museum of Cheese in Rome, New York, and an intriguing old map he had seen there. We took a trip to Rome to explore the museum, refresh our knowledge of local

The Adirondack Crescent. *The map we saw in the New York State Museum of Cheese. A larger image and explanation are presented opposite page 1.*

New York State Museum of Cheese

history, and learn a little more about cheese in the region.

The museum is part of the Erie Canal Village, through which the namesake canal runs. Melody Milewski, the curator, told us that Rome was the site of the world's very first cheese factory, built by Jesse Williams in 1851. The world's first cheese factory had been right in our childhood backyards. We picked up a diagram of the layout of the village with descriptions of the various buildings. Dodging raindrops we set off to explore this charmingly informal historical site with Jake, our golden retriever, in the lead.

Across a little footbridge over the canal was a big barn-like cheese factory. It had been moved to the site and restored as the museum. Inside, among photos of early cheesemakers and their cheeses and the displays of cheesemaking paraphernalia, we found what Hakim had described: a four-by-four-foot map of New York State with a dot marking the location of each 1899 cheese factory. The remarkably abundant dots clustering around the north, west, and south sides of the Adirondacks formed what the article described as a "c" shape. But to us, being more into breakfast pastries and Adirondack moonlit nights than geometry, it looked like a crescent. From then on, it became our Adirondack Cheese Crescent.

Both the museum and the map led us to wonder why, at the beginning of the twentieth century, 618 cheese factories were crowded into this crescent-shaped cluster around the Adirondacks. What happened here? Where did those factories come from, and where did they go? Almost all of them seemed to be gone, and we were curious to know if the new American cheesemakers were replacing them.

Having sorted through our memories of childhood cheese, vegetable gardening, and natural food, we could see that our fascination with the new American cheese fit a pattern we had not actually been aware existed in our life. Having reconnected with the Adirondacks and discovered the Adirondack Crescent, we began to integrate our geographic roots with

our growing interest in foods. Our past was helping us understand new American cheeses.

Then another idea struck. Maybe like people did in the old days, we could make some cheese by hand in our own kitchen just for the fun of it. It would certainly be another way to learn about cheese.

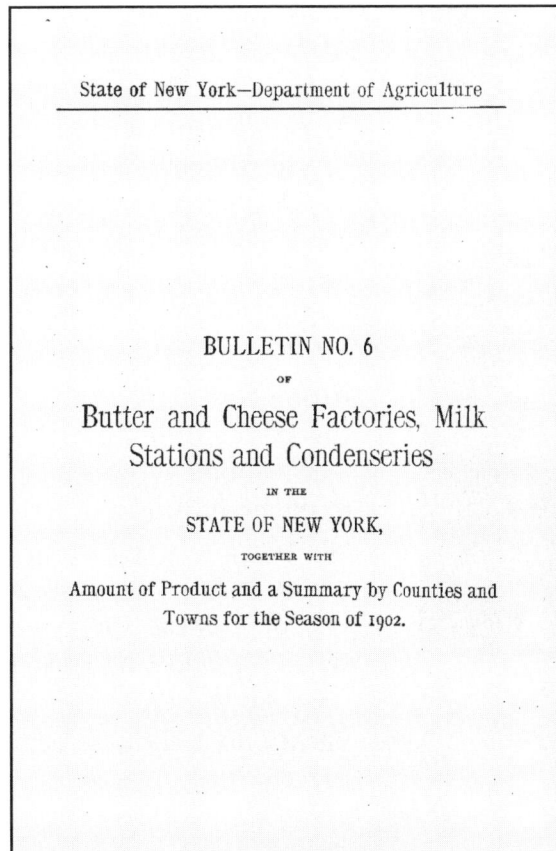

State of New York—Department of Agriculture

BULLETIN NO. 6

OF

Butter and Cheese Factories, Milk Stations and Condenseries

IN THE

STATE OF NEW YORK,

TOGETHER WITH

Amount of Product and a Summary by Counties and Towns for the Season of 1902.

Statistics on cheese production. After discovering the Adirondack Crescent, we obtained a copy of this statistical analysis, providing detailed information on the 1,140 New York State cheese factories reporting to the state Department of Agriculture in 1902.

Visitors are welcome. *Nevertheless in recent years Star Lake has few services available for travelers.*

View of Star Lake. *Except for the disappearance of resort hotels, the lake and its immediate surroundings have changed little in 100 years.*

Ruins of the Benson Mines plant. *Near Star Lake, the operation was abandoned in the late 1970s.*

Short Take: Star Lake and the Cheese Connection

Our connection with the Adirondacks, and ultimately with cheese, began when we returned to Star Lake. We had not been back to Star Lake in more than 35 years, since Russ's dad retired from the now closed iron mine and his parents moved away from the cold northern winters. But since a friend arm-twisted us into attending the 40th reunion of Russ's high-school class, we have been visiting each summer. In this we are like many former schoolmates who have been returning—not just to attend reunion festivities—but to stay and reconnect with the place.

Russ grew up there before the iron ore mine and the paper mill closed, before the school shrunk from about a thousand K-12 students to fewer than three hundred. Everyone knew everyone. It is a place where teenagers came of age on skis—water skiing all summer and snow skiing all winter—where the parents all worked together, where nobody had extended family close by so neighbors and co-workers and their families spent vacations, holidays, birthdays, and anniversaries together.

This sparsely populated area on the western side of the Adirondack Park is mostly designated as "Forever Wild." Star Lake itself—not the town but the lake—is glacier-formed, cold, in some places 60-feet deep. Teens in this town spent their off-ski hours fishing, swimming, hiking and exploring wilderness.

Four of Russ's father's colleagues from the mine bought adjacent lakefront lots and built camps (the Adirondack word for <u>cottage</u>) on them. They lived in "company houses" and wanted little places of their own. It is to one of those camps that we go in the summer. There is no cell phone service and no Internet service. The camp does not have a telephone line, a television, town water, or heat.

We listen to North Country NPR on the radio and buy drinking water at the Nice and Easy. When it is colder than 50 degrees at night, we put on an extra blanket and try to conjure up the feeling of Florida's August heat.

Star Lake is miserably cold in the winter, which lasts a very long time. There are no jobs to be had. The churches mostly have already been consolidated out of town. Its hospital is the smallest in the state and always at risk of being closed. On an "average" day it has less than a single patient (0.7 to be precise).

People love it and hate it. We are lucky to have a place like this to go, and lucky that we do not have to live there all the time. Surrounded by the ghosts of more than six hundred cheese factories, it seemed a wonderful jumping-off place for anyone interested in learning more about cheese.

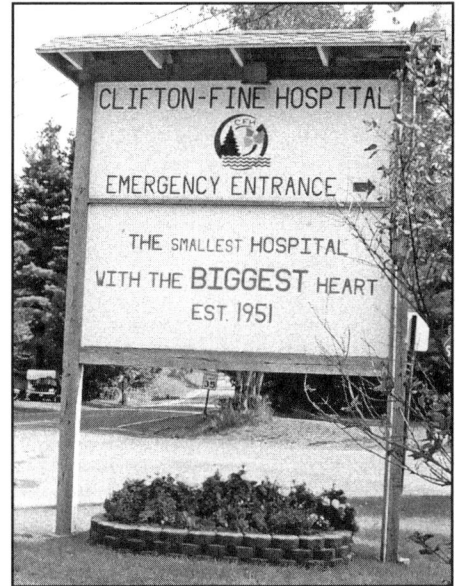

Smallest hospital. *Ms. Joan Leffert of Star Lake took this photo for us.*

Lake scene. *This is the view from the dock of the place where we stay in the summer.*

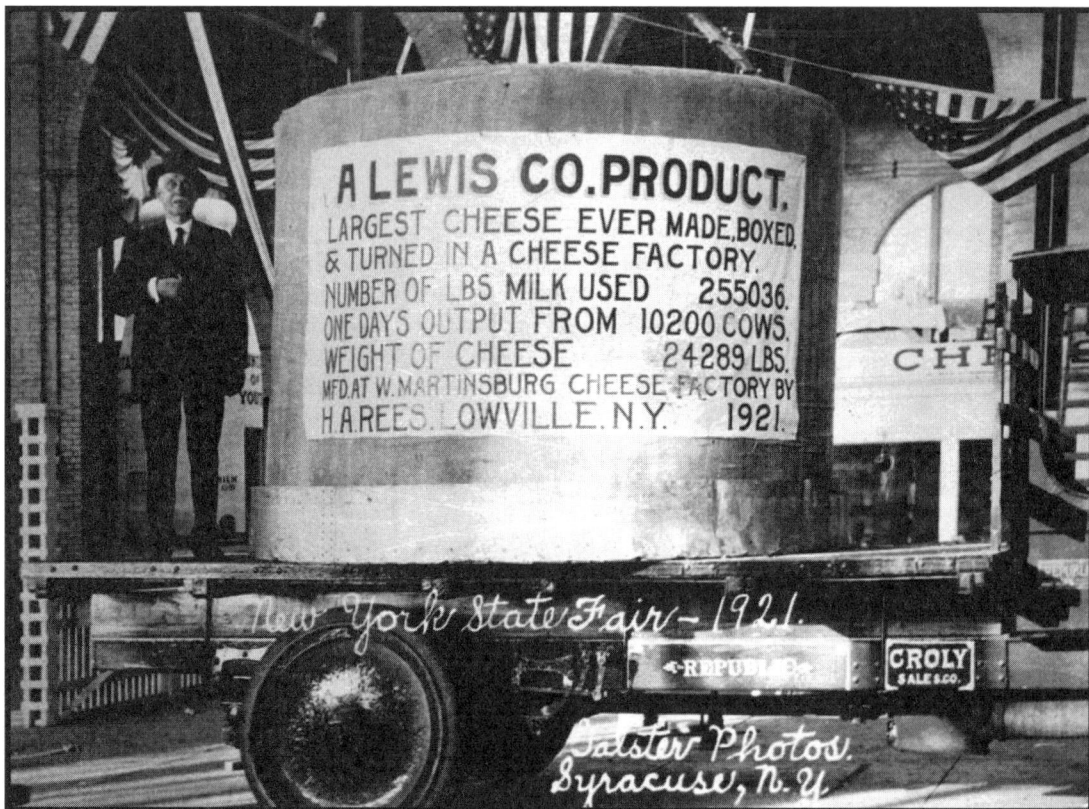

A big cheese. *Outsize cheeses were often used to generate publicity, sometimes being donated to presidents and other prominent individuals. The term "Big Cheese" came into use to refer to such persons. This cheese, from Lewis County New York, was made from the equivalent of the daily production of more than 10,000 cows and was displayed at the 1921 New York State Fair.* Image courtesy of the New York State Museum of Cheese.

Part Two:

Nuts, Bolts, Recollections,

and Fermentations

as told by Russ

As a youth I avidly read the stirring accounts of Louis Pasteur and other scientific heroes in *The Microbe Hunters*, and later I became a biologist. Because of this background I understood that, contrary to intuition and legend, the making of cheese is not a mystery. The process is an ancient one that in modern times has become well-known to science. I knew I could and decided I would learn all about cheese and how it is made.

In college I loved all my biology courses, and at one point I even thought I might specialize in microbiology. On a holiday visit home, I told the local high school science teacher that I couldn't decide whether I wanted to become a microbiologist or an ecologist. "That should be an easy decision," he said. "Would you rather work in fields and forests, or deal with smelly little dishes in a laboratory?" I took his point and opted for ecology, a decision I have never regretted.

Nevertheless, several decades blurred past, and microbiology still had not completely lost its allure. I relished getting into the nuts and bolts of

Louis Pasteur in his laboratory.

cheesemaking; learning more about it was to be only a minor challenge and a welcome one at that. My strategy would be first to learn what I could from what professionals and experts had to say in books. Then if all went well, I would try making cheese in our kitchen; I knew it could be done because I had seen books of instructions written for hobbyists. And it would be almost like getting transported back to my microbiology courses and the not-quite-forgotten adventure of putting my book learning and those friendly little microbes to work in the laboratory.

I recalled a recent e-mail message from the wife of a friend. He is a retired chemist and now a serious amateur wine-maker. "Arnold is very busy with his wine," she said. "The basement looks like a lab, and I think he is happy."

Her words made me wonder if something very like that friend's devotion to his cellar had helped to stoke my interest in food. Maybe the allure of the kitchen was a bigger part of the attraction than I had realized. And was it possible that I have always liked working in the kitchen because unconsciously it reminds me of a laboratory?

Whatever layers of motivation might be involved, I decided to hit the books and then head off to the kitchen for some fun.

What, If Anything, Is Cheese?

In my days as a scientist, I came across an article with the title "What, If Anything, Is a Rabbit?" The point of the article was that rabbits and their few close relatives are so unlike any other mammals that it is difficult to place them within the larger classification scheme. The author wanted to locate rabbits on the proper branch of the mammalian family tree, next to their closest relatives. This was problematic because they resembled any potential relatives so little. I liked the title and have borrowed from it here, but the problem of classifying cheese is quite different from classifying rabbits. Cheese has lots of relatives and near-relatives, and it exists in so many varieties that coming up with a concise and accurate definition is nearly impossible. Even if one omits outliers like so-called cheeses made from extracts of soybeans, the problem persists.

Thumbing through our small collection of books about cheese, I found that neither the technical nor the popular ones attempted to define cheese. They seemed to assume—correctly it appears—that all of us have a sense of the essence of cheese and don't really require being told what it is.

A search of the Web was a bit more productive but didn't really solve the problem. The simple dictionary definitions for cheese—for example,

a solid food prepared from the pressed curd of milk

—were often repeated, not particularly informative, and technically inadequate. Some seemed on the right track—for example,

a food made from coagulated milk curd

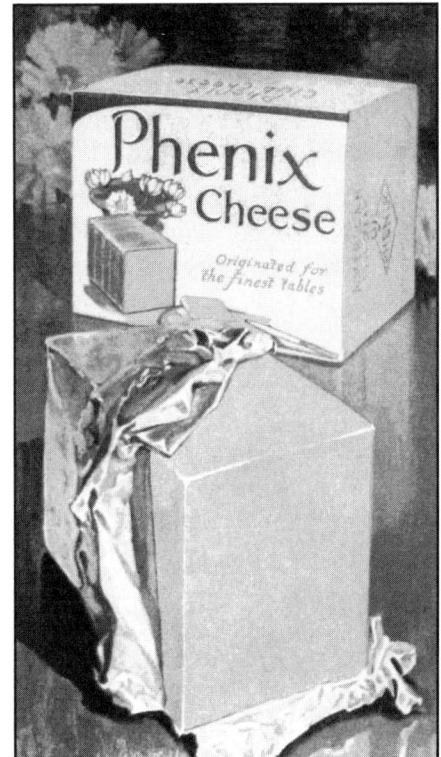

Another Lost Cheese. *This old advertisement features another brand of cheese no longer produced in America.* Image courtesy of the New York State Museum of Cheese.

Men at an old cheese vat. *Although technology has brought advances to cheesemaking, the basic processes used date from antiquity.* Image courtesy of the New York State Museum of Cheese.

—is more or less technically correct. Cheeses can be made without pressing and as I was later to learn, some cheeses are made without bacteria. But all are certainly made from milk and all of them involve coagulation to form curds. However, this definition would not be particularly informative to a native of a desert island who had never experienced cheese. Other definitions I came across were obviously narrow ones applying to specific areas of interest— for example,

> *a food produced industrially by the precipitation of milk protein and capable of acting as a vector of animal disease caused by resistant bacteria but especially by viruses, especially foot-and-mouth disease*

—which clearly was coined by someone primarily interested in disease transmission. Another—

> *a nutritious food consisting primarily of the curd or the semisolid substance formed when milk coagulates*

—although also the product of a health-related organization, appeared to come from the nutrition department rather than the pathology department.

Surprisingly, government agencies seemed not to have a general definition for cheese, although the USDA has extensive definitions for varieties sold in commodity markets, specifying what constitutes a cheddar, a mozzarella, and so on. And it also has a definition for what cheese is not, requiring adulterated cheese products to be called "cheese food."

The most useful definition I found—

> *Cheese, a concentrated dairy food made from milk, is defined as the fresh or matured product obtained by draining the whey (the moisture or serum of the original milk) after coagulation of casein, milk's major protein. Casein is coagulated by acid produced by select microorganisms and/*

or by coagulating enzymes resulting in curd formation. Milk may also be acidified by adding food-grade acidulants in the manufacture of certain varieties of cheese, such as cottage cheese.

—comes from the National Dairy Council and, of course, it doesn't really tell us what cheese is but guides us through a few high points in the process of production.

The search left me troubled. How could I represent myself as a cheese enthusiast without being able to answer the simplest of questions? What if some troublemaker posed the bombshell question "Exactly what is cheese?" Could I give a satisfying answer? I might try "Well, we all know it is made from milk because it is usually found in the dairy coolers in supermarkets," but an answer like that would humiliate me and probably embarrass the questioner.

Like most people, I thought I knew cheese when I saw it and usually when I tasted it, but explaining that wouldn't answer the nettlesome questions. Where does it come from, and how does it differ from other related products? Although I knew it fit into the category of dairy products, I was more than a bit vague on how it differed from yogurt, for example. I remembered making yogurt when our children were little. Was that really different from making cheese? And how can there be an almost infinite variety of cheeses? Hmm... these questions led me to the books. Confident that anyone learning about how it is made would have at least a notion of what cheese is, like the National Dairy Council, I found myself looking for an explanation of how it is made.

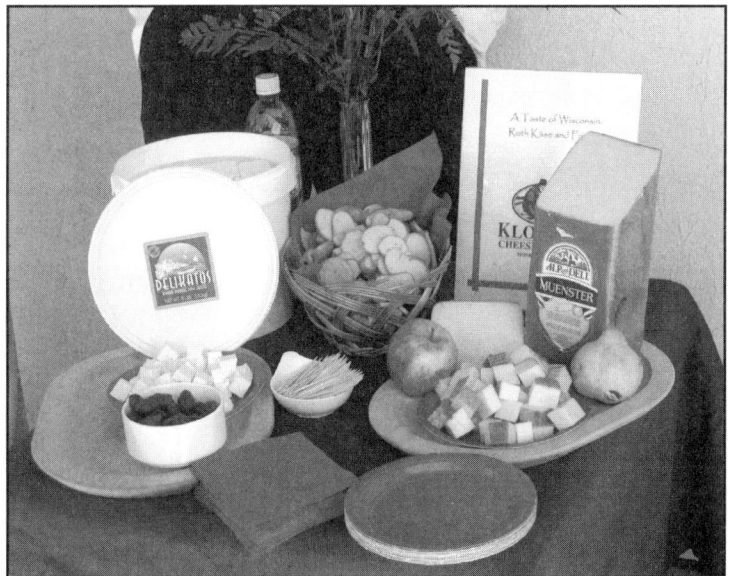

Cheese display. *This array of Roth Käse products welcomed American Cheese Society members arriving for a factory tour. The tour was offered as a field trip arranged as part of the Society's 2008 annual conference.*

Excellent books by Kindstedt, Kosikowski and Mistry, and McGee (cited in the Literature section) provided me with a detailed, if far from simple introduction. They were about cheese at the most fundamental level, and, like everything else in our cheese quest, reading them involved a string of discoveries.

Because cheeses are products of milk, I learned, in order to understand cheeses, some rudimentary understanding of the composition of various milks is necessary. Essentially, the production of cheeses from milk involves the removal of some constituents and the transformation of others. The production of most cheeses is mediated by bacteria, which transform milk by fermentation—a type of chemical reaction occurring in the absence of oxygen. The process releases energy, enabling the bacteria to grow and reproduce. You actually can eliminate the bacteria and produce some kinds of cheeses by chemical means using vinegar or lemon juice, but most familiar cheeses are produced by bacterial fermentation, and cheeses produced by other methods are relatively minor exceptions.

Curds, Whey, Protein, Fat, and Milk Sugar, But No Spiders

Informed in part by decades of advertising by dairy interests (I recall being bombarded with what was even then the sappy and not altogether convincing "Milk is nature's most nearly perfect food"), I knew that all milks provide complete nutrition to babies and other young mammals. My reading initially bore this out by stating that milks contain the three basic biochemical constituents providing the bulk of most foods and, of course, the composition of living bodies. These are proteins, lipids (or fats), and carbohydrates (sugars and starches). Milk can be visualized (Kindstedt's book has nice diagrams) as a soup in which butterfat globules are held within a weak structure formed by dissolved proteins. Those of us old enough to remember milk that was not homogenized realize that the fat globules are only weakly held. We know this because they tended to rise to the surface when resting for a while.

Homogenization breaks butterfat into smaller, less buoyant particles. The most abundant carbohydrate present in milk is lactose, also known as milk sugar, a complex sugar that can be broken down into glucose, the basic fuel that powers most living things. Various proteins are present, but the important one is casein.

In reading and thinking about bacteria, it struck me how fortunate it was that as ten-year-olds happily munching on cheese curds we had been unaware that cheese is made by bacteria. Nor would we have been pleased to learn that we were actually consuming untold millions of them with every bite. In childhood we were constantly reminded that bacteria were sinister agents to be avoided at all costs. After all, weren't bacteria the same as germs? Germs cause illness, make things rot, and eat up the dead bodies of human and beast alike. I remember as a four-year-old my mother telling me that the floor was covered with germs, and then imagining I must be killing dozens of them each time I walked across a room, picturing them being squashed by my hard-soled shoes. And there was my aunt who could not be convinced that any amount of scrubbing would remove the germs from the skin of a peach, imbedded as they were in the fuzzy covering. She would never let Cousin Charlene eat an unpeeled peach. Yes, bacteria were not our friends, and only very much later, in college courses, would their rehabilitation begin.

Peg came across a fascinating paper by Heather Paxson of the Massachusetts Institute of Technology (see list of Literature mentioned in the text). Paxson, a cultural anthropologist, relates what she and many others believe to be an excessive public concern in the United States about "germs" and sanitation. Her observations fit nicely with what we already knew about ongoing battles concerning the potential positive and negative health effects of eating raw milk cheeses (more about this later).

In elementary school we were taught that pasteurization controls bacteria normally present in milk that will multiply and eventually cause it to spoil. It took some reading to relate that information

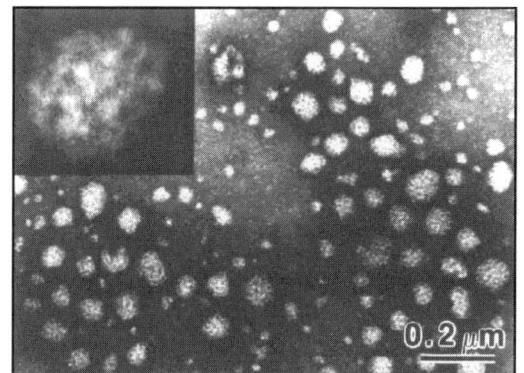

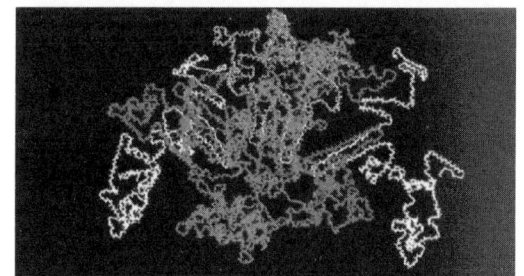

Casein micelles. *Scientists at the USDA Dairy Products and Processing Research unit in Wyndmoor, Pennsylvania are conducting research on the structure of milk. The upper images are electron micrographs of the actual micelles, the lower image is a model developed to show the structure of the protein subunits. The micelles encase butterfat globules in a loose framework. In cheesemaking the proteins coagulate, forcing out liquid components and holding the fat in a more rigid framework.*

Cheese knives. *These can be seen when looking into a modern closed vat at the Roth Käse USA plant in Wisconsin. The arm holding them will rotate, coursing the blades through the curd. Cutting of the curd accelerates expulsion of whey.*

to the cheesemaking process, but bit by bit it came together. The processes involved in spoilage and those involved in souring — as occurs in cheesemaking — are quite different.

Spoilage bacteria tend to break down the proteins in milk. In a bottle of thoroughly spoiled milk, the remnants of the proteins and fats become little white lumps, floating in the expelled liquid — an unsavory yellowish fluid.

Having seen the results of milk spoilage, I was pleased to learn that the bacteria responsible for spoilage are not the same ones responsible for souring, and the products are far different.

Bacteria involved in cheesemaking break down the sugar lactose into lactic acid. When these bacteria multiply explosively, with more and more lactose converting to lactic acid, the milk becomes increasingly acidic. This acidification is acting on the protein framework and causing it to become deformed and to shrink — coagulation (in the words of some of those definitions) — is occurring. The shrinking framework encases and squeezes the fat globules more closely, forcing out liquid components, like a foam rubber sponge being squeezed.

Nor is the yellowish fluid seen in the bottle of spoiled milk the same as the residue from cheesemaking. According to the National Dairy Council definition, the liquid squeezed out by the growth of the bacteria is a mixture of water, lactic acid, and soluble proteins known as "whey." And, the semisolid, yogurtlike remainder is the "curd." This separation of liquids and solids in cheesemaking is "curdling."

Cheesemakers control the bacterial action in at least three ways. First, they inoculate cheese milk with overwhelming numbers of lactic acid producing bacteria, which reproduce rapidly and outcompete less desirable kinds. Second they heat the milk to temperatures most favorable for growth of the desired bacteria. And third, they add a substance known as rennet relatively early in the process of forcing out liquids and making the cheese more solid. Rennet is an enzyme traditionally derived from the fourth stomach of calves or the young of other ruminant mammals. Once again, I was led down a short path in the subject of mammalian biology; the presence of rennet, I learned, helps suckling calves, kids, lambs, and such to digest milk. In cheesemaking, rennet takes over one part of the process that the bacteria began. It speeds up the expulsion of whey and development of the semisolid curd. Cutting up and "cooking" the curd — actually just heating it to 100 °F, more or less — also help to remove more of the whey.

I might never have taken my first taste of cheese if I had known that it contained a product derived from the stomach lining of a dead calf. "Hmm," I might have said, wondering what other disgusting facts remained to be learned. Back in the 1950s not much was said about "natural" foods. As children we preferred to believe that if milk did not arise spontaneously in bottles, at least it was purified by pasteurization, homogenization, and perhaps other processes. We knew intellectually that the milk we consumed was produced by cows, but we didn't dwell on that knowledge. However on a visit to an aunt, I did get to visit a dairy barn at milking time, and I could never think about milk in quite the same way after that experience. As with our naïve childhood concept of where our milk came from, most of us were comforted by the wishful belief that cheese was a manufactured product miraculously issuing from gleaming sterilized machinery. Grass, cattle, udders, bacteria, and the massive, ever-present quantities of fly-infested manure in the milking barn were all far from our innocent minds as we nibbled our Velveeta.

Once the whey is drained off, the curd is relatively solid; again picture something a bit firmer than the contents of one of those little plastic containers of yogurt. Depending on how it is drained, pressed, salted, inoculated, or treated subsequently, the curd will become one of the many varieties of cheese.

"What is cheese?" Looking for a short answer to that question, one could truthfully say that (with some exceptions) it is a fermented dairy product (i.e., some kind of milk modified by particular microbial

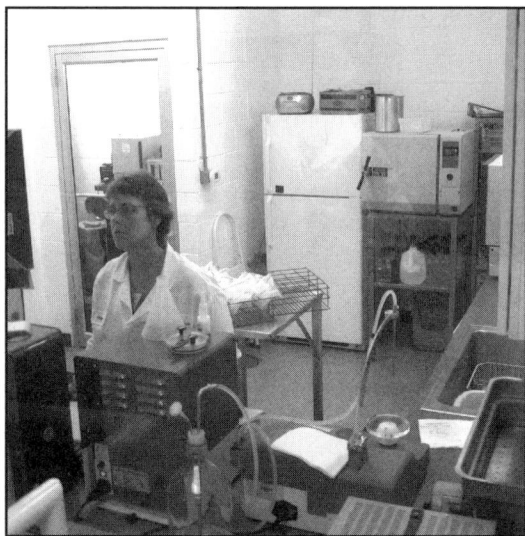

Laboratory in a cheese factory. *A technician analyzes samples in the laboratory of the Roth Käse USA factory in Wisconsin. Every cheesemaking operation, from those with large laboratories to those with instruments in the corner of a tiny cheese room must perform certain tests to ensure safety and quality.*

reactions). A somewhat longer and perhaps more informative answer would be that it is a fermented dairy product in which most water and water-soluble constituents have been removed, leaving globules of butterfat encased in a variably solid protein framework. I liked that latter definition, believing I had made some progress in coming up with a definition that would apply to most, if not all, kinds of cheese. And, of course, I now had a scientifically valid and reasonably dignified way to answer that potentially embarrassing question.

However, while getting to this point provided a "generic" answer, it was hardly an adequate one because it told nothing about how cheese can exist in so many forms and bring to us so many enchanting flavors. I needed to know more. Why, exactly, can there be so many kinds of cheese?

How Curds Turn into So Many Types of Cheese

Having learned about many kinds of cheeses and having tried what seemed like hundreds of them at cheese festivals like those we attended in Warwick and Burlington, it came as a surprise to me to learn in my readings that there are only a few unique kinds of cheeses—Kosikowski and Mistry mention eighteen, and Kindstedt believes there may be only twenty truly unique kinds. Much variation, I learned, results from relatively minor tweaking of the basic processes used. Armed with this information, I set out to learn what these basic kinds are and to get a notion about the source and reasons for the variety. Alas, the subject proved more complex than what I had been prepared to tackle. I learned that there are indeed only a few basic processes, but these overlap and interact in complex ways. Although various simple classifications are possible, like most simplistic things, they have little power to enlighten. Let me try to explain.

Of course cheese is made from milk, and even before you get to the "curd stage," one basic difference in cheeses results from the kinds of milk used. Most familiar cheeses are made from cow, goat, or sheep milk, and others use buffalo, camel, or other milks.

The milks differ in composition and flavor and produce distinctive, different-tasting cheeses. Some cheeses are even made from combinations of milks or from milk fortified by addition of extra cream. Also, the particular milk used can differ seasonally and as a result of what the animals are eating. So, one broad classification of cheeses—goat cheese, sheep cheese, cow cheese—is based on the animals producing the milks used, and perhaps more finely on the particular environmental factors encountered by these animals. Even the results of subtle environmental differences can alter the composition of milks.

Another broad classification of cheeses is based on whether they are soft, hard, very hard, and so on. It is useful for some purposes, but I found it less than satisfying. Other things may be involved, but most of what makes a cheese soft or hard is based on whether and how it is aged. As ripening proceeds, moisture tends to be lost, and proteins and fats are broken down into smaller and denser compounds, producing ever harder cheeses. (By the way, "ripening" is often used as a synonym for "aging," and the terms are frequently used interchangeably.) The nature of the aging or ripening process is the most important—and most interesting—way that cheese gets to exist in so many different varieties, and provides the most reasonable basis for classifying them.

So here's how it works: After the bacteria do their thing, breaking lactose down into lactic acid, and the milk reaches the curds-and-whey stage, it can be drained and packaged right away, as a "fresh" cheese, or it can be aged. Fresh cheeses such as chèvre and Neufchatel differ substantially from aged cheeses such as cheddar, Gouda, and alpine types. Arguably the most basic way of dividing cheeses is between those consumed when they are fresh and those consumed after they have been transformed during the ripening process.

The constituents of fresh cheeses are largely fats and long-chain proteins. These cheeses, for the most part, are soft in texture and relatively bland in flavor. During aging, microbes break the long-chain compounds into smaller units, which may alter the

Cheddaring. In this old photo, men are stacking slabs of cheese curd in the bottom of a vat. The process helps expel whey and encourages knitting of the proteins that will provide the structure of the final product. Image courtesy of the New York State Museum of Cheese.

texture and, most important, result in an array of flavors. The final texture and flavor of a cheese will depend on (1) the specific microorganisms (bacteria and molds) responsible for ripening, (2) the manner in which the ripening microbes are applied to the cheese, (3) the conditions in which aging occurs, and 4) and the length of time the cheese is aged.

By tweaking these four variables, cheesemakers have an almost endless source of variation in aging options that permit them to produce a wide array of distinctive cheeses. Nevertheless, it is possible to distinguish basic styles, as shown in the following table:

How Ripening Agents Are Introduced	Ripening Agents			
	Bacteria		Molds	
Spread on Surface (surface ripened)	"washed rind cheeses"	e.g., Munster; Limburger	"bloomy rind cheeses"	e.g., Brie; Camembert
Innoculated into Cheese Milk (grow in crevases in cheese)			"blue-veined cheeses"	e.g., Blue; Roquefort
Dispersed in Cheese (present in cheese milk)	most others	e.g., Cheddar; Romano		

The different processes produce fundamentally different cheeses. For example, in bloomy-rind cheeses, like Brie and Camembert, surface-growing molds (the white stuff that forms the edible layer on their surface) are the primary agents of aging, and are responsible for flavor and texture development. Molds are also responsible for aging in blue-veined cheeses like Danish blue and Roquefort, but in these cheeses the molds (the greenish-blue stuff in the middle) are usually introduced by innoculation into the the cheese milk, and they grow in interior crevices. In washed-rind cheeses like Munster and Limburger (often called the "stinky" cheeses), bacteria (rather than molds) grow on the surface, often as a thin reddish film, and perform the aging function. The term "washed rind" refers to the frequent moistening of cheese surfaces during aging to encourage the growth of bacteria.

In both kinds of the surface-ripened cheeses (bloomy and washed rind), the microbes do not penetrate the body of the cheese, but enzymes they produce diffuse inward from the surface. This has two effects: (1) the cheeses can't be too large or too thick, or the enzymes won't penetrate fast enough to make cheeses that are reasonably uniform throughout; (2) flavors and textures differ, depending on sizes and shapes of the cheeses. For example, a surface-ripened cheese made in the shape of a hockey puck and another made in the shape of a little pyramid may develop differently, even though agents and conditions used in their aging were identical.

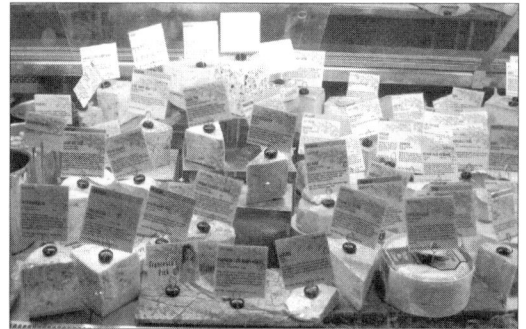

A multitude of cheeses. *Some of the many kinds of cheeses offered by one shop.*

In most cheeses that are not of the surface-ripened or blue-veined styles, the bacteria naturally present in the milk from the beginning, and those introduced by the cheesemaker before curd formation, remain in the cheese as it ages and are responsible for ripening. Bacteria reproduce rapidly for a brief period during curd formation; in later stages their reproduction is slowed considerably by loss of moisture, addition of salt, lowering of the temperature, and sometimes competition from other micoorganisms. Some bacteria may remain alive throughout the aging process, but their activity decreases drastically. Even after they die, the enzymes left behind by burst bacterial cells remain biochemically active and continue for many months to work on breaking down other components during aging and developing the flavors and textures. Some bacteria may survive indefinitely in aged cheeses, and they may be important in flavor development. However, their kinds and numbers may vary, based on whether the cheese milk was pasteurized. The role of diverse populations of bacteria and their importance are hotly debated in some quarters along the fault lines created by diverging views on the pasteurization issue (see Short Take: The Pasteurization Issue).

So, the second "simple" way to classify cheeses (the first being by the kinds of milk used), by the aging

Cave in a cheese shop. This window into the temperature- and humidity-controlled storage unit permits customers to view cheeses as they age naturally.

process, distinguishes the cheeses by the ripening agents used—molds or bacteria –with subcategories developed for the various means of introduction—on the surface or into the interior.

I had heard that cheese is a living thing that will change over time, even after you have purchased it. This seemed to be a cool idea, but my research on aging revealed that this may be only partly true and truer of some kinds of cheese than others, depending on the treatment processes.

The kinds of agents and the manner of their introduction are important, but still more minor variations in processing can result in significant differences in the cheeses produced. I learned that the temperatures to which cheeses are subjected in processing is important, as is the amount of salt added to them and the manner in which it is administered. As a means of reducing acidity, some kinds of cheeses have the curds washed by the addition of water. Others are milled—chopped or ground up after the curd knits—and the manner in which this is done influences the outcome. Still other cheeses such as cheddars, mozzarella, and provolone are subjected to manipulations in the curd stage, and this affects the texture of the final product. Curds for cheddars are stacked in slabs as a means of draining whey and knitting their proteins, and mozzarella and provolone are stretched to align their proteins into long, elastic fibers. Minor as these variations in processing may be, they contribute to the tremendous variety we see in the cheeses available to us.

And of course, there is *terroir*—in the narrow sense, the effects of the land on this product that comes ultimately from the land. Different types of soil, different patterns of rainfall, and differences in the kinds of plants on which dairy animals forage all can contribute to subtle differences in cheeses. However, in a broader sense, *terroir* may involve other local variations that make cheeses distinctive. For example, essentially similar cheeses might be produced in Wisconsin and in North Carolina, but in one region the cheese might be aged in natural caves while in the other aging takes place in mechanical coolers. The resulting tastes may be subtly—or substantially—different.

Of course processed cheese has played prominently in the cheese experiences of most Americans, and I needed to learn about it too, even though I assumed it is practically the antithesis of the new American cheese. Processed cheese is made by grinding up un-aged (fresh or "green") cheeses and aged cheeses and gluing them together to form a smooth, uniform texture. Various other manipulations are possible, including the addition of flavoring materials and flavor enhancers, as well as the substitution of vegetable oils for butterfat. Amen on the subject of processed cheese.

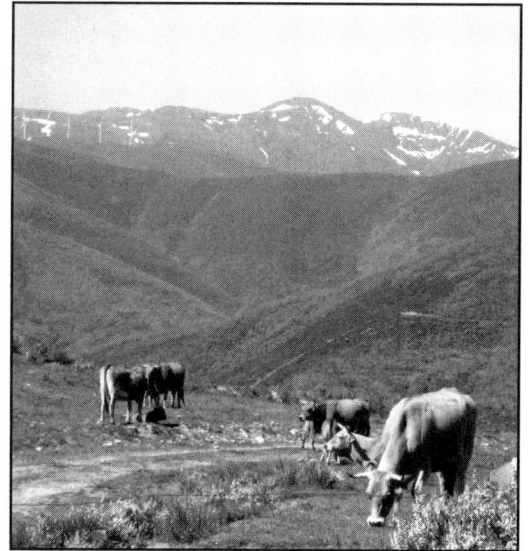

Alpine pasture. *Some breeds of cattle— those in this image appear to be Brown Swiss—are reputed to be well adapted to alpine climates.*

Informed by Kindstedt's book and others, I engaged in a little mind game, asking myself to think about all the differences in conditions and practices that could lead to two radically different kinds of cheeses. I chose Brie and alpine types—the latter commonly sold in the North America as "Swiss cheese." Although neither of these namesake cheeses is produced in America, their styles have been widely adapted by the new American cheesemakers.

Like Brie, alpine types (including Comté and Emmenthal) are also produced in parts of France. Brie tends to be made in the lowlands, and obviously the alpine types are made in the mountains. Both are normally made from cow milk, but quite possibly the breeds of cattle differ as might the amount of butterfat and other components in their milks. Of course forage plants would differ also, possibly resulting in subtle flavor differences in milks. More important, human populations and farms are relatively dense and evenly distributed in the lowlands, and consumers of Brie are close to farms where the cheeses are made. There is no need to keep cheese for long periods to transport it to consumers, as they are nearby and usually consume it within a few weeks. Alpine types, on the other hand, are made from the milk of cows driven into high mountain pastures in the summer, where the cheese is made. Cheeses must not only survive the return to villages in the valleys at the end of summer but must last long enough to feed people throughout the year. Thus, Bries are soft and quite perishable, whereas alpine cheeses are more robust and long lasting. Bries are aged by the action of molds growing on the surface, and this dictates that they be quite small so that enzymes produced by the molds can diffuse into the center of the mass. Alpine cheeses, on the other hand, are ripened by bacteria dispersed more or less evenly throughout and therefore can be quite large. As if these differences weren't enough, Kindstedt points out that the amount of salt used in the production of alpine cheeses is less than in most others because of the difficulty of carrying it up to the high pastures. Lower salt requires higher cooking temperatures and strains of bacteria that can tolerate them. These factors combine to produce the distinctive qualities of alpine cheeses.

Although these two cheeses differ extremely from one another, the effects of different environmental conditions and the practices developed to deal with them can be found in all kinds of cheeses. And knowledge of the effects of such conditions and practices has inspired the new American cheesemakers to experiment and be creative.

Having read about how things like the aging effects of surface molds and the influence of cooking temperature result in different types of cheese, the urge to make some cheese of our own was stronger than ever. I felt I was ready to take to the kitchen. Cheese would be more than the search for a definition, a series of concepts gotten from books, or a sought-after treat in the marketplace. It would be something developing before my eyes.

Short Take: How Many Kinds of Cheese?

USDA Handbook Number 54, Cheese Varieties and Descriptions, published in 1953, describes over 400 named varieties of cheeses. The document actually mentions more than 800 names, but many are considered to be synonyms. The handbook author attributes this great number of recognized kinds mostly to local variations on what he considers to be only 18 truly distinct styles. Examples considered typical of the 18 basic kinds are the following:

Brick	Camembert	Cheddar
Cottage	Cream	Edam
Gouda	Hand[1]	Limburger
Neufchâtel	Parmesan	Provolone
Romano	Roquefort	Sapsago[2]
Swiss	Trappist[3]	Whey[4]

[1] Known as Handkâse in German

[2] A flavored grating cheese made by the Swiss

[3] Better known today as Port-Salut

[4] Myost and ricotta mentioned

This list differs in important ways from similar lists prepared by other experts, although there are substantial areas of agreement. Despite differences on what they are, the number of 18-20 basic kinds of cheeses seems to be an area of general agreement. It is a sign of the great amount of innovation and rapid evolution in the new world of cheese that the handbook fails to recognize many newer types that are reasonably familiar today.

The handbook is available for downloading from the USDA Website. The URL is http://www.nal.usda.gov/ref/USDApubs/aghandbk.htm

Short Take: The Pasteurization Issue

The issue of pasteurization was hotly debated in certain places we visited along our cheese trail, particularly in forums at American Cheese Society conferences. We later learned that the debates about raw milk swirl far beyond cheese circles, with zealots on both sides. We even passed a car in Pennsylvania with a license plate frame declaring that Pennsylvania is "The Raw Milk State." Broad areas of disagreement among proponents and critics include the nature of good health, and the causes and prevention of disease. A growing chorus of advocates claims that pasteurized milk is less healthful than raw milk. Our interest was and is in cheese, however, and we will leave it to others to engage in the larger controversy concerning the risks and benefits of consuming raw milk.

Raw milk cheeses may be sold in the United States only if they are aged 60 days or more. Disease-causing microorganisms in raw milk may be transferred to cheeses made with them, but the biochemical transformations occurring during the 60-day aging virtually guarantee that no disease-producing microorganisms can survive. Although the timing is somewhat arbitrary, 60-day-old cheeses are generally regarded as adequately aged.

Many favorite kinds of European cheeses are traditionally made with raw milk and aged less than 60 days, and these cannot be imported into the United States. Canada has strict laws requiring pasteurization, and parents can even face criminal charges there for giving raw milk to their children. Canadian health authorities proposed a total ban on raw milk cheeses but relented in the face of protests by cheese enthusiasts.

The purpose of pasteurization is to kill any bacteria that might cause disease, and a secondary benefit is that it can greatly increase the shelf life of liquid milk. The temperature to which milk is heated and the length of time it is maintained at that temperature vary inversely. The primary positive effect is the measure

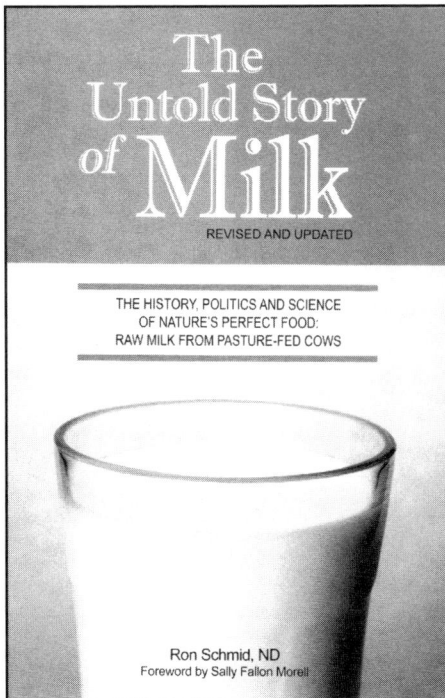

The Untold Story of Milk. *In this book, author Dr. Ron Schmid presents a long series of highly technical arguments addressing the health benefits of raw milk. Most cheesemakers are concerned instead with the flavor-enhancing qualities of the diverse bacterial flora in raw milk.*

of safety provided (again, this is debated). Negative effects for cheesemaking include imparting a "cooked" flavor to milks, which can be transferred to cheeses made with them, and killing bacteria that could be important in producing complex flavors developed in the aging process. In fresh cheeses, the first effect is most important and can be partially overcome by pasteurization for longer periods at relatively lower temperatures. Aged cheeses present another story. The primary argument among cheesemakers swirls around the loss of bacterial diversity. If a few kinds of bacteria can produce a certain cocktail of flavor compounds in aging, then more kinds of bacteria should be able to produce a much greater variety of flavor components and more complex cheeses.

Some health officials urge pasteurization for all cheese milks, seeing the 60-day rule as a risky loophole. Universal pasteurization would be a surer guarantee of the public health, they contend. Opponents see a conspiracy perpetrated by some mainstream cheesemakers to deny a competitive advantage to the new cheesemakers. In fact, only a minority of the new American cheeses are made from raw milk. Many cheesemakers seem to view required pasteurization as they do other regulations having to do with health—something affording them a measure of protection.

Even among the new cheesemakers, the advantages conferred by using raw milk are not taken for granted. We participated at a tasting where raw- and pasteurized-milk cheeses were compared in a blind test. None of the participants could reliably identify the raw versus pasteurized milk cheeses. However, there were too many variables to make the comparisons valid; some cheeses were made from milk from grass-fed cows, while others were made from grain- and silage-fed animals, and each of the cheeses was made by a different cheesemaker.

In a curious twist revealed at the 2007 American Cheese Society conference, an industrial group promoting the use of ionizing radiation as a means of sterilizing foods unwittingly provided a potential benefit to those wishing to make raw-milk cheeses. In a late-night session of Congress, lobbyists for the radiation group convinced lawmakers to redefine pasteurization as

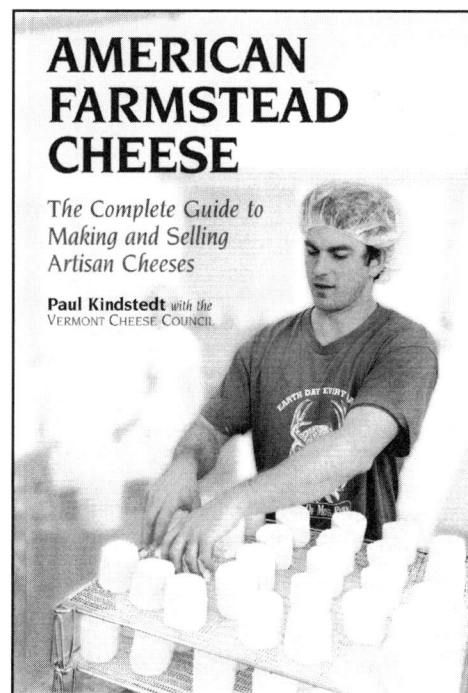

"The Pasteurization Dilemma," a chapter in Kindstedt's book written by Catherine W. Donnelly, Ph.D., addresses pasteurization and the alternatives to pasteurization by which the safety of raw milk cheeses can be ensured.

Goat

Milk

& Cheese

For pet consumption only

Pricey pet food. This sign was posted by a vendor at a farmers market near our home in Florida. State law dictates that unpasteurized milk can be sold only for consumption by pets. A week after we took this photo the cheesemaker was temporarily banned from the market until his case could be reviewed by the market's board of directors. He argued that he was operating entirely within the law and that the directors' concern about liability was spurious because they could be sued by anyone claiming to have been made ill by any vegetable or other product sold at the market.

part of the 2002 farm bill. Here is the text:

> *The term "pasteurization" is redefined to include other processes for eliminating microbial pathogens besides heat treatment, potentially allowing foods treated with irradiation, high pressure, or ultraviolet light to be labeled as pasteurized.*

While intended to support a narrow business interest, the redefinition may have had an unintended consequence. If *other processes for eliminating microbial pathogens* meets the legal definition of pasteurization, it can be argued that 60 days of aging *is* pasteurization. So there is at least a glimmer of hope that the proponents of the old model of universal pasteurization will not further impose their will on the new American cheesemakers.

ABSOLUTELY
PURE

BOTTLED MILK

Bricks, Shortening Cans, Dented Sinks, and Plastic Caves

Armed with my rudimentary knowledge of cheeses and how they are made, I wanted to start from the bottom, so to speak. I was ready to try making cheese at home. I wanted to share the experiences that have been, and continue to be, familiar to all cheesemakers. And, I hoped, what I would learn along the way would add to my understanding and ultimately to my appreciation of the new and the old worlds of cheese.

I knew now that the preliminary and basic steps in cheesemaking are common to almost all cheeses. It would be fun to see milk turn into curd, but I thought these first steps would be relatively uninteresting, compared to the later steps, such as aging. Later I was to discover that the technically interesting business of aging was in practice rather tedious, compared to the first few intense hours in the process.

As for providing answers to the two big questions— "What is cheese?" and "How is it made?"—all I expected those first steps to teach me was how to progress from milk stage to the rather bland product just beyond the curd stage that is a cheese in name, but that has almost none of the qualities we like about cheese. I knew the initial steps in the cheesemaking process would not let me create the subtle variations that give rise to the many of kinds of cheeses with their myriad flavors.

Although one idea was to start out making the edible kind of cheese curds we favored as children, I did not find a recipe right away. My first adventures began with instructions gotten from an appendix in Edith Stamm's *The History of Cheese Making in New York State*. Contributed by staff at the Genesee County

Cheesemaking materials. *I was able to make my first cheese with items found around the house, including large pots and a candy thermometer. The milks, fabrics, and plastic shortening container were obtained especially for the purpose. Only the rennet tablets could not be obtained locally.*

Museum, the recipe provided an easily accessible way for novices to begin. With one exception, I could obtain locally everything I needed.

I visited the local supermarket with a shopping list in hand that included one pound of store-brand vegetable shortening in a plastic container, two gallons of milk, some buttermilk, a twelve-ounce can of tuna fish, and cheesecloth. Most of these I found easily. I had to look harder for the cheesecloth, which was sold out in the fabric store I visited. Eventually I found it on the supermarket aisle containing cleaning supplies. I also needed unbleached muslin. The fabric store didn't have that either, and of course it was not available (and not expected) in the supermarket. I was impatient, however, and substituted a kitchen towel I found at the market; it looked as if it might have been made of muslin.

I later learned that the kind of cheesecloth I had purchased was not what a real cheesemaker would have used and also that I should have sought out a fabric known as "butter muslin." Neither of the genuine products was available for the first cheese, but I got them from cheesemaking supply houses for my subsequent cheesemaking experiments. The one essential item for the first cheesemaking attempt that I could not obtain locally was the rennet. I sent off an order and waited impatiently for the six-pack of vegetable rennet enzyme tablets.

Of course, the two gallons of milk would provide the basic raw material for the cheese. A very small amount of the buttermilk would be added as the source of live bacteria to initiate fermentation; the rest of it I would use for buttermilk soup, a favorite. Special strains of bacteria to produce various kinds of cheeses are available from suppliers, but most strains are closely related, and it turns out that the bacteria responsible for making cultured buttermilk are perfectly capable of producing cheese.

Following the instructions at hand, I opened and removed the contents from the plastic shortening container, discarding the shortening. I cleaned the container thoroughly and drilled holes in the bottom.

This was to be my cheese mold, or "hoop," in the jargon of cheesemaking. I cut the edges off the rather flimsy top so it would fit inside the mold, and thus it became the "follower," the part that would go on top of the cheese curds and press them down in the mold. The can of tuna fish was to be used unopened to help with pressing duties; it would sit atop the follower and hold the weights that would press down on the cheese. Anytime after the can had completed its duties in cheesemaking, we could open it and eat its contents.

The remainder of my cheesemaking apparatus consisted of everyday items already found around the house. They included a stainless steel stockpot that held slightly more than eight quarts, a 21½ - quart enameled steel canner, a candy thermometer, a large stainless-steel colander, a stainless-steel spatula of the kind used for slicing cakes, and a nylon spoon for a stirrer. The stockpot would receive the milk and serve as my cheese vat. I placed it inside the water-filled canner, which functioned as a water bath, allowing me to gently increase and maintain prescribed temperatures of the milk. To press the cheese in my shortening-can mold, I added weights on top of the tuna can on the follower. I used bricks for pressing weights, as recommended in the instructions, and I wrapped them in plastic to keep dust from contaminating the cheese. The first cheese was to be a "farmer" or "farmhouse cheddar" cheese.

Over the next twelve months I made eight different cheeses, and as I progressed my equipment and operating procedures became more sophisticated. I substituted an electronic model with an alarm for the candy thermometer used at first, I ordered special bacterial cultures, I got the appropriate kinds of cheesecloth and butter muslin, I acquired a pH meter, and ultimately I opted for a commercial cheese press. Actually, the results of my efforts were not greatly influenced by this increasing sophistication. Some cheeses succeeded, some failed, and none were particularly superior to those first attempts carried out with primitive equipment. Even some early mistakes did not seem to noticeably affect the

Warming the milk. Once it reached 90°F, a small amount of buttermilk was mixed in as a source of bacteria. After an hour, bacteria have reproduced explosively, converted much of the lactose to lactic acid, and begun the process of expulsion of liquid components, collectively known as whey.

Cut curd. After the addition of rennet and another period of rest, the curd is a solid mass having the consistency of sour cream. Cutting the curd into small cubes increases the surface area and accelerates the expulsion of whey.

Cooking the curd. *A slow increase in temperature to 100°F and gentle stirring for thirty minutes completes the separation of the solid components of the curd from the liquid whey.*

Draining the curd. *The whey is drained and discarded. It can be used for a variety of purposes, including making of certain kinds of cheeses. When discharged from industrial cheesemaking processes, it can be a significant pollutant. Up to this point, the processes for making most kinds of cheeses are very similar.*

results. On the first attempt I used too much rennet. I also dissolved the rennet tablet in chlorinated water, and later salted the cheese curds with iodized salt. I learned these were no-no's and corrected them in later attempts. Perhaps others would have noticed the results of these mistakes in the cheeses, but I detected only inconsistent differences.

The accompanying series of photos and captions illustrates the making of my first cheeses. Rather than describe the various steps separately, I will just relate what turned out to be the only real frustration. The cheese curds in the plastic mold, the follower and tuna can on top, and the weights used for pressing proved to be quite unstable. Lacking enough weight with the bricks at hand, I got creative and added a weight in the form of a gallon-size can of mushrooms. To this I added the bricks, ultimately four of them. Balancing this tower of weights atop the cheese mold was a challenge. It was possible, however. By carefully shifting the can and each brick, the perfect distribution of weights could be obtained so that all would remain upright and more or less even pressure could be applied to the curds.

Alas, success was short lived. As the curds pressed down and knitted together, slight shifts from side to side were inevitable. Ten or fifteen minutes after seeing that all was aligned and balanced, I would be greeted by a loud crash. Rushing to the kitchen sink, where the pressing was underway, I would find a jumble of cheese mold and weights scattered in the basin. One such crash brought down a brick with enough force to dent the stainless steel sink. In later attempts I placed my cheese press in a more durable fiberglass laundry tub.

Also for a later cheese, I had a flash of inspiration—real creativity this time—and substituted a cast-iron stockpot for the mushroom can. I could set the stockpot upside down, with the tuna can connecting with its inverted bottom, concentrating much of its weight lower and lowering the center of gravity of the weight complex. It worked better but was no panacea; it crashed also, and my continuing problems with pressing ultimately induced me to procure the commercial press.

I also obtained new instructions. Rikki Carroll's *Home Cheese Making* and Margaret Morris's *The Cheesemaker's Manual* provided me with recipes for different varieties of cheese. They were very helpful in increasing my knowledge of the kinds of cheeses and how differences in manufacture lead to the almost endless range of variation.

With one exception I aged all the cheeses I made for at least 60 days. Even though I used pasteurized milks, the 60-day aging period required by U.S. Department of Agriculture regulations for raw milk cheeses seemed an appropriate benchmark for aging my cheeses.

Finding a suitable environment for aging my cheeses proved to be my second major challenge. In the garage we had an old refrigerator, which was used primarily for beverages and occasional overflow from the refrigerator in the kitchen. I found that by turning the temperature control to its warmest position, I could maintain a temperature within the acceptable range for aging but still colder than the desired 55°F. Nevertheless, in winter when temperatures in the garage sometimes fell below 50° the temperature inside the refrigerator sometimes fell back into the 40s.

Worse, the humidity inside my improvised aging "cave" tended to be far lower than the 65% said to be in the ideal range for aging. I partially solved that problem with a shopping trip for a clear plastic storage box with a lid. I put the cheeses inside the box with an open bowl of water. When I did this, the humidity rapidly shot up to 90%. That was too high, and what followed was a constant tinkering, by wedging little pieces of wood—toothpicks, chopsticks, pencils—under the edge of the inverted storage box, seeking to let just enough outside air in to attain the desired humidity. Of course even when I seemed to have it just right, all might go askew each day when, per the instructions, I opened my little apparatus to turn over the cheeses. I own a wireless weather station

Curds in the mold or "hoop." In the upper image, the curds have been packed into the shortening container, shown on its side. In the lower, my tuna can and follower are shown in place. They will transfer pressure from weights to the curds, expelling liquid and helping them to knit together.

Pressing. *The series of images above shows successive attempts to solve the problem of pressing the curds. The first two attempts (top and middle) used combinations of bricks and an unopened large can of mushrooms to press down on the curds in the hoop. Both were highly unstable. The middle image shows an upside-down cast-iron stockpot added weight with a lower center of gravity — better but still unstable. The ultimate solution was purchase of a commercial cheese press (bottom).*

and was able to keep track of the temperature and humidity inside the aging chamber by putting the transmitting unit in with the cheeses. I got readouts on my computer screen and thus was alerted to times when additional adjustments were necessary.

The problem of controlling humidity brought me back to memories of graduate school, where I wanted to control humidity in an experiment in which I was incubating lizard eggs in glass containers. After my first series of cheeses, I remembered the lizard egg problem and hearing at the time of a way to control humidity in a closed container by including an open vessel inside with water and glycerol mixed in prescribed proportions. I never got to try the technique and don't know if any cheesemakers have ever tried it. I will have to look up the instructions and perhaps try it someday.

My first cheese was delightful when we sampled it two months after its production. A critic would have declared it too hard, probably because of my excessive use of rennet, but the flavor was pleasing and we ate the entire cheese, apart from the edges that had hardened excessively. In making the second cheese I followed the same instructions I had used with the first, correcting some of the deficiencies of the first try. With this cheese I may have overcorrected some of the problems encountered with the first, for it seemed to retain too much moisture. Perhaps I had pressed it too little. In any event, it was pleasing to taste, with a creamy, buttery flavor. Like the first, we and our guests eagerly consumed it.

My third and fourth cheeses attempted to improve on the first two. They were based on the same recipe and basically the same utensils, and the fourth differed from the others by being flavored with green peppercorns. For reasons I was unable to determine (perhaps that iodized salt was at fault?), the third was less than fully successful. It was excessively hard and crumbly, had a texture with relatively large crevices, and tasted somewhat acidic. In contrast, cheese #4 had a good texture and a pleasing flavor, although the flavor of the peppercorns may have overpowered any imperfections in the cheese.

In the interlude between my fourth and fifth cheeses, I finally decided to try my hand at cheese curds. I went through an elaborate recipe found on the Internet. It included cheddaring, the traditional process of stacking slabs of the curd after the whey was expelled, and milling the cheddared curd (i.e., cutting it into even-size pieces.) Unfortunately, the product was a disappointment. Although tasty, my cheese curds had the pasty color of cottage cheese and a smooth, slimy texture quite unlike the rubbery, squeaky cheese curds with which we are familiar. By that time I had even purchased a pH meter to help in determining the precise times to take critical steps in preparation, so it was not lack of technical sophistication that doomed this project. It could be that the protein strands in the curd did not knit properly because I performed the cheddaring incorrectly. Perhaps I gave up too soon, but that was my one and only attempt at making cheese curds.

Carroll's and Morris's recipe books gave me the opportunity to try making some different kinds of cheeses, and I next tried a traditional cheddar, made by a process much more involved than the one used for the farmhouse cheddars I had made previously. In succession I made a Colby, a Monterey jack, and a Gouda.

The Colby and Gouda were aged for 60 days, more or less, and were reasonably successful, or so it seemed. At any rate they were remarked upon favorably by guests, perhaps expressing pleasure and perhaps just politeness or kindness.

The traditional cheddar and the Monterey jack I tried aging for a full year, with poor results. The longer they aged, the more opportunity there was for something to go wrong. In both cases, the wax covering on them was insufficient to prevent the invasion of molds. The cheddar was partly salvageable and quite tasty, but the Monterey jack had spoiled completely.

To make better cheeses and to produce more reliably acceptable products, I need to solve the aging problem. Our ancient refrigerator wasn't suitable and even if modified with one of the available specialized

Out of the press. *After 24 hours of pressing, the curds have knitted into something beginning to look like a cheese.*

Waxing. *Some later cheeses were waxed, unlike the first, which was aged while wrapped in cheesecloth smeared with butter. In the waxing, a homemade double boiler keeps the wax from overheating.*

Aging cave. *My first cheese can be seen in its modified plastic storage box in a spare refrigerator. The thermometer permitted me to keep track of temperature and humidity, although regulating both proved to be a problem. My first cheeses were aged just over sixty days.*

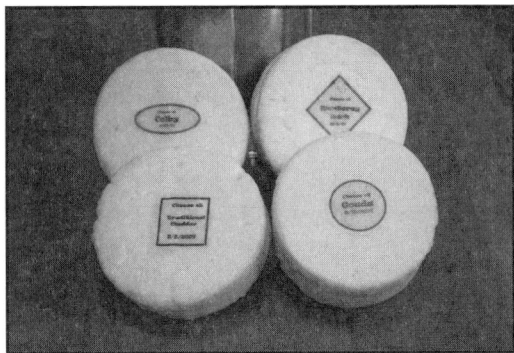

Waxed cheeses. *Later cheeses included several different types, shown here freshly waxed.*

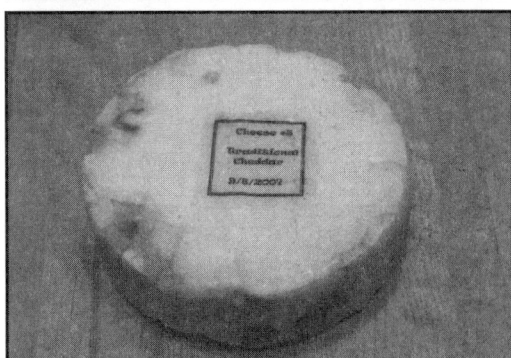

Inconsistent results. *Most of my cheeses were edible, including the cut peppercorn cheese in the upper image, which was quite good. The one below it was attacked by molds and was chalked up as a learning experience rather than a tasting one.*

controls, probably would be unable to overcome the wide variations in temperature in our Florida garage. I thought I could probably do much better with a wine cooler or compact refrigerator that could be kept inside the house. With minor adjustments, I thought I could probably overcome the humidity problem also. As appealing as the idea seemed, I have yet to find what I think will be an appropriate unit. In the meantime, the old garage refrigerator has been abandoned in the name of energy efficiency, and my making of aged cheeses is on hold until I find the right product.

In all these cheesemaking efforts I had wanted to get as complete a picture of its several aspects as I could, so I deliberately chose to make kinds of cheeses that involved all the processes commonly used. Otherwise, starting out with a simpler cheese might have been a better choice. Making fromage blanc, for example, is the essence of simplicity. A gallon of milk, a packet of commercial starter culture, and a stockpot in which to heat the milk are all that is needed. Perhaps a small amount of buttermilk could substitute for the starter culture. (Later I tried this and made not fromage blanc but instead a product very like buttermilk. It is probably worth the expense to purchase the specialized culture.) No cutting of curd, cooking, salting, pressing, or aging are involved. One simply heats the milk to 86°F, mixes in the starter culture, removes the pot from the heat, and lets the covered pot sit at room temperature for twelve hours. It is then drained in butter muslin (surely other fabrics would work) for up to twelve more hours, and voila! a simple fresh cheese is there for your use. I realized I had learned much more by making cheddars and other hard cheeses, but I had never tried making a fresh cheese. Perhaps I had missed something. Making fromage blanc would be a step backward—going from the difficult cheeses to an easy one. However, a minimum of effort would be required, I wouldn't have to solve my aging problem (my cheese aging problem, that is), and some readers might be encouraged by my experiences to try making this simple cheese themselves. It was late in my cheesemaking career, but I decided to give fromage blanc a try.

I followed the instructions, planning ahead so I wouldn't have to wake up in the middle of the night to start the draining. This time I tried using the trick we had learned from a would-be artisanal cheesemaker: I made my own nonhomogenized milk by mixing skim milk and heavy cream.

The process was as simple as promised, no glitches developed, and after very little effort and an inconsequential wait, the fromage blanc was ready. I found the hardest part of this cheesemaking exercise to be cleaning up. The product, regrettably but predictably, was not particularly interesting. It tasted like cheese curd—not the rubbery, salty kinds made after cheddaring but rather the pasty and sourish curd reminiscent of the early stages of hard cheesemaking. And now I had three-quarters of a pound of it and didn't know what I would do with it. Ricki Carroll's recipe suggested adding herbs or spices, but nothing came to mind right away. Dill weed? I couldn't decide. I resolved to try mixing some of it with diced green chiles and use it as a filling for enchiladas. If that proved to be edible, maybe some other use would come to mind.

As it turned out, the fromage blanc proved to be an excellent filling for enchiladas. I mixed about a half pound of it with a four-ounce can of chiles, added a bit of juice from pickled jalapeños, rolled the mixture in flour tortillas, and topped all with store-bought enchilada sauce before it went in the oven. The concoction came out great, and we loved it. The remaining cheese we turned into a spread by mixing it with rehydrated sun-dried tomatoes and a bit more of the jalapeño pickling juice. It was good also, and sometime soon we'll probably try making more fromage blanc.

Now I was through with cheesemaking, and it was time to get out of the kitchen again for a while.

Fromage blanc. The draining curd is shown in the image on the left and the finished cheese is seen on the right on the opened sac of muslin after draining for twelve hours. While arguably a cheese, fromage blanc only barely merits the designation.

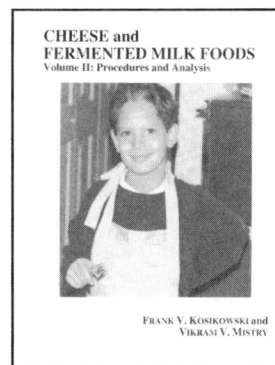

Instructions. Ricki Carroll's (top), is intended for home cheesemakers, and the two-volume reference by Kosikowski and Mistry (bottom) is focused on industrial cheesemaking.

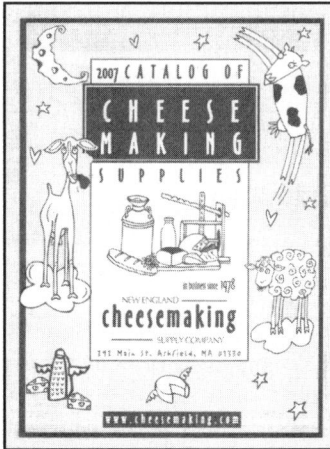

Supply catalog. *One of the catalogs regularly put out by New England Cheese Making Supply.*

Our pH meter. *It seemed to work fine but did not noticeably affect the quality of our cheeses.*

Short Take: A Renaissance in Cheesemaking Suppliers?

Without making any effort to do an exhaustive search, we discovered a surprising number and variety of companies whose business it is to supply cheesemakers with the equipment and materials needed. When we noted the number of such establishments catering to small-scale cheesemakers and hobbyists, we became convinced not only that farmstead and artisanal cheesemaking is far from a fringe activity but that the growing interest in cheese extends from the largest factory to the smallest kitchen.

Perhaps the most familiar and most accessible of the suppliers to home cheesemakers is the New England Cheesemaking Supply Company. Operated for the past thirty years by author and home cheesemaking guru Ricki Carroll, it caters to novices and very small cheesemakers, while at the same time providing easy-to-understand technical advice and high-quality merchandise needed by artisanal cheesemakers engaged in the serious business of earning a living. Those beginners just wanting to try cheesemaking without first coming up to speed on needed equipment, supplies, and materials can purchase kits, complete with printed instructions or informational DVDs.

Although probably the best-known purveyor of things needed by small-scale cheesemakers, Carroll is far being from the only one. Other firms fill similar roles. Some, like Carroll, specialize solely in cheesemaking and closely related activities such as making yogurt. Other suppliers include cheesemaking supplies in a range of farm and food-preparation materials. And still others specialize in supplying small cow or goat farms where cheeses are produced primarily for on-site or local consumption. The overlap is significant, but we noted some focused on cheesemaking as a hobby, others primarily serving those for whom cheesemaking is a business, and a broad range between them. For example, one can purchase from author/teacher/supplier Margaret Morris's Glengarry Cheesemaking and Dairy Supply, Ltd. in Canada, a 2-gallon home pasteurizer for less than $350, or a 50-gallon batch pasteurizer for more than $20,000. Likewise, one can get a pasteurizer as small as 25 gallons from Fromagex, another Canadian supplier, and a range of other batch pasteurizers in sizes up to 525 gallons. Larger pasteurizers tend to work on a flow-through rather than a batch process, and the largest cheesemakers would use these. Danlac, still another Canadian supplier, offers products for home, farm, and industry and separates them on the basis of the volumes of milk handled. In their classification scheme, home cheesemakers handle 1–10 liters (0.3–2.6 gallons), farm cheesemakers 10–500 liters (2.6–132 gallons), and industrial cheesemakers more than 500 liters (132 gallons).

One example of the continuum is provided by Dairy Connection, Inc. Beginning as a home-based supplier of cultures for home and hobbyist cheesemakers, the company has expanded to fill the needs of a rapidly expanding artisanal cheese movement. It provides smaller cheesemakers with cultures produced by Danisco, a Denmark-based multinational. Thus, technology available to the largest and most progressive European and American cheesemakers is also available for small-scale and home use. Research and product development underway by leaders in agricultural microbiology such as Danisco and Cargill employ biotechnology to "engineer" desired flavors in aged cheeses. It is possible that cultures designed to produce particular combinations of flavors in cheeses may soon be available for home use. Many farmstead and traditionalist cheesemakers might eschew the use of bioengineered cultures and could even be horrified by the prospect, but it seems democratic that the capability of producing designer cheeses is available to anyone willing and able to pay the price.

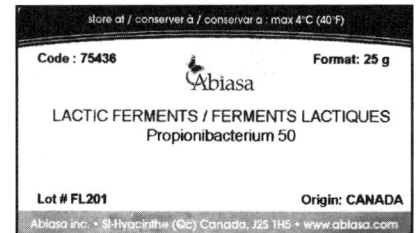

C6 - PROPIONIC SHERMANII

This bacteria is responsible for the taste and small eye formation in Swiss type cheeses. Add 1/16th tsp. directly into your milk for each gallon you are using. May be stored in the freezer for up to 1 year.

New England Cheesemaking Supply
85 Main St., Ashfield, MA 01330 Tele: 413-628-3808
www.cheesemaking.com

store at / conserver à / conservar a : max 4°C (40°F)

Code : 75436   Format: 25 g

Abiasa

LACTIC FERMENTS / FERMENTS LACTIQUES
Propionibacterium 50

Lot # FL201   Origin: CANADA

Abiasa inc. • St-Hyacinthe (Qc) Canada, J2S 1H5 • www.abiasa.com

Cheesemaking cultures. These are labels from a culture packet purchased for home cheesemaking. This packet contains Propionic shermanii, a bacterium responsible for generating the Carbon dioxide that produces the holes in Swiss-type cheeses.

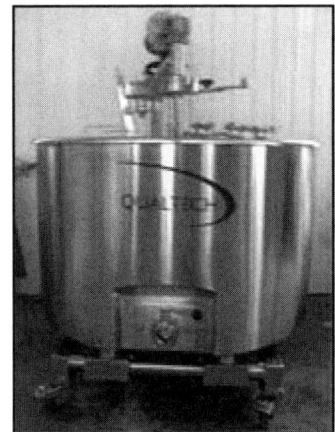

Small pasteurizer. This size might be used by small commercial cheesemakers.

Sampling homemade cheeses. *Friends and family were offered the opportunity to sample some of our cheeses. Some at least, evoked favorable reactions as can be seen in the images above. To our knowledge, no one suffered any serious health problems from eating our cheeses.*

Part Three:

Mainstream Cheesemaking

as told by Russ

To put the new American cheese into perspective, we felt we first had to learn more about the other kind—mainstream—cheesemaking and discover what it had become. We knew a bit about the history, with its rush to enlarge and consolidate, but we lacked any real knowledge of the state of corporate cheesemaking in the twenty-first century.

We were fortunate to get a sense of the business by visits to five cheese factories at which we either took factory tours or interviewed managers in their offices. Later we interviewed another manager by phone. The first section of Part Three describes our initial chance encounter with the business of cheesemaking. Visiting the others, we were surprised by the diversity we found, and our findings are the subjects of the second section. Finally, in readings and discussions with individuals, we learned of some of the challenges faced by the industry. Those challenges, with special emphasis on smaller cheese factories in the Adirondack Crescent, we relate in the third section.

Large scale cheesemaking. *Milk storage silos at a large cheese factory we visited. A steady stream of tanker trucks brought milk to this facility.*

Changing landscapes. *One of a large number of abandoned and deteriorating farm buildings in the Adirondack Crescent.*

The Summer with No Cheese Curds

On one of our annual visits to the Adirondacks we again found ourselves driving the 50 miles from Star Lake in the western foothills to tiny Heuvelton in the St. Lawrence River valley. Our first visit had piqued our interest in cheesemaking and we wanted to learn more. Also, we were looking for cheese curds and hoped to track them down at the source.

Passing through what had long been prime dairy land, we were more engaged with our surroundings than on our earlier visit. We expected to see lush pastures dotted almost everywhere with black and white cows. Instead, we drove past farm after farm with barns and silos falling down, overgrown and long unused, and we saw almost no cattle. Most houses seemed to be occupied, but only at a few could we detect any evidence of farming. Perhaps one in five or ten appeared to have herds and to be actively engaged in dairying. Although we saw small

The Heritage Cheese House. Seen here as it appeared during our later successful run to bring back cheese curds. We also loaded up on extra sharp cheddar.

General store in Wanakena, New York. No cheese curds were available here in the summer of 2006.

groups of beef cattle here and there, dairy cows in pastures were scarce. Some barns we saw were in good condition and might have been jam-packed with cows, and we thought a few farmers could be practicing confined feeding.

I thought it might be interesting to conduct an informal survey of dairy farms along our route, estimating how many remained active and how many had been abandoned. But I quickly gave up. Most of the time, I couldn't tell if the farmhouse and its farm were still connected in any economic or organic sense. Houses often had pickup trucks parked in the driveways, but I knew that didn't mean anybody was using them for farm chores. As in other rural areas, trucks are more common than cars whether their owners do any farming or work only in town. We guessed more than a few of the homes might belong to retired farmers who had sold off their herds and lands but kept their houses.

As we drove on, the scenery changed a bit. Occasional well-maintained farms with small herds of cattle in pastures and austere houses came at first as a surprise. We began to understand, however, when one of us saw a black buggy and soon after we noticed that parked near most of the better-looking farms were horse-drawn buggies or wagons, and sometimes children in nineteenth century garb could be seen helping with chores. We had entered Amish country.

On visits in other years we had bought cheese curds at the IGA in Star Lake and at the Wanakena General Store, a few miles up Route 3. Failing to find them at either place this time, we attached ourselves to the grapevine and picked up a rumor that the primary supplier, the little cheese factory in Heuvelton, had closed. Once before we had stopped in Heuvelton to visit the factory store, curious to see the place and sample what it had to offer. We had met the cheesemaker himself on that trip and heard that almost all of his milk came from local Amish farmers.

This year of no cheese curds, the rumor circulating

in Star Lake and Wanakena was of a split within the Amish community. One informant speculated that the cheesemaker was Amish—a problem because Old Order Amish are forbidden by their traditions from using electricity or electrically powered machinery. The community, the rumor held, was sharply divided over whether it was acceptable for one of its members to be operating the factory, with its modern machinery. That disagreement led to the resignation of the cheesemaker and shutdown of the factory. Without the factory to accept their milk, the Amish farmers were dumping it— just spilling it on the ground—because they had nowhere to sell it.

Being somewhat familiar with the factory, when we heard the rumor we couldn't resist driving over to Heuvelton to check it all out. Someone had told us the store connected to the factory was still open, selling off its stock of cheeses. The possibility that some cheeses remained would have been reason enough to go, but a possible opportunity to learn something we could contribute to the grapevine was also a strong motivator.

Amish buggy. *This was parked near the entrance to the Heritage Cheese factory store in Heuvelton, New York.*

After passing by the Village of Heuvelton welcome sign, the gas station and convenience store, the fire house, and a few blocks of prim houses, we arrived at the main intersection. Turning right we passed the tiny Protestant and Catholic churches, and in a quarter mile or so we saw a sign: Heritage Cheese House. We hadn't noticed the sign when we visited the factory earlier. It announced a little complex of buildings: the cheese factory, now dark; a store selling furniture and other products handmade on the Amish farms; and the cheese store, which we were happy to see was indeed open.

Inside the approximately 10' x 20' store, we learned only hard cheeses were left. As reported, not a cheese curd was to be found. We asked the clerk which cheeses had been made on site and then picked out two large pieces—a three-pound chunk of extra sharp cheddar and a smaller wedge of raw milk cheddar —from the cooler on the left, skipping the one on the right with cheeses brought in from other factories in

Heritage Cheese. *The welcoming sign along state route 812 in Heuvelton.*

the region. We said something like "We heard the factory might be closed," hoping to get a blow-by-blow account of what had been happening so we could satisfy our curiosity with new bits of data.

All the clerk gave us (besides a bag of ice to keep our cheese fresh in the cooler we had brought for the return trip) was the information that the factory was in the midst of a "change of ownership."

Later we were to learn more. Conversations with acquaintances in the area told us there had been an influx of Amish to the St. Lawrence Valley. They were said to be escaping urbanization elsewhere and taking advantage of rich and undervalued dairy land set in a depressed and distressed local economy. Most local people welcomed the newcomers because they bought and continued to operate farms the former owners had struggled and failed to operate profitably. These new Amish owners were making a go of it and thereby giving a lift to the local economy. And by all accounts, arrival in this place was beneficial to the new owners as well; local lore had it that the calcium-rich soils of the St. Lawrence Valley produced forage unequaled as nourishment for cows making cheese milk.

Reports we later found in newspaper archives shed a little different, less dramatic light on the story and a less conflict-laden take on the closing than the one the rumor mill had provided. They told of an earlier cheese factory in the region that had relied on the Amish milk. It had folded, and this one had opened to replace it. They reported that volatility in the cheese business, excessive inventories, and an overworked cheesemaker had caused the Heuvelton factory to close, rather than disagreement among the Amish. Like many rumors, there was at least a hint of truth in the one we had heard. The Amish farmers were in a bind. Dependent on the factory, they could not operate it themselves and needed to find an outsider who would run it for them. One newspaper article, dated in early July 2006, told that the factory would be reopening under new management in early August. We thought that curious; the suggestion that the factory might not be economically viable and the news it would be reopening under new management didn't add up. We figured there must be more to the story.

Regardless of what had caused the problem that led to our not eating any cheese curds that summer, the temporary closing had a large regional impact. The plant was essential to the economic well-being and sustainability of the 95 Amish-operated dairy farms in the area. Their milk, never being refrigerated, is salable only if it can be used locally and promptly. Their handling practices do not meet government regulatory standards for sanitation and storage of "Grade A" milk, only "Grade B." We learned that the most difficult Grade A requirement was to refrigerate the milk within two hours after harvesting. Grade B milk cannot be sold directly to consumers. It can be used only in "manufactured dairy products," with cheese production being one of the few viable alternatives.

Luckily for the region, the closing was indeed only temporary. The factory had been reopened by the time we went back a year later. We never got the whole story of the closing, but we bought aged cheese and curds and heard how the immediate problem for the Amish farmers was solved by the establishment of an entity called the Heuvelton Community Irrevocable Trust. Taking over operation of the factory, the trust received substantial funding from the farmers and from outside sources having vested interests in the future of the community. The trust hired a cheesemaker and managed the business. The Amish farmers were able to hold equity interests in the trust and thereby in Heritage Cheese, but factory operations were the responsibility of non-Amish employees of the trust. It was a clever, unique solution to keep the factory and its milk suppliers afloat.

Only later did it strike us that the problems faced by the Amish farmers because they eschew modern technology were in no small part the same ones faced by early dairy farmers in the region. And, as with

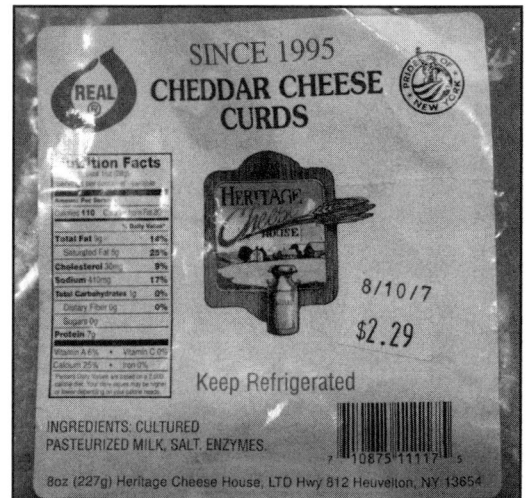

Cheese curds. *A package of the sought-after curds, obtained when they were once again available in the summer of 2007.*

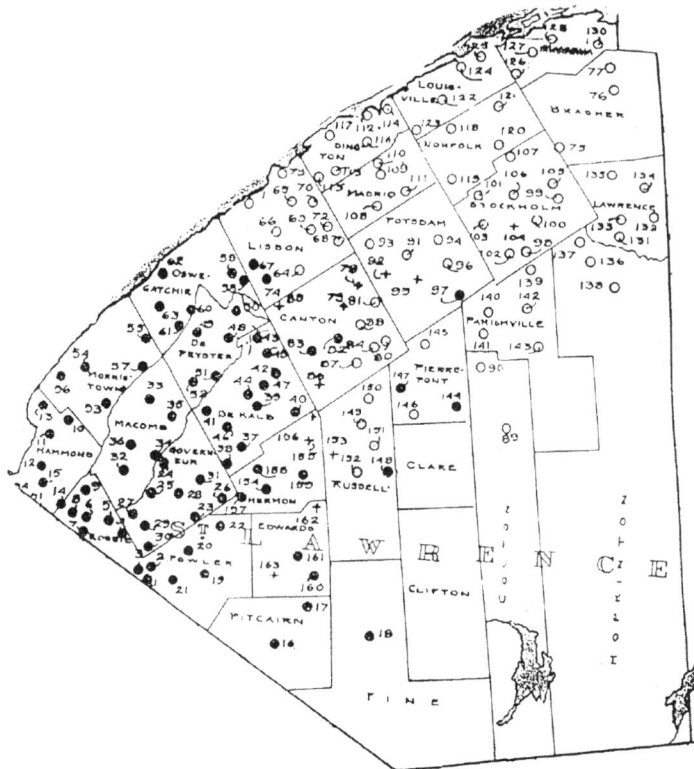

Cheese map. *This map shows the locations of cheese (solid circles), butter (open circles), and cheese and butter (plus signs) factories in St. Lawrence County, New York. This county map appears to be a tracing of the statewide map, a copy of which we saw in the New York State Museum of Cheese. Cheese factories were not developed in the southern part of the county because the mountainous Adirondacks were unsuitable for dairy farming. The northern part of the county is in the St. Lawrence River valley. Note that cheese factories are concentrated in the southwestern portion of the valley and butter factories in the north-eastern portion. We could not discover what became of the skim milk left over from production in the butter factories. Some of it could have been passed on to nearby cheese factories, but it seems that rail transportation would have been necessary to transport it the 30+ miles from the northeastern corner of the county to the nearest cheese factory.*

the modern Amish, solutions in the nineteenth century frequently involved cheese factories.

That the Amish dairy farmers were in a time warp—caught somewhere in historical crosscurrents—became clearer to us after we did some research on the history of cheesemaking in the region.

A fortunate early find was the excellent *The History of Cheese-Making in New York State*, published by Eunice R. Stamm in 1991. It is packed with detailed information that begins with the earliest Dutch settlers in the Hudson Valley and extends all the way to the time of its publication. We discovered some bland volumes of agricultural statistics and general historical accounts to be helpful also.

A few pieces of our still frameless cheese puzzle began to fit together. The revolution that was to transform cheesemaking in the Adirondack Crescent and far beyond began in Rome, New York, in 1851 with Jesse Williams's decision to pool milk from his dairy with that of his son, and later with other nearby farms, and to centralize local cheese production in a single factory. His factory changed everything because all cheeses had formerly been produced at individual farms. Williams freely shared his ideas and the technical developments that made them work, and we found it fascinating because this tradition of sharing seems somehow to have been passed down to the new American cheesemakers (more about this later). Because of Williams's insights and his willingness to share them, by 1900 the number of factories in the area was more than 600 and formed the traces on the landscape that we have dubbed the Adirondack Crescent. It was no arbitrary choice that placed the New York State Museum of Cheese in the city of Rome, where it all began.

With the factory system came economies in the purchases of equipment and supplies and in the storage, transport, and marketing of finished cheeses. Full-time cheesemakers managed the factories, performing the delicate tasks needed to ensure high-quality cheeses. No longer were farm families part-time cheesemakers. Various authors have noted that what had formerly been a home-centered almost exclusively female undertaking, along with cooking, canning, and preserving, became the province of factory employees, who were mostly men.

We learned with the help of century-old state-compiled statistics that in 1902 the 618 factories in the Adirondack Crescent produced a total of 67,275,922

The New York State Museum of Cheese, in Erie Canal Village in Rome, New York. Near the site of Jesse Williams's first cheese factory, it was moved from another site in the vicinity. Being adjacent to the canal facilitated transport: milk was brought in by wagons, but cheeses could be shipped to distant population centers via the canal. The restored building contains numerous displays depicting the history of cheesemaking in New York.

pounds of cheese. That's a bit more than 100,000 pounds per factory. The number of factories was large because basic problems of isolation and inadequate transportation still had not been overcome 50 years after the factory system began. Thus, "crossroads cheese factories" dotted the dairying landscape, in a regular and almost ubiquitous distribution, providing ready access for farms. A somewhat smaller, but still significant, concentration of cheese factories grew up in southwestern New York State. Like the Heuvelton Amish, dairy farmers of the early twentieth century needed nearby factories where they could take their milk in horse-drawn wagons before it spoiled.

Only when motorized transportation became widely available in the early decades of the twentieth century could milk travel relatively long distances. The advent of the railroads had a significant effect on cheesemaking by creating larger markets for fluid milk. Instead of bringing milk to the cheese factory, a farmer could bring it to a nearby railhead. Loading their milk onto trains gave farmers an alternative market, and often a more lucrative one. Even today, when most milk is no longer transported by train, the term "milk runs" is still used to describe routes with many stops over relatively short distances.

Once milk could be transported quickly by train all the way from the farm to the milk-drinking public in cities, consumption increased dramatically and markets for milk became competitive. Cheese was no longer the only game in town. Trains also made it possible to consolidate cheese production. Cheese factories could be farther than a wagon ride from farms. They could be larger and more strategically located, resulting in economies of scale in production and in marketing efficiencies. As these advantages came into play, it became difficult for small factories to overcome the advantages of larger ones.

We could see why the number of small factories declined precipitously in the Adirondack Crescent. Railroads killed the "crossroads factories," and progressively larger factories outcompeted the smaller ones on costs.

Milk delivery. *Wagonloads of milk in cans are arriving at what may be either a cheese factory or, more likely, a rail stop.* Image courtesy of the New York State Museum of Cheese.

A cheesemaking couple loaned us a copy of the 2001 *St. Lawrence County Agricultural Development Plan*. It might sound like a dull read, but it gave us a unique overview of past and present agriculture in the Adirondack Crescent. Of particular interest was a section by county historian Trent Turlock that gives a broad overview of the role of cheesemaking within the development of the agricultural economy in the region. He tells of the explosive growth of cheesemaking in the county; the first factory was built in 1863, and by 1900 there were 99 cheese factories, 67 butter factories, and 20 butter and cheese factories. Encased in its unpretentious three-ring binder, this account was another fortunate find. It made us mindful of the sweep of history and its role in the things we were discovering. We celebrated its finding by nibbling on cheese curds, washed down with glasses of red wine.

The strict regulatory environment that limits the uses to which milk produced by present-day Amish dairy farmers can be put also has historical connections with trends within the dairy industry. Beginning in the

Although cheese production in St. Lawrence County was never completely abandoned, and continues today, the following statement suggests that the great majority of the 8,000 farms in the county in 1900 began shifting to fluid milk marketing within a decade.

"Beginning in about 1910 this butter and cheese making gave way to the production of fluid milk production for the New York Market. This is the situation today. Right or wrong, the section turned wholly to the production of milk for sale in various forms. St. Lawrence County is the largest milk producing county in the state."

[Webster, 1945, *St. Lawrence County: Past and Present.* Quoted in the St. Lawrence County Agricultural Plan.]

earliest decades of the twentieth century, regulations enforcing standards to protect quality and ensure consumer safety became another major factor in the decline of small factories. Meeting these regulations was burdensome to small and large factories alike. Deficient equipment or unsophisticated operators existed at both. But the larger factories were better able to raise the capital needed for improvements and to acquire more technical expertise. Smaller factories had trouble operating economically while paying for upgrades. Many went out of business or were bought out by competitors.

We found that in the first years of the twenty-first century, 100 years after the dots representing the 600 plus cheese factories formed our crescent around the Adirondacks, the number of factories in that region had dwindled to only a handful. Some of the largest were owned by multinational corporations or conglomerates best known for their tobacco products. Despite their small numbers, the large factories turned out millions of pounds of cheeses annually compared to the thousands of pounds produced by each "crossroads" predecessor.

In more recent times the larger factories' business advantages have not completely protected them from the economic realities which are becoming more severe in the newest century. The big fish that ate the little fish were falling prey to even bigger fish. Early in the twenty-first century, most of the large factories in the region surrounding the Adirondacks, like their crossroads predecessors, were disappearing.

St. Lawrence County's little Heritage Cheese House had become for us a Rosetta stone, helping us to understand more fully the economic and cultural shifts that took cheese from farms to factories. At the same time, we saw its products and its very existence cherished by a new wave of cheese lovers who valued its links to the ascendant local and artisanal food traditions. Having more in common with Jesse Williams's first cheese factory than with modern corporate giants, and poised to serve a discerning twenty-first-century clientele, it seemed to span 150 years of change. Part of of the little factory seemed rooted in the days of the earliest cheese factories, and the other part was emerging with the pioneers who were bringing us the new American cheeses.

Cicero, New York cheese factory in 1968. *Many old-style cheese factories persisted until the mid-twentieth century, often producing specialty cheeses with limited markets. This one, producing mozzarella and pizza cheese, was soon overtaken when the corporate giants discovered a growing market for these cheeses.* Image courtesy of the Town of Cicero historian.

Fine, N. Y. *June 21* 191 *5*

Mr. *Loyd Ward*

IN ACCOUNT WITH

White Clover Cheese Factory

No. of Sale. *10*

Cheese sold from. *June 8* to. *17*

No. of Boxes in Sale. *135*

Local Sales *261 # Butter @ 27*

No. Pounds Cheese in Sale. *10456*

Price per Pound. *14⅞*

Amount received for Sale, $. *1547.38*

Expense of Sale, $. *161.96*

No. Pounds Milk to Pound of Cheese. *9.09*

Your Milk *1423*

Net per Hundred, $. *1.3388*

Butter Drawn Out by You. *10#*

Balance Due You, $. *16.35*

F. ROY KILBOURN, Sec'y and Treas.

Short Take: The White Clover Cheese Factory

Here are an undated photograph of the White Clover Cheese Factory, Town of Fine, St. Lawrence County, New York, and a receipt from the same factory, dated June 21, 1915. As we struggled to make out the entries on the receipt, we concluded that Loyd Ward was receiving payment for the portion of milk from his dairy used in the production of 135 boxes of cheese totaling 10,456 pounds. The factory operator received $1,547.38 for the sale, from which he deducted $161.96 to cover his operating expenses. We calculated that at 9.09 pounds of milk for each pound of cheese produced, on the order of 95,000 pounds of milk would have been consumed. Of this total, Mr. Ward's milk contributed a relatively minor 1,423 pounds. For this he received $16.35. Also in the mix are some transactions involving butter. Apparently the factory partially skimmed the milk, withdrawing 261 pounds of fat to make butter. Mr. Ward took 10 pounds of this for his own use. Mr. Ward's proceeds therefore were $19.05 for the milk, at 1.3388 cents per pound, minus $2.70 for 10 pounds of butter at 27 cents per pound. We aren't sure that he got a good deal on the butter, as the butterfat content in his own milk appears not to have been taken into account.

Note that the receipt shows June 8 to 17 as dates when 10,456 pounds of cheese were sold, not made. The same plant produced only 66,564 pounds of cheese in all of 1902, and it seems likely that cheeses sold during the period on the receipt were produced over a much longer period. Note also that the $161.96 withdrawn by the factory for operating expenses was apparently a fixed amount, rather than a portion of the sale price.

We thank Jean Grimm, Town of Fine Historian, for copies of the photograph and receipt.

Short Take: Cheesemaking
and Social Progress

We got wind of and later obtained a copy of the scholarly *Transforming Rural Life* by Sally McMurry. The author explains the social effects of historical changes in the cheese business, specifically the arrival of cheese factories. Her studies focus on New York State's Oneida County, on the southern flank of the Adirondack Crescent. One effect she explores in depth is the way in which the advent of factories changed the lives of farm women. Arrival of the factories freed them from cheesemaking, which had been one of their most demanding chores. This newfound freedom led ultimately to a whole range of advances in the status of American women in general—for example, in the growth of women's colleges. She mentions Mount Holyoke College as one example.

In a curious twist, with much justification, many people credit the rebirth of American cheese to the return of women to cheesemaking. We might still be awaiting the arrival of the new American cheese had it not been for the influence of pioneers like Laura Chenel, Mary Keehn, Allison Hooper, and Paula Lambert. So perhaps it was men who nearly ruined American cheese!

Cheese room. *This one appears to be in a farm-based dairy.* Image courtesy of the New York State Museum of Cheese.

Short Take: Cheesemaking and Dairyland History

In a chapter prepared for the *St. Lawrence County Agricultural Development Plan*, County Historian Trent Turlock recognizes four eras in the development of the agricultural economy of St. Lawrence County, New York. The St. Lawrence valley may not equally represent all parts of the Adirondack Crescent; some counties were clearly more isolated than others and slower to feel the benefits of improvements in transportation. Nevertheless, if one takes into account these differences, Turlock's eras probably apply generally all across the region because the counties are similar geographically and demographically.

St. Lawrence County cheese factory. The date of this photo is unknown. Month and days can be made out but no year is visible on the poster for the county fair. Image courtesy of the New York State Museum of Cheese.

The first he calls the <u>Ash</u> era. As land was being cleared for agriculture, it was possible to derive income from the manufacture and sale of potash. Potash is the name given to a family of potassium containing compounds that are a byproduct of clearing land for cultivation. Produced from burning wood, these chemical compounds were used for a variety of purposes— for example, in making lye for soap production. Potash was easier to transport than lumber, and, shipped to Montreal and sold, it was an important source of cash.

This era was followed by one Turlock simply calls Sheep. Sheep-herding was the dominant agricultural activity in St. Lawrence County between 1845 and 1865. Like potash, wool was not perishable and could be shipped to distant markets using the relatively poor transportation infrastructure of the time.

The era of Cheese Factories began in the second half of the nineteenth century and became the primary agricultural activity in the county by 1865. The importance of dairying grew rapidly with the coming of the cheese factories, and dairying continues today as the mainstay of local agriculture.

Turlock's final era, which began early in the twentieth century and still persists, he calls Milk-Marketing. This era resulted from the arrival of improvements in transportation and technology. Consequently, markets for fluid milk, rather than for cheese, are the forces driving local agriculture. Unfortunately, milk marketing nationwide, and particularly in the Northeast, is experiencing hard times, and it has been a fading source of wealth for the region for several decades.

Short Take: A Century-Old Cheese Transaction

It is a strange feeling to look at a financial document more than 125 years old and find oneself examining it using the exact patterns employed while examining a modern tax statement, medical bill, or real estate settlement sheet. Of course times were simpler in the nineteenth century, but not so simple as to avoid the necessity of making sure the numbers add up properly.

Thanks to Town of Cicero, New York, historian Thomas Mafrici, we obtained this copy of a May 28, 1883, sales record. It records a transaction in which dairyman John Matchie (if we read his name correctly) received payment for milk he delivered to this Madison County factory. In this instance as in others we observed, the factory was a cooperative; dairymen received payment based on a portion of the sales price of the cheese produced, with factory managers deducting amounts needed for processing

of the milk into cheese. We were struck with the apparent longevity of this process; it resembles contemporary practices in which USDA–determined "make allowances" set the remittances commodity cheesemakers receive from cheese sales. As in Matchie's long-gone century, the benefits and burdens of fluctuations in market prices are borne by the farmers.

The handwriting on the Bridgeport document is faded, but it appears that the factory sold 50 cheeses weighing a total of 2,841 pounds. They were made from May 1 to May 14 (inclusive), and 32,739 pounds of milk were consumed in the process. Thus, each pound of cheese required 11.57 pounds of milk. The factory received 11⅝ cents per pound for the cheese, for a gross income of $330.27.

Mr. Matchie provided 1,982 pounds of milk of the total used. Operators of the factory deducted $1.35 for each 100 pounds of cheese produced. After deduction of this amount, the net amount due Mr. Matchie was $17.82. We could not discover the significance of the 16.36 written after the initials at the bottom of the document.

We tried two different ways of going through the calculations, arriving at $17.67 due to Mr. Matchie when calculated on the basis of the amount of milk provided and $17.58 when based on the amount of cheese sold. It is possible that he was overpaid by a few cents, but more likely we incorrectly interpreted some of the smudged numbers.

Factory Cheesemaking

Milk storage silos. *These are part of a cheese factory in Ogdensburg, New York as they appeared during a visit in 2009.*

At first we saw the new independent, artisan cheesemakers, as a product of—or a reaction to—more than a century of changes in the production of American cheeses. The crescent of dots on the map we had seen that day at the New York State Museum of Cheese in Rome was clearly gone. We imagined the ever-larger factories that obliterated the Adirondack Crescent as giants gobbling up its dots. This led us to wonder about the current status of factory cheesemaking in the Adirondack Crescent and elsewhere. Were the larger factories really predators? Where were the descendents of all those Adirondack Crescent cheese factories, and what was happening to them? Could we hang onto our faint notion that perhaps the cheese industry, after thoroughly transforming itself from farms to factories, was even now reinventing itself in response to the evolving preferences of the American public?

Thus factory cheesemaking captured our interest. We didn't have a good idea what modern cheese factories were like, but we felt they were an essential part of the story we were tracking down.

We expected to see a great deal of daylight between factory cheesemakers and the newly emerging artisanal and farmstead cheese producers. Despite our lack of hard knowledge, we thought we had a good idea what had become of the Adirondack Crescent's cheesemakers. The successors to Jesse Williams's first cheese factory would be huge facilities, receiving milk from hundreds of farms. Likely, they would be turning out ton after ton of cheddar, mozzarella, or other familiar cheeses, sending out some good cheeses and some mostly bland and often undistinguished— but always predictable—products to the far corners of the nation and the world. Much of their cheese, we guessed, would go on to other factories where it would be processed into products valued for their convenience, be sprayed on crackers, or otherwise become an ingredient in snack food.

We were not to be disappointed. We did find examples at least superficially fitting those stereotyped assumptions. More intriguingly, few of the factory cheesemakers we encountered seemed to fit nicely into the neat categories we had prepared for them. The lines between the old, the new, the industrial, and the artisanal were much less sharply drawn than we had imagined. And the reality provided a better story than the one we had imagined. Creativity, it appears, is not confined to the artisan's studio, and it certainly is not absent from some factory floors.

We visited five cheese factories, two large, two small, and one somewhere in between. They varied, of course, in degree of specialization, division of labor, and automation. Some fit well our notion of what we call mainstream cheese factories. Others were operated by "new" cheesemakers and were quite unlike our expectations. Most people would recognize them as factories without hesitation; nevertheless, their products would meet consumers' expectations of artisanal cheeses—those made in relatively small batches under the close supervision of master cheesemakers. Factories were sometimes making artisanal-style cheeses, and artisanal cheesemakers were sometimes using factory processes.

Three of our factory visits were field trips offered during the American Cheese Society annual conferences we attended. They were guided tours of the Cabot Creamery and Vermont Butter and Cheese facilities, both in Vermont, and the Roth Käse USA factory in Wisconsin. The other two were interviews with managers at McCadam Cheese and the Heritage Cheese House, both in New York State. (Later we got to interview a representative of another New York State factory cheesemaker, and we tell what we learned from her at the end of Part Three.)

Cabot is a very large factory and Heritage a very small one. The number of kinds of cheeses produced in the factories ranged from many at Roth Käse and McCadam to few at Heritage. We believed we saw the most innovation at Roth Käse and Vermont Butter and Cheese. Surprisingly, the variety of cheeses produced and degree of automation at factories seemed to be unrelated. Cabot, McCadam, and Heritage came closest to what we considered mainstream in terms of their products and methods. Vermont Butter and Cheese was farthest from the mainstream. Larger factories had few things in common with each other, smaller factories little resembled other small factories, and so forth.

We visited the Cabot Creamery's home plant in Cabot, Vermont. Cabot is part of a large, 1,000-plus-member dairy cooperative and is unabashedly an industrial operation. Cabot's managers were gracious hosts; we received cheese snacks and samples of microbrewery beers that were more than welcome when we toured on a warm midsummer day. They gave us an overview and then a detailed tour.

We toured the plant in street clothes while separated from the cheesemaking by glass partitions. Despite this separation, we had a good view of the operations and seemed not to be isolated from the atmosphere of the cheese rooms; it was hot and humid, and the concrete floors on which we walked seemed perpetually damp. The smells, obviously filtered by the plant's air-handling equipment, were a strange mixture with faint traces of cheese and machine oil. Muffled sounds of machines and people penetrated the glass.

This plant produces cheddar cheese, and during our visit was also turning out sour cream. We watched the sour cream containers as they traveled along on a conveyor belt after being filled by a machine. Don't be surprised, the tour leader told us, when you note that the names on the labels don't say Cabot. They bore instead the name of another well-known dairy products company. The practice apparently is common and a poorly kept trade secret; a Cabot product in a supermarket and a usually less expensive store brand beside it might have come from this same

Cheese vat. *These are in the Cabot factory in Cabot, Vermont. Cheddar cheeses have traditionally been made in open vats because the process of cheddaring requires that slabs of curd be manually stacked and restacked in the vat bottoms to facilitate drainage of whey.*

Cheddar ready for aging. *Blocks of cheese, each weighing 40 pounds at the Cabot plant. Cube-shaped blocks are wrapped in a special plastic material, then placed in corrugated cardboard cartons. They will be aged in these containers before being cut and packaged for sale.*

Cheese hoops. *These molds with packed curds are shown being pressed in the Cabot plant. Old-style round cheeses are made 100 or more at a time for cut-to-order cheese shops.*

factory or even the same batch. The packages showing the identity of the non-Cabot brand sour cream were the only things in the plant we were asked not to photograph.

As in all cheesemaking, the Cabot factory produces its cheese in batches, rather than in a strict assembly-line manner. As far as we could discover, no one has yet been able to make cheese by continuously feeding milk into one end of a series of machines and having a steady stream of cheese come out the other. The classic *I Love Lucy* show where Lucy can't keep up with the conveyor belt of candy could have been filmed in the packing department of a cheese factory, but not in its cheesemaking departments. Nevertheless, even though machines did not do everything, various things in the Cabot plant were moving about on conveyors, making it look and feel like an industrial operation.

We learned the plant we visited is not Cabot's biggest. A larger one in Middlebury, Vermont is capable of producing 150,000 pounds of cheddar cheese each day. By way of comparison, I had been playing around with some old statistics and realized that this *daily* amount is greater than the average *annual* production of each of the 1,140 cheese factories operating in the whole of New York State in 1902. I did some rough calculations and figured the Middlebury Cabot plant's annual production might actually exceed the annual output of nearly half of all those early twentieth-century plants. And we had USDA figures showing that the annual production of 11 Vermont cheesemakers in 2008 was in excess of 149 million pounds. In contrast, our calculations based on the old statistics showed that in 1902 the 1,140 New York State factories produced less than 119 million pounds. Thus, the output of each modern plant is more than 1,000 times the output of those old factories.

Everything about the operation of the plant we visited seemed to us to say "large." Most of its cheddar cheese ends up in 40-pound cube-shaped boxes. Curds are pressed, vacuum wrapped in plastic film, and encased in corrugated cardboard boxes, all in an assembly-line fashion. The cheese is actually aged in those boxes. The cube shape facilitates efficient storage during aging, and then during transport, and makes it easier to cut the 40-pound blocks into smaller packages. From the big cubes come the familiar bricks of Cabot cheese we buy at the grocery store — 80 eight-ounce packages.

Unlike grocery stores, retail cheese shops usually cut and wrap cheeses on site and prefer traditional wheels of cheese. The Cabot factory also has banks of hydraulic gang presses, capable of pressing hundreds of wheels simultaneously. Large production volumes, a small number of similar products — the cheeses differ primarily in the length of time they are aged — and a high degree of organization characterized the plant.

I was surprised to see that Cabot used old-style rectangular, open cheese vats. Perhaps it kept them in part, I thought, because they give visitors like us a much more detailed and informative view of the cheesemaking process than modern enclosed vats would. This naïve notion was brushed away when I recalled that the traditional process of cheddaring requires slabs of cheese curd to be cut, stacked, and restacked in the bottom of vats to help separate curds from whey and encourage knitting of their protein framework. Later I did read of plants in which draining, matting, and cheddaring are done in a closed vat, presumably by an automated process, but Cabot was using traditional processes.

I mentioned that the factory was producing both cheddar cheese and sour cream the day we visited. I might have expected this but had not. It seems that many large cheese factories are parts of even larger entities often called "dairy products plants." They may manufacture other dairy products such as butter, sour cream, yogurt, and ice cream as well as cheese. Some may even bottle fluid milk. This diversification of products permits them to respond efficiently to changes in supply and demand. Supply, that is to say the milk that cows or other dairy animals produce,

Sizes of 1140 Cheese Factories
in New York State in 1902
(pounds produced annually)

Average = 104,092
(smallest 1,232; largest 1,454,123)

90% between 30,000 and 207,869

75% between 45,000 and 155,000

59% less than 100,000

is not easily controlled by cheesemakers. Farmers may have some ability to increase or decrease the amounts of milk produced by their herds, but this is not as simple or as rapid as turning a spigot. The cows have to be milked, the milk sold if possible, and somehow both farmers and cheesemakers have to manage things so they can operate at a profit.

Factories can manage fluctuations in demand by diverting the flow of arriving milk from cheesemaking to other products. If cheese is accumulating faster than it's being sold, switching to the production of yogurt, for example, might help to balance inventories.

After we'd observed this diversification at a couple of factories, a news item appearing on the Web cast it in a broader light. The ability of the factories to deal with supply and demand problems is a value both to them and to dairy farmers, but it is often not enough. The article told of a huge increase in the government stockpile of powdered milk. It said that the U.S. government purchases powdered milk, a dairy product with a very long storage life, in order to help damp down fluctuations in supply and demand, thereby stabilizing prices dairy farmers receive. Any cheesemaker who had to turn every pound of milk delivered into cheese might suffer out-of-control inventories in times of slack demand. One option would be to stop buying milk, but this would be a difficult choice, particularly when a dairy cooperative was the factory owner or when some other special relationship had been developed between the cheesemakers and the dairies supplying them.

I had heard of the government buying surplus cheese as part of some commodity stabilization program, and I remember hearing that some of it was provided for school lunches and used in nutrition programs for low-income families. (We were amused when we came across a music video called *Commodity Cheese Blues*. Made on the Menominee Indian Reservation in Wisconsin, it appears to have been inspired by the large and numbing role this food has in reservation cuisine.)

I was led to wonder, however, what would be done with all the powdered milk the government has been stockpiling. I was aware that it can be used in some kinds of cheesemaking as a way of fortifying fluid milk but doubted this could handle the huge volumes held by the government. And powdered milk seems to have relatively little use as a consumer product; we usually have some of the stuff around the house to use in emergencies, such as when we're out of milk needed for a recipe and don't feel like going to the store for it. But it was difficult to imagine using it more than a few times each year. It would have only very limited use as an animal feed because humans are the only adult mammals able to digest lactose. I vaguely remember hearing of some of it being shipped abroad to alleviate famine. Maybe at this very moment shiploads of it are on their way to hunger-stricken parts of Africa.

Even though Cabot is unquestionably a large cheesemaker, I was later in for a surprise when I came across some USDA statistics on the production of cheeses by state. In 2008 Vermont did not rank among the top five cheese-producing states, and indeed was number eleven, annually turning out only about 6% or 7% percent as many pounds of cheese as either of the leaders, Wisconsin and California. I would expect the leading states to have more factories than tiny Vermont, and probably some larger ones also. Perhaps if we were to visit some of them we would have to readjust upward our notion of what constitutes a large cheese factory.

We visited the second cheese factory on the same day we visited Cabot. Websterville, home of the Vermont Butter and Cheese Company, is only 25 miles from Cabot.

The Vermont Butter & Cheese factory is a fraction of the size of Cabot, receiving its milks from 20 independently owned farms. We were plied with goodies on this visit also—cheeses and samples of local wines in this case—and in this plant too we were separated from cheesemaking operations by

Vermont Butter & Cheese. *Milk storage tanks at the factory in Websterville, Vermont. A fraction of the size of the large cheese factories visited, it perhaps should not be included in the same category with them.*

glass partitions. There, however, any resemblance to Cabot ended. We found this factory to be a study in contrasts. Although producing hand-made and specialty products, much of the operation, with about 30 employees, seemed quasi-industrial—it looked and felt like a factory, albeit a small one. There were bulk storage tanks for milk, a testing laboratory, and a warehouse area. Cheeses, butters, and other products moved along conveyor belts, were produced in fairly large quantities, and were packaged for shipment to distant markets. On the other hand, goat and French-style cheeses were produced in a modern, technologically sophisticated facility where they were hand-crafted. While conveying some impressions of a mainstream cheese factory, the visit to Vermont Butter & Cheese also convinced us that its core mission is far different from what we had come to understand as the mainstream. Indeed, the term "artisanal" is used to describe some of its products. Moreover, we knew that Alison Hooper, founder and co-owner of Vermont Butter & Cheese, is regarded as one of the pioneers of the new American cheese, having learned cheesemaking in France and translated her knowledge into a thriving and much imitated business venture.

We arrived at the Roth Käse factory in Monroe, Wisconsin, a year later in 2008, after a long bus ride from downtown Chicago. I looked for cattle along the way and saw none. Though we passed through vast fields of corn and soybeans, I did not spot one cow until we were almost in Monroe. The bus was a microcosm of the larger conference; a dozen different conversations—all of them different but all about cheese—were underway simultaneously. One nearby conversation involved a cheesemaker who milked hundreds of goats and a young husband and wife team who were attending the conference to get information; they were thinking about starting up a goat farm, and were looking for expert advice. Somehow the scene reminded me of early school bus rides when we callow seventh graders were able to get inviting peeks into the lives of the upperclassmen on the bus.

The bus ride brought up other connections. Our route took us past the iconic Chrysler Corporation Belvedere, Illinois, assembly plant. The plant clearly was not idle, but forlorn looking nevertheless. Knowing that the American cheese business was in the midst of sea changes, the scene out the bus window provided yet another reminder that change was underway all around us.

We didn't realize until later that getting to Monroe was a short trip when compared with our grueling three-hour return trip to Chicago, which featured long periods of inching along in snarled traffic.

At Roth Käse we were entertained lavishly, being offered a variety of cheeses, locally made wines, and a luncheon that included local entertainers and little shooters of a traditional Swiss firewater—a concoction similar to schnapps.

Here, we got to enter the factory floor without the intrusion of glass barriers, but not before we had donned lab coats, plastic booties, and shower caps and gone through disinfecting treatments. Much of the cheesemaking went on in closed vats, and milks and curds were piped from one stage to the next in closed circuits of gleaming stainless steel vessels. We did get to see curds being spread into molds and visit the plant's extensive aging caves. And we got an unadulterated dose of the moist, pungent atmosphere, leaving us with little doubt that we were surrounded, and nearly engulfed by cheese in all its stages.

In Roth Käse we had found a factory smaller than Cabot and larger than Vermont Butter & Cheese, and one that was more automated than either. Our tour leader told us this was a "specialty cheese" plant. Providing the plant with advanced equipment from Europe, the American and later the Swiss owners had set it up to produce a variety of kinds of cheeses in relatively small batches. Their methods permit them to produce 40 different cheeses under 10 distinct brands, representing traditional European and Latin American kinds, as well as original creations. Whatever inefficiency resulted from the company's diverse mix of products and relatively short production runs was presumably balanced by its computer-driven automation. Also because of this diversity of products, it likely benefited from engagement in markets with relatively little competition and received much higher prices than were commanded by commodity cheeses.

Roth Käse cheese vat. *The closed vats are computer controlled and permit production of a variety of types of cheeses.*

We were surprised to learn in the Roth Käse plant that cheese milk was "standardized." In a process probably long practiced in most cheese factories, butterfat is removed so that its content reaches some lowest common denominator; then production of all cheeses begins from a common starting point. Possibly the removed butterfat is sold to be turned into butter or more likely, it is added to milks used in making some kinds of cheese such as Butterkäse.

The Roth Käse factory reminded us of Cabot in the total volume of cheeses produced and Vermont Butter & Cheese in the variety of cheeses produced and the size of production runs. That this Swiss-owned factory in the rural heart of "America's Dairyland" was truly an international affair was underscored not only by the variety of its cheeses but also by our observation that many of the factory's workers appeared to be immigrants from Latin America.

The next cheese factory we were to visit was the large McCadam factory in Chateaugay, New York. Big-rig milk carriers were streaming into and out of the plant compound when we arrived, unloading their liquid cargo in`to a cluster of refrigerated silos. This was no small operation.

The McCadam plant seemed to combine some of the qualities of Cabot and Roth Käse. We learned that McCadam had recently been acquired by Agri-Mark, the dairy cooperative that owns Cabot. In the northeastern part of the Adirondack Crescent, Chateaugay is less than 45 miles from Vermont, and the newly combined cooperative includes farms in New York and all six New England States. We never learned whether McCadam's New York State cheddars and Cabot's Vermont cheddars came only from factories and herds in their namesake states. One part of the McCadam plant produces large quantities of cheddar. Another, established by Valio, its former Finnish owner, is equipped for producing a variety of European-type cheeses. The McCadam Website indicates that the plant is capable of producing 20 different kinds of cheeses. Depending on such things as commodity prices, currency fluctuations, and taxation, we were told, European corporations at various times have found it more profitable to produce cheeses for the U.S. market and even for their home markets by establishing or purchasing factories in the United States.

Our final cheese factory, visited again in 2008, is one already featured in our earliest journey in the world of cheese. Heritage Cheese in Heuvelton, New York,

Cream separator. *This is used in the Roth Käse plant for standardizing milk.*

Aging "cave." *Some Roth Käse cheeses are adaptations of European types and must be turned frequently during the aging process. We were asked not to photograph a state-of-the-art mechanism used in the factory that obviates the need to laboriously turn them by hand.*

The McCadam plant. The depot where milk haulers unload at the plant was undergoing improvements when we took this photo.

was producing only one basic kind of cheese—a cheddar style cheese—and producing it by what we are calling mainstream methods. We had a very pleasant chat with three of the factory's managers and came away with a far different impression than we had gotten at any of the other factories. If McCadam was the antithesis of a small operation, this seemed in contrast to be a caricature of one.

We met with managers in the tiny attic-like office over the factory store. Although at one time the Heritage factory had received milk from 95 dairies, by the time of this visit the number had dwindled. The dairies still were small, mostly Amish farms. The plant's 15 employees included some who were part-time. Its small size and relative lack of high-technology equipment, and the fact that it was producing cheeses little different from those available from high-volume factories, apparently put it at a competitive disadvantage. We learned from newspaper accounts that concerns about its financial viability continued to arise, as they had repeatedly since its opening in 1995.

Sizes and scales of operations of the factories we visited varied tremendously in such metrics as number of dairies supplying milk, production volume, and number of employees. Two we would call large (Cabot and McCadam), one we would classify as medium (Roth Käse), and two were small (Vermont Butter & Cheese and Heritage). Nevertheless each of the five was unique. We were really interested in what we were calling mainstream cheese factories, and clearly Vermont Butter & Cheese didn't fit. We weren't sure about Roth Käse. Despite some remaining uncertainty, we had learned a lot, and we decided to forge ahead.

What about trends? Had we detected any? Visiting only five would probably not be adequate to reveal trends in an entire industry, so we weren't sure. We really couldn't call it a trend, but we thought one of the factories at least appeared to have a sound business plan. Roth Käse appeared to have moved up the food chain—pursuing lucrative markets for foreign-style and unique cheeses—and taking optimal advantage of automation. Perhaps these would be successful strategies in the years to come.

As we looked back on our factory visits and interviews, we felt we had gotten an essential, albeit somewhat superficial view of factory cheesemaking. Although we believed the visits to factories and interviews with managers had given us a good feel for the diversity of factory cheesemaking, we really had learned little about its current status and trends. What large forces were shaping these successors to the early crossroads cheese factories? And what were the prospects for the future? The people we had talked with had seemed upbeat and definitely content with their situations. Nevertheless, we had heard rumblings about unstable markets and occasional hardships. And we knew that factories had closed, been downsized, or had a succession of owners. It would take more research before we would get a glimpse of the big picture.

CIRCULAR No. 187

New York State Agricultural Experiment Station

Geneva, N. Y.

———

FOREIGN-TYPE CHEESES THAT SHOULD BE MORE GENERALLY MADE AND CONSUMED IN AMERICA*

———

AMERICANS who visit Europe invariably return with a greater appreciation of certain European foods, particularly cheese. So accustomed are we to one English type cheese that cheese to most of us is just this one type whether it appears as store cheese, as creamed and pasteurized old English cheddar, as club cheese, or in the familiar pasteurized and processed form.

Few realize that many other types of English, French, Dutch, Belgian, Swiss, and Italian cheeses have been made in the United

ALPINE CHEESE FACTORY.

———

*Compiled from a series of articles appearing in *Farm Research* during 1936, 1937, and 1938 under the authorship of R. S. Breed, C. D. Kelly, J. C. Marquardt, and J. A. de Tomasi. Several of the original articles are now out of print.

Title page of state agricultural circular 187.

Short Take: Foreign-Type Cheeses

The cover page of a 1939 New York State Agricultural Experiment Station publication is shown on the facing page. As is evident from its title, it seeks to diversify products the American, and most certainly the New York State, cheese industries. The authors systematically examined cheeses made in France, Canada, England, Holland, Germany, Switzerland, Italy, and the "near-east," evaluating kinds that might be acceptable to American conditions and tastes. They may have been encouraged by Governor (and Adirondack Crescent native) Roswell P. Flower. They quote him as saying,

> "Why should farmers cater to English tastes by exporting cheese at 8 cents a pound when there is an abundant home market for fancy cheeses bringing many times that price?"

Having associated early cheesemaking in the Adirondack Crescent with cheddar, we were surprised to learn from a statistical compilation that already in 1902 New York State factories were producing Limburger, domestic Swiss, Neufchâtel, Fromage de Brie, Munster, Square (i.e., Philadelphia cream cheese), kosher, Weiner, and imitation English cheddar. Another variety called D'Isigny was, despite its name, an American original production attempting to emulate Camembert. Together with a handful of other distinctive, non-cheddar varieties, the foreign types constituted more than 10% of total production.

Pounds of Non-Cheddar Cheeses Produced in New York in 1902	
Limburger	4,233,051
Domestic Swiss	879,588
Neufchatel	1,605,042
Sage	520,680
D'Isigny	1,292,992
Fromage de Brie	510,312
Munster	546,002
Square Cream (=Philadelphia)	1,446,229
Kosher	438,687
Weiner	4,000
Imitation English Cheddar	816,150
Club	Not recorded
Pineapple	157,960
Total Non-Cheddar	12,450,693
% of All Cheeses	10.5%

Non-cheddar New York cheeses. *State Agricultural Commission statistics from 1902, indicated that New York State cheesemakers were not "stuck in a cheddar rut."*

Traditional?

Industrial?

Corporate?

Commodity?

Mainstream?

Short Take: The Name Game

Even though we'd already begun to find evidence that the cheesemakers didn't fall neatly into categories, we still wanted to distinguish between what we regarded as the old American cheese and the new American cheese. But what words could we use to describe them? For some reason, "old versus new" seemed vague, misleading, and wholly inadequate. If we said "old" you might think we meant the cheese and cheesemakers of the crossroads factories, or even way back in the farm kitchens, when we really meant those of the cheese factories that swallowed up the Adirondack Crescent and similar places.

In the beginning we wanted to call them "traditional." They exemplified cheese and cheesemaking as, until recently, we expected them to be—associated with factories having refrigerated silo-like tanks, one or more smokestacks, a mix of skilled and unskilled workers, and facilities to unload refrigerated milk trucks and ship out pallet after pallet of cheese in large boxes. But we sensed a problem. If we used the word <u>traditional</u> for them, whose tradition would we be referencing? Was it our own tradition of thinking food products come from factories, mostly owned by large corporations? Also it seemed perhaps we should reserve the term for the other traditions, the cheesemaking traditions still being rediscovered. We gave up and decided to leave the word <u>traditional</u> alone.

We tried other terms, such as "industrial," "corporate," and "commodity," but none seemed to convey the sense of what we had perceived cheese and cheesemaking were like for most of the second half of the twentieth century.

In the end we settled on the term "mainstream" to apply to those old, more or less familiar, cheeses and cheesemakers. Not that the term had a precise meaning, but it carried no hint of anything novel or pioneering. When we visited factories and learned they were sometimes making artisanal-style cheeses and artisan cheesemakers were sometimes using factory processes, we felt our mainstream terminology had redeemed itself because its imprecision fit well with the complex mix we observed.

Within the new American cheese, terminology may also cause confusion. The terms "artisan" and "artisanal" are generally accepted within the cheesemaking community as applying to cheeses manufactured by hand using the traditional craftsmanship of skilled cheesemakers. However, no regulations require that this meaning be used in the marketplace, and undoubtedly it is often used too loosely. In fact, factory cheesemakers and other industrial food producers may, and sometimes do, tout their products as artisanal.

Liz Thorpe in *The Cheese Chronicles* proposes an interesting definition that provides an objective criterion for use of the term. "Artisanal cheesemakers change their recipe and technique, to accommodate the shifting fluid medium that is milk." Regrettably, her good efforts seem unlikely to change the overuse and misuse of the term.

The term "farmstead" is less controversial and is recognized by the American Cheese Society and others as applying only to those cheeses made on a farm using only the milk of animals residing on that farm.

Artisanal?

Farmstead?

A so-called artisan product. We enjoyed these crackers, but doubt that they are produced by artisans. The label states, "Wisconsin Colby cheese from America's heartland, known for its mild, gentle flavor and smooth texture, is baked into Wheat Thins Artisan Cheese Crackers." We saw nothing on the label suggesting that the Colby cheese came from anywhere other than a factory. Indeed, the crackers are a product of Kraft Foods, surely well-known for its popular line of factory-made cheeses.

More big cheeses. *Particularly in the days of small cheese factories, producing outsize cheeses for the State Fair was a source of publicity. Moreover, if a factory's cheeses were prize winners, it was provided with a competitive advantage.* Image courtesy of the New York State Museum of Cheese.

Times and Trials in the Cheese Business

Our experiences at American Cheese Society conferences suggested that the cheese business in America has never been healthier—at least not for a century or more. However, despite the upbeat words and apparent contentment of cheesemakers we were meeting in our travels, we kept receiving unmistakable signals that being in the cheese business—the mainstream cheese business at least—may be a nerve-wracking series of financial ups and downs. While the nation's love affair with cheese appears to be building, we could not avoid stumbling over tales of closures, buyouts, and sagging profits among factory producers of cheese. Part of the problem, we thought, might result from the position of cheesemaking within the larger dairy industry, in which supply and demand problems seem to be chronic.

Mainstream American cheese is a commodity product depending on milk—another commodity product—and both suffer supply and demand problems and regular fluctuations in price. These erode profits or, at worst, cause producers to receive less in exchange than it cost them to produce the milk or the cheese. Also, in both dairying and mainstream cheesemaking, competition and low profit margins demand economies of scale and significant capital investments, putting small and mid-size dairies and cheesemakers at great risk. The problem is particularly acute in the northeastern states and neighboring provinces in Canada, where further consolidation and industrialization are limited by climate, landscape, and the agricultural traditions historically developed in response to them.

While the story of economic woes seemed to be an

Facility in poor repair. *Streaks of rust stain the white-painted silos of the cheese factory in Ogdensburg, New York. The factory has had a succession of owners and a poor record of profitability.*

"Growing cheese demand has been one of the most important forces shaping the U.S. dairy industry. Per capita cheese use is twice the level of 25 years ago and shows no signs of leveling. Increasing cheese consumption has been aided by ready availability of a wider variety of cheeses, increased away-from-home eating, and greater popularity of ethnic cuisines that employ cheese as a major ingredient."

USDA 2009

important one, we did not want to become experts on the economics of the cheese business. Nevertheless, we could not ignore all that we heard and read about what, despite close regulation by governmental bodies, seems to be an extremely volatile and highly competitive business. And when we took a brief, tentative peek at the economics of cheese, the exercise was bewildering and humbling. We understood little of what we read and at first felt too unsophisticated in economic matters to make any sense of it. However, we regained some of our self-esteem when, while Web surfing, we happened upon an undated statement by an organization called Citizens Against Government Waste. Describing (USDA) policies related to the pricing of dairy products, they wrote: "The program's tangled web of mind-numbing pricing schemes has metastasized into a multilayered, incomprehensible, intrusive labyrinth increasingly divorced from economic realities and market forces."

So, we learned that we were probably no more stupid than many others. This, however, did little to offset the bad news—our discovery that much of the system responsible for putting cheese on our table is seriously broken, resulting in hardship for many people and the communities in which they live.

What was happening? Why was the greatest part of the cheese industry in America undergoing some sort of crisis? We thought some important issues were at stake for cheesemakers, so we decided to delve a bit deeper and try to make what little sense we could of economic driving forces and their effects. Agricultural commodity prices, we learned, are determined by the USDA by a series of formulas. These seemed on the surface to be bizarre, but we had to assume the USDA had decent motives and worthy goals. However, as in other regulated areas, those affecting factory cheesemakers seem to be plagued by unintended consequences. A regulation developed with the intention of helping dairy farmers in one part of the country might hurt those in another part, or it could in the end harm cheesemakers relying on the farmers for milk. And, in an effort to redress this problem, putting the cheesemakers in firmer financial situations might have unwanted negative effects on the ability of dairy farmers to earn a living. Unintended negative effects might go one way or the other, and the further tragedy is that they seemed capable of pitting dairymen and cheesemakers— groups we thought should be natural allies—against each other.

The dilemma in implementing regulated prices came home to the Adirondack Crescent in our readings. We discovered testimony offered at a USDA hearing in which Kraft Foods cited USDA pricing regulations as part of the rationale for closure of its cheese factory in nearby Canton, New York. Producing commodity cheddar cheese, the plant suffered among other things from a "make-allowance" regulation that fixed the price cheesemakers received for each pound of cheese produced. When conditions such as costs of energy or labor changed, Kraft and other cheesemakers had to absorb the increased costs. And if the price paid for the cheese by the consumer increased, the increased income would go not to the cheesemaker but to the dairies supplying the milk. We found the following

Abandoned factory. The former Kraft cheese factory in Canton, New York. We did not visit the site until after reading about its closure. We were surprised at its apparent good condition and its size — it did not fit our image of a "smaller" cheese factory. Not completely abandoned, a Kraft subcontractor occupied the plant after Kraft left, re-employing 15 of the 65 laid-off workers to make containers for cheese.

transcript (altered only as indicated by brackets) of testimony given by a representative of Kraft Foods, relating the role of the regulatory environment in the decision to close the Canton plant.

> With a nationwide network of manufacturing plants and suppliers, we continually analyze costs of internal manufacturing versus purchasing from an external source. One example of this analysis is the cheese plant we used to operate in Canton, NY which made 640 lb. Cheddar blocks. On January 27, 2004, Kraft announced the closure of the Canton plant. Instead of making the cheese internally, Kraft would procure the cheese from other locations in the US, notably regions with a less onerous regulatory environment (e.g. ID) or outside the Federal Order system (e.g. CA).

> As a small plant, Canton [did not] benefit from economies of scale that could help lower overall costs and make it competitive with cheese plants elsewhere in the U.S. Plus, [it lacked] profitable means to process whey, a byproduct of cheese-making.

> In its last year of operation, the total cost of making cheese was $0.23/lb which is well above the make allowance in the USDA milk formula. We use this example to point out the inherent dangers of product formulas and make allowances that do not cover smaller, less efficient plants. Our experience has shown these types of plants are not competitive in the long run, and the industry risks losing a significant number of these plants if economic conditions do not improve."

So in the example of the closed Canton cheese

factory, the unintended consequence of a well-intended regulation aimed at saving dairy farms was the demise of smaller cheese plants. In Canton, 65 employees lost their jobs, presumably a number of local dairies also lost markets for their milk, and the regional economy suffered a significant setback.

Not all plant closures and consolidations are the direct result of USDA regulations. We also learned that the giant Canada cheese conglomerate Saputo has closed many plants, citing market conditions in the three Western Hemisphere countries in which it operates. Nor could the USDA be implicated in the collapse of the giant Italian-based multinational Parmalat. Having acquired dairy, cheese, and other food products companies in many countries, Parmalat entered bankruptcy in 2003 because of the combined effects of overly leveraged buyouts, poor profits or operating losses, and massive corporate fraud. The affair continued to garner headlines in 2009 because of lawsuits filed by the reorganized company against Bank of America and other financial institutions alleging it had abetted and enabled the malfeasance.

As we stayed attuned to happenings in the world of

Ogdensburg, New York cheese factory. *Although active cheesemaking was underway when we visited, it appeared that only a fraction of the facility was in use. Most of the buildings and silos appeared to be in poor repair. We found the scene to be sobering.*

cheese and the Adirondack Crescent in particular, we could not help time after time encountering new episodes in the saga of the cheese factory in Ogdensburg, New York. Like Canton and Heuvelton, it is in our familiar St. Lawrence County. Over a 30-year period, the Ogdensburg plant had a rocky history, with four different owners or operators, each ultimately giving up or moving its operations elsewhere. Problems of disposal of whey were nearly constant, with fines levied or payments demanded by the city for discharges overwhelming the municipal sewage treatment system. That profits were slim or nonexistent was indicated by occasional failures to pay taxes. In 2004, together with another factory in Lowville, New York, the idle factory was acquired by Ahava, one of the nation's largest kosher food producers. Kosher foods are in their own competitive environment and, as specialty products with a relatively secure market, they may be less subject to prevailing economic pressures than other products. Specifically, some consumers might be willing to pay premium prices for kosher foods, thereby negating or minimizing the economic advantages accruing to mass producers that enjoy economies of scale, marketing muscle, or other factors favoring their survival on slim profit margins.

That the kosher cheese operation in Ogdensburg was up against hard times was evident soon after its inception. Ahava, a California company, went into bankruptcy, and creditors threatened to take it over. The Ogdensburg city manager saw the future of the plant and the welfare of the community as closely intertwined and understood the marketing benefits of this being operated as a kosher cheese plant.

Commenting on this problem, he said, according to the *Watertown Daily Times*, "We also need a specialized niche market for this cheese, because there is no way that a small plant in upstate New York would be able to compete with such industry giants as Kraft Cheese. The kosher market provides the perfect niche market so that this plant could survive."

In response to the threatened closure of the factory,

the city acquired the plant in lieu of unpaid taxes and leased it back to the company — the goal being to keep the plant in operation and thereby preserve the more than 50 jobs and the market for milk produced by local dairy farmers.

However, things did not go well. Rumors reaching us from local people familiar with cheese production in the region told of employees being forced to work uncompensated hours, given slave wages, and enduring unsafe working conditions. Regardless of the specifics and whatever exaggeration might have attended the reports we received, the implication seemed clear that the operators of the factory were desperately exploiting employees, as well as creditors. Evidently whistle-blowers came forward, Occupational Health and Safety Health Administration inspections were conducted, and the plant was cited and fined for numerous flagrant violations of health and safety regulations.

Other lurking problems soon were in the open. For months the city received no rent payments. Nor were utility bills and taxes paid. The city had a lien placed on the cheesemaking equipment in lieu of unpaid rents and ultimately was awarded ownership. With bankruptcies and defaults in the background, the plant continued to operate long after its serious problems became known. Despite mounting unpaid rents and utility bills, the city did everything it could to keep the plant going, in early 2009 serving eviction notices to the operators while desperately seeking a buyer able to keep the plant open and its remaining 30 full-time workers employed. The plant did close, however, when in February 2009 inspectors from the State Department of Agriculture and Markets detected contaminated cheese, seized a large stockpile, and ordered the plant shut down to ensure the safety of the public. A new buyer was found for the plant and equipment, and it was reported that the plant resumed production of kosher cheese and milk in late April 2009.

We visited the site in mid-2009 and were struck by the appearance of the plant. Although clearly in operation, it seemed obvious that only a small fraction of the facility, which occupies most of a square block, was in use. Rust-stained silos, unused equipment strewed around the grounds, and a general air of decrepitude told of a long series of struggles and decline that would not be quickly or easily reversed.

We later learned of plans underway to build a new kosher cheese factory in the village of Auburn, in central New York. That one, which would cater to the needs of members of a Hasidic sect with uncommonly strict dietary rules, was to receive significant funding and other incentives from state and local governments. This development suggests that the plan in Ogdensburg is perhaps a viable one.

More abandoned facilities. Views of two former McCadam facilities in Heuvelton, New York. The plants were closed as a result of the 2003 buyout of McCadam by the cooperative that owns Cabot. Operations formerly housed in these facilities were consolidated in other McCadam and Cabot plants.

We did not have to leave St. Lawrence County to learn of more woes of cheesemakers in the Adirondack Crescent. As alluded to already, Agri-Mark, a large dairy cooperative headquartered in New England, bought McCadam Cheese in 2003. The new owners decided to close the Heuvelton McCadam plant, consolidating its operations with its Chateaugay, New York plant and its Cabot Cheese facilities in Vermont. Chateaugay is also in the Adirondack Crescent, more than 75 miles from Heuvelton. The closure cost the jobs of 115 employees and ended

McCadam's presence at a cheese factory that had operated continuously for 125 years.

A few years earlier, the county had suffered a loss of 50 jobs when Losurdo Cheese, also in Heuvelton, announced the transfer of production of some kinds of cheeses to other plants and the reduction of its workforce. Like the others, Losurdo had experienced whey disposal problems and in 2003 had set a date for closing the plant. The plant reduced its operations by half, and only a negotiated agreement with the village regarding the whey disposal problem kept it open.

Closure of Kraft's Canton plant and McCadam's Heuvelton plant, and finally the rocky history and temporary closure of the Ogdensburg factory suggest that St. Lawrence County could be left with only the diminished Losurdo factory and the tiny Heritage Cheese House, which for most of its existence had hung on slender threads. The number of factories had gone from 119 in 1900 to just three 109 years later, with prospects that the number could easily tumble to zero. With these events came the realization that one of the pillars of the local economy had all but crumbled.

We know people like cheese and will continue to demand it, but that seems to have little bearing on the question of whether it is possible in the twenty-first century to make money by producing it in the Adirondack Crescent. And if specialty markets like that for kosher cheese or the cachet of Amish cheese were unable to overcome the economic handicaps, what could save cheesemaking in the Adirondack Crescent or anywhere else in the Northeast?

Could farmstead and artisanal cheese be part of the answer?

———

In the summer of 2009 we found ourselves driving along Interstate Route 81 in northern New York. We were passing the village of Adams and, knowing of the Great Lakes Cheese factory not far from the

Losurdo cheese plant. Two views are shown of the cheese plant in Heuvelton, New York. Losurdo continued to operate its Heuvelton facilities in mid-2009, despite past problems with whey disposal. Its workforce had been reduced to about one-half of former levels.

highway, we decided to drive over and take a photo, on the chance that we might find a use for it. There was another connection, albeit a weak one. I am a one time local resident; between my first and third birthdays, my family lived in Adams (population 1,600).

To our surprise, when we saw the complex it little resembled the one we had visited a few years earlier. Then we had stopped to buy cheese at a retail store attached to the factory. We knew the store was long gone but were nevertheless surprised to see a row of portable toilets and obvious heavy construction underway. The expansion appeared to be significant, perhaps doubling the size of the factory.

What could be going on? The three cheese factories in St. Lawrence County were either gone or struggling to preserve scraps of their former existence, and this one in adjacent Jefferson County was preparing for a future of growth. The contrasts were extreme, for example with the Ogdensburg factory, where only subsidies by local governments kept an underutilized facility minimally active. What was it? How had the managers of Great Lakes Cheese been able to overcome the built-in disadvantages faced by other northern New York cheesemakers? And if they had succeeded in doing so, why had the others failed?

We were later able to obtain some degree of understanding by interviewing an agreeable and forthcoming company representative. Great Lakes Cheese is a large company headquartered in Ohio that both distributes and manufactures cheese. They are indeed doubling the capacity of the Adams factory, we learned, and installing whey drying towers, which can convert a difficult disposal problem into a product that can be sold at a profit.

We learned that the Adams plant is the only facility in which Great Lakes manufactures cheddar cheese, and Adams Reserve is its flagship brand. The company has a strong commitment to cheddar and is confident that demands for its products will continue to grow. It also buys cheeses from other manufacturers and

packages and distributes them for "private label" brands — for example, the cheeses supermarkets sell under their own names. The company is committed to quality and sells only naturally-aged cheeses — those in which aging is not accelerated by the addition of enzymes during manufacture.

We were told that one can visit a high-end chain supermarket and buy Adams Reserve at the deli counter and Great Lakes-supplied store-brand cheeses in the dairy case.

What a business plan, we thought. Great Lakes Cheese is tapping into the market for upscale cheeses with Adams Reserve — the same market now propelling the growth of other specialty American cheeses. At the same time it is supplying the market for everyday cheeses. We didn't hear it from the company representative but guessed that when the company is making more Adams Reserve than it can sell, it might divert the excess into the private-label stream. And by outsourcing supplies of most private-label cheeses, it can avoid the problem of excessive inventories.

Adams Reserve. Seen here is the plant in Adams, New York. When we visited, construction activity was significantly increasing the size of the factory. Somehow this company had managed to buck the trends negatively affecting its counterparts in neighboring St. Lawrence County.

So, we believed we had our answer. Keys to the Adams Reserve success were a great business strategy, a commitment to quality, and the financial resources to build a production facility capable of efficiently turning out high-quality products.

CREAM CHEESE FESTIVAL

Saturday, September 19
11am - 6pm
Downtown Lowville
FREE ADMISSION

Live Music ✳ Delicious Food ✳ Local Artists
Contests for Children & Adults with Cash Prizes
✳ Largest Cheesecake in the United States ✳
✳ Children's Discovery/Fun Park ✳
✳ Cream Cheese Festival Souvenir Store ✳

Sponsored by Kraft Foods, Reality Check, Village of Lowville, The Lowville
Business Association and Lewis County Chamber of Commerce
Media Sponsor: North Country Public Radio

For more information visit www.creamcheesefestival.com

Lowville plant. The Kraft plant in Lowville, New York may be another exception to the pattern that has brought decline to many Adirondack crescent cheese factories. We did not visit this plant. It produces Philadelphia Cream Cheese and appears to be thriving. This 2009 announcement celebrates the bond between the factory and the community.

Short Take: Four Decades of Change in Industrial Cheese Production
(Source: USDA reports)

Top Five Cheese Producing States and Production (millions of pounds)							
1978		1988		1998		2008	
WI	1,232	WI	1,901	WI	2,116	WI	2,524
MI	450	MN	635	CA	1,243	CA	2,113
NY	283	CA	540	NY	631	ID	805
IA	179	NY	509	MN	617	NY	716
CA	137	IA	259	ID	515	MN	642
US Total	3,519		5,571		7,330		9,777

Trends in Production Totals:

1) The relentless growth of California on its way to becoming the largest American producer of cheese.

2) The decline in the relative importance of the Midwest and Northeast. Michigan, Iowa, and Minnesota all lost ground or remained static in production. Even Wisconsin, though it retained a slim hold on the number-one ranking, went from producing nearly 38% of all U.S. cheese in 1978 to less than 26% in 2008. New York, the only northeastern state in the top five, failed to keep pace with the leaders.

3) The rise of the West. The growth of California was matched by the sudden appearance and rapid growth of Idaho (credited to a favorable regulatory environment by a Kraft representative). Not shown in the tables is the rise of New Mexico, which at 603 million pounds in 2008 was just behind Minnesota.

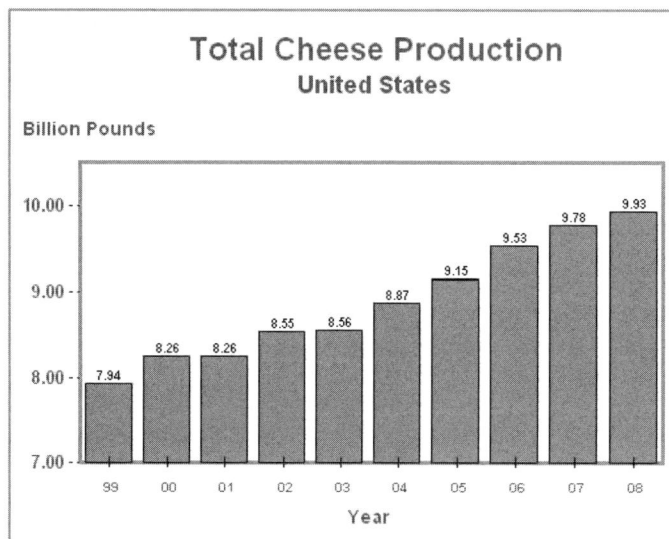

Total Cheese Production
United States

Billion Pounds

Year	99	00	01	02	03	04	05	06	07	08
	7.94	8.26	8.26	8.55	8.56	8.87	9.15	9.53	9.78	9.93

Cheese Production
Percent by Type 1978

Cheese Production
Percent by Type 2008

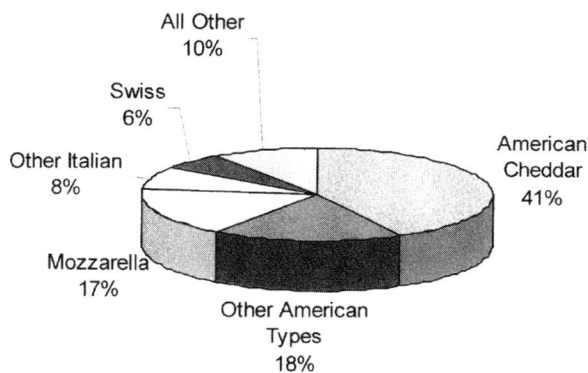

All Other
10%

Swiss
6%

Other Italian
8%

Mozzarella
17%

Other American
Types
18%

American
Cheddar
41%

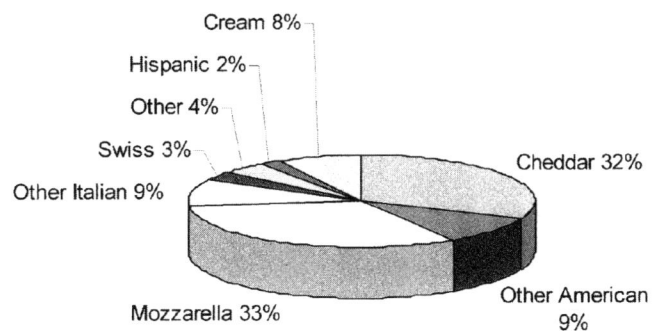

Cream 8%

Hispanic 2%

Other 4%

Swiss 3%

Other Italian 9%

Mozzarella 33%

Cheddar 32%

Other American
9%

Trends in Kinds of Cheeses Produced
1978 versus 2008

Original figures from USDA reports for 1978 and 2008 are shown above. Apparent trends are:

1) A significant shift away from cheddar and related American types. If these categories are totaled, they decrease from 61% in 1978 to 41% three decades later.

2) A near doubling of the amount of mozzarella produced; by 2008 production of mozzarella exceeded that of cheddar.

3) A general shift from harder to softer cheeses. Cheddar and Swiss are hard cheeses, whereas mozzarella and some of the "other" cheeses (e.g., cream and so-called Hispanic-- presumably Latin American—types) tend to be softer. Part of the increase in this shift from lower-moisture to higher-moisture cheeses includes more water in the finished products. Thus the increase in production is less dramatic than the numbers suggest.

4) A greater variety of cheeses made it into the statistical summary in 2008, suggesting an expansion of American tastes.

Short Take: Hard Times Down on the Farm

Our interest in cheese got us reading widely about farms and the current precarious economics of dairy farming. The story is clearly troubling, as problems seem to be serious and growing worse. In late 2009, as we are writing this, the bottom has fallen out of the milk market, prices paid for milk are less than costs to produce it, and a fresh round of farm closures seems imminent. Northern New York isn't alone, as the problems appear to be nationwide and are echoed in the countries of the European Union. If troubles with economics weren't enough, regulatory changes are now piling on, with additional serious economic consequences.

"Local agricultural agencies see the new state permits for Concentrated Animal Feeding Operations [CAFOs] potentially as a nail in the coffin for local farms," stated a July 17, 2009, article in the *Watertown Daily Times*. At issue was a tightening of environmental regulations regarding discharges of waste materials from the CAFOs. Already reeling from the sagging market for milk and escalating feed prices, farmers were said to be losing tens of thousands of dollars per month. Under the new regulations, dairy farming, or at least a large part of it as it is now practiced, would be treated as are most other economic activities. Complying with the new regulations could run into the hundreds of thousands if dollars. Many farmers would soon be taking steps to sell off their herds and get out of the farming business, the article said.

What's wrong, we wondered. How did things get to this point?

We had read that children don't drink as much milk as they used to, in part because of the popularity of carbonated soft drinks. And there aren't as many children as in past decades of more rapid population growth. Adults weren't drinking as much milk or using as much butter either, primarily based on perceived health concerns. And although the appreciation for cheese among all age groups seems to be growing, the new American cheese was mostly coming from small farms and would not be doing much to bail out the farmers who operate large CAFOs.

It's the CAFOs, we concluded. Housing large numbers of cows in closed facilities and bringing food to them may not be the only cause, but the practice is surely an important component and an unquestionable symptom of all that has gone wrong. Hundreds of cows standing in confined spaces produce vast quantities of waste materials. We are not used to thinking of farms in the same terms as so-called industries, but if their production of pollutants is similar, why should they be treated differently? Putting cows in a CAFO and feeding them grain achieves increased productivity on the basis of pounds of milk produced per cow. But that apparent efficiency is real only when we do not take into account the costs of dealing with the wastes they produce.

We already knew that farms had been getting fewer and larger for more than 50 years. And even though the total number of cows had declined over the decades, the total production of milk continued to rise. This was possible, we speculated, because cows were being fed high-energy grains instead of grasses and were expending less of the energy they consumed because they were standing around in barns all day, instead of taking care of themselves outdoors. Also, it might be that as the number of CAFOs increased, selective breeding could favor cows that were top producers of milk, even if this meant they were less fit to fend for themselves.

We thought we saw the big picture. Whatever gains had been achieved over the decades, they came at significant costs and they exposed the system and the people who depended on it to significant risks. Once a dairy becomes dependent on feed purchased from others, it also finds itself at the mercy of forces beyond its control. As has happened, in creating competition for corn for production of motor fuel, global energy demand creates a crisis that devastates the dairy industry. And this is even before anyone has reckoned with the costs needed to deal with wastes.

Dairy farming, once a way to make a living for millions of families and individuals, became an industry. And becoming an industry exposed it to all the impersonal forces that buffer other industries, including the tyranny of the global marketplace.

We wonder if it would still be possible to make some kind of living on a dairy farm with 20 cows or fewer. The cows would eat only grass and the hay we would harvest, and we would expect at times the milk produced to be scarce. But what if we turned it into cheese? Making and selling aged cheeses would damp out the seasonal fluctuations in the milk supply, and maybe we would be able to add enough value and get enough money from selling it to cover our expenses. Entirely different forces would be at work than those faced by farmers 200 years ago, but nevertheless we would have in common with the dairy farmers of the early nineteenth century the need to make cheese because there were no viable markets for our milk.

Short Take: Changing Rural Landscapes

Changes in rural landscapes occurring over the past several decades may be irreversible.

We got a hint of this in a conversation we had with a northern New York cheesemaking couple and their neighbor over cups of coffee. The neighbor revealed that he was a local native who had grown up on a farm and worked in a now-closed cheese factory.

"Are some of the good things about farming as it was practiced in the past being recaptured?" We asked this, thinking that this setting — in the home of a farmstead cheesemaker — might be a hopeful sign.

"It's gone for good," the neighbor replied, despairingly.

The reason, he said, is in the way patterns of land ownership have changed. Dairy farms began consolidating in the 1950s. Farmhouses were sold with a few acres of land to be used as residences and separated from most of the farm lands. Coming into the ownership of other farms, or owned by someone else and rented, the lands might be operated by larger farms for pasture, hay, or row crops. Or they might have been taken out of production entirely. This happened repeatedly, farms were divided and their lands consolidated with other large spreads, and he could think of no circumstances in which the original farmsteads might be reconstituted. Nothing convinced him that these trends would do anything but continue.

We later learned from the *St. Lawrence County Agricultural Development Plan* that the number of farms in the county had declined from more than 5,000 in 1950 to just over 1,600 in 1998. Acres of land devoted to farming and the number of dairy cattle in the county had each declined approximately 50% in the same period. We got out pencil and paper and calculated that in the last 20 years of that period, the number of cattle had declined 20%. Other statistics showed that while farms and numbers of cattle were decreasing, total production of milk had increased by nearly 20%.

Yet another look at the statistics made it clear to us what was going on. While land devoted to farming and number of cattle were decreasing, there was a huge increase in the production of feed corn. That same 20-year period saw more than a 100% increase in corn produced as grain. Cattle were producing more milk in part because they were relying less on pasturage and more on corn. We had read much about corn—and were well aware that it is the quintessential agricultural commodity.

Dairy farmers, we realized, were under exactly the same pressures that had forced massive consolidation in the cheese business. Milk is a commodity, and to survive in a commodity business, one has to achieve economies of scale, marketing muscle, and all the other traits helping to maintain competitiveness. And one way to do this is to engage in the production of yet another commodity — corn.

Returning to the changes underway in rural landscapes, could the new cheesemakers possibly help to save the few remaining traditional dairy farms? Surely adding value to their milk by turning it into cheese and eliminating layers of middlemen could dramatically improve the financial balance sheets of dairy farms. And whether cheesemaking is art or a science, adding an element of creativity to make unique and highly sought-after products could create lucrative markets where none existed before. Perhaps cheesemakers could help to drive a rural renaissance by achieving prosperity in landscapes where it has become elusive.

Lester Brown in his book *Plan B 3.0* reported government statistics revealing that the United States recently had 960,000 farmers and 2 million prison inmates. While these numbers are not directly related, Brown took the justaposition to be a sign of some fundamental problems with American society. We found it difficult to dispute that the dwindling numbers of people responsible for feeding all of us is a problem, and is one made all the more evident by the contrast between the farmers who are producers and the prisoners, who are judged not as assets, but liabilities and burdens on society.

Part Four:
The New American
Cheesemakers

as told by Peg

During my last six months of being employed, which were Russ's first six months of being retired, I lived full time, and he part time, in Prague. The experience had its own cheese adventures. When we were both there we experimented with the stinky mild Czech cheese tvarůžky; the crumb-covered, fried, soft cheese comfort food smažák; and the braided, salty sheep milk cheese Korbáčiky that Czechs import from neighboring Slovakia. While I was there alone teaching at the university, Russ was home in Florida doing our first cheesemaking experiments. When I got home and joined him in retirement, we decided as a next step we wanted to go to cheese festivals and conferences we had heard and read about and to interview cheesemakers.

We were curious to see what cheese events were like, and we wondered how our images of the cheesemakers would match the reality of their lives. We expected cheesemakers to have passion for cheese and for farm life. We imagined some might be former city dwellers who had given up intense desk jobs and wanted to spend more time outdoors. We imagined others who had always been farmers and had taken up cheesemaking as a way of keeping the farm afloat. In the next several months, we began our conversations with cheesemakers. They were wonderfully cordial and welcoming.

Olomoucké tvarůžky.
This is a pungent cheese made in Moravia, a region of the Czech Republic.

But, before the interviews came a festival and two conferences. They were our sensory introduction to the abundance of the new American cheeses.

Prague. *A view of the Karlův most (Charles Bridge), a celebrated site in Prague, the capital of the Czech Republic.*

Tasting a Thousand Varieties of New American Cheeses

Three times in our explorations—in Warwick, Burlington, and Chicago—we found ourselves surrounded by more cheese than we could have imagined. Having read about the *Festival des Fromages de Warwick*, we decided to go check it out. Warwick is southwest of Quebec and northeast of Montreal, in a region referred to as "subfluvial" Canada between the St. Lawrence River on the north and the Vermont border on the south. The region has gentle, rolling hills like sand dunes. Your eye travels over what seems like miles of open fields. The land has a prosperous-farm look, reminiscent of an era in the United States before the consolidation of family farms into agribusinesses.

While driving through open farmland on our way to Warwick in June 2007, we were awestruck by the expansive lushness of the fields. We could see many farms simultaneously. At one crossroads, we counted thirty-two silos in view. Nevertheless, we saw few cattle. The presence of silos and the absence of cattle suggested that although the dairy business was doing well, the cows were not eating grass but perhaps silage and corn instead.

We found Warwick. We followed the signs past a squat, blue, metal-clad cheese factory on the main street. Cars filled its parking lot. People were making cheese, even as the rest of the town was celebrating it. Written on the store window in front of the factory, with that easily removed paint I have always wanted to try, were ads for cheese curds, fresh yogurt, and ice cream. I put in a vote for a stop there after the main event of the day.

We found the parking lot for the festival in an open field and parked on the mown weeds. We got in line under the collection of past and current festival

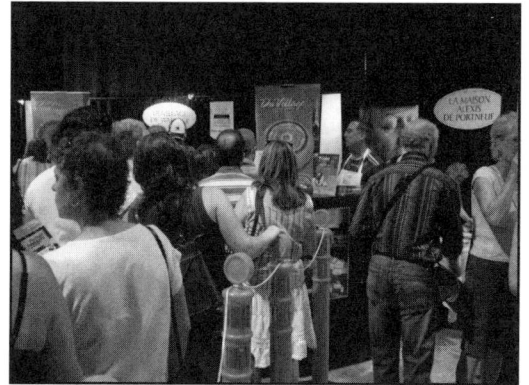

Warwick. *Visitors queued up to sample cheeses at the Festival des Fromages de Warwick.*

We had gone to Canada for a week-long, homestay and immersion class in French. Working to recapture my college French was another retirement activity, and one that might help with interviewing cheesemakers. We were also beginning to consider a future hike on El Camino de Santiago de Compostela. We wanted to each have some skills in French and in Spanish. I would take the lead in French and Russ in Spanish. We later took Speed Spanish on Internet. Finding a cheese festival was a big bonus for this trip to Quebec, and we would be ready to shop for cheeses in France and Spain.

posters. At least two pole barns were in sight, with a large tented area between them. Under the tent were a stage and dozens of round tables with eight or ten chairs at each. Soft drink and sandwich vendors were setting up. Several ticket booths were getting ready for all of us.

In addition to paying a modest entry fee of less than $15 apiece at the booth, we bought tickets for sampling. We were clueless as to what we would find inside or how many sampling tickets we should buy. Our slight disorientation was increased by the shock of seeing so many people lining up for a cheese event. The mood was festive. It seemed to be the gathering place for all the people from the rural towns for miles around and probably a large number of city people out for a day in the country. "Il fait chaud," remarked someone behind us. Being Floridians, we hadn't noticed the heat.

When we entered the festival buildings, we estimated more than a hundred exhibitors were set up. A rope line maintaining a one-way flow of traffic guided people past each of the vendors, at least until the crowds swelled to huge about two hours after the doors opened. Being Canada, not Florida, there was no air conditioning. We started to notice the heat.

About a third of the exhibitors were artisanal and farmstead cheesemakers, but we also met soap makers, honey producers, and wine and cider makers. The cheese samples were about as big as the dice in a board game. They were mounded on cutting boards and platters or piled on an uncut wheel of the same cheese and spilling over its sides.

We smelled, tasted, compared, and contrasted cheese in a way we had never done before. The building was damp, even though it was a dry, hot day. The cheese and food smells collided with each other, though not unpleasantly. Perhaps because of all the display props, it smelled a bit like cut grass and bails of hay. The milky cheese smell was there too.

I asked a cheesemaker if a sample I was trying was

made with cow milk. She gave me an early lesson in noting the differences among cheeses when she responded, "You can usually tell by the color. Goat milk cheeses tend to be quite white, like what you are sampling. A cow cheese would likely be quite a bit more yellow."

The variety of types of cheese was visually overwhelming. Our eyes joined our taste buds in trying to differentiate among the cheeses. There were cow milk, goat milk, and sheep milk products. There were soft, semi-soft, and hard cheeses. There were fresh and aged cheeses and cheeses made from pasteurized and raw milk. Every booth was hosted by cheesemakers eager to have us sample — and buy. It was not until later, when we had pulled together all our book learning, that we came to understand everything we saw and tasted at this, our first, cheese festival.

Artwork in cheese. A carving made with different colors of cheese celebrating Vermont cheesemaking at the American Cheese Society's 2007 Annual Conference.

On our first venture around the pavilion, which took about an hour and a half, we tried primarily to give ourselves a sense of what was there. As the crowd grew, it was easy to see that the cheesemakers could not afford to give away their samples for free. This throng would consume mountains of cheese. We went out and bought many more sampling tickets, planning to head right back into the fray since waiting for the crowd to thin out didn't look like it would work. Besides, it was great fun to be experiencing so much cheese all at one time.

On second thought, we decided to hang out in the tent outside the pavilion for a while. We bought a cheese plate, of course, and iced tea. We listened to the live music, rested, and compared notes about what we each had tasted and seen the first time through. Then we headed back inside. The second time through took longer. We didn't care a bit. We sampled and sampled. We listened to all the discussions around us, in French and English, about people's favorite cheeses and cheesemakers. After we'd had our fill, we bought chunks of our favorites to bring home.

Aroma wheel. Developed in France to describe the aromas of cheeses, the French descriptors classify the basic aromas into eight groups. A version of this graphic was presented for American audiences at the 2007 American Cheese Society Conference.

If we had any residual doubt in our minds about

the new American cheese being a phenomenon worthy of attention, *Festival des Fromages de Warwick* banished them and also, we thought, would set us up for our first visit to an American Cheese Society (ACS) conference a few weeks later.

The ACS conference that year was in Burlington, Vermont. Our vegetarian daughter was already a fully committed cheese enthusiast and attended the conference with us. We drove across the Adirondack Park from Star Lake and crossed Lake Champlain on a ferry.

Burlington proved to be a pleasant enough place to visit, but it was stretched to its limits by the popularity of the conference. More than half the 1,400 ACS members attended and were almost more than the town could handle. The conference hotel filled up, then the other local hotels, motels, and bed and breakfasts filled to capacity, and finally the University of Vermont opened student quarters vacant for the summer to help accommodate the overflow crowds. The burgeoning interest in cheese was signaled unequivocally by the numbers streaming into Burlington.

About three hundred conference attendees were cheesemakers. People who sell cheese were the next largest group. The remainder were people like us—enthusiasts and writers. Informative sessions abounded. We split up and covered most of the workshops, with such wide-ranging topics as "American Artisanal Cheese: Is the Sun Setting or Rising?" "Developing a Sensory Profile for Your Cheese," "How Big Is Big Enough?: Getting at Size for Farmstead Sustainability," and "Of Grass and Fermentations: The Marriage of Beer and Cheese." That last one particularly appealed to me after my months in the Czech Republic, where beer is considered food, not beverage, and treated with such respect that it is always served in a glass or mug. Serving it in the bottle is considered rude to the beer.

In conversations over our cheese-filled breakfasts and dinners, we caught up on what each of us had learned. For example, because the U.S. Army requested a system for sensory analysis of food after soldiers in the 1950s complained their rations were tasteless, there is now a way to describe how cheese smells. A wheel of 75 aromas in eight cheese aroma families—lactic, herbaceous, floral, fruity, roasted, animal, spicy, and other—was later developed to describe cheese.

The 2008 American Cheese Society Festival of Cheese. *Cheeses and cheese samplers filled the large hotel ballroom.*

Traditionally, the conference highlight is the Festival of Cheeses on the final evening. I was waiting for this. After seeing the spectacular array from the thirty or so cheesemakers in Warwick, I could not wait to see all the cheeses that three hundred cheesemakers might bring to this event.

Sculptor. *She is rendering a cow in cheese, at the American Cheese Society 2008 Annual Conference.*

Warwick had not begun to prepare us for the bounty of the Burlington Festival of Cheeses. We walked into an entire hotel ballroom filled with tables of cheese. More than 1,200 cheeses were displayed. The tables were landscaped with bales of hay and dried wildflowers as backdrops for the plates of cheese samples. Each table held only one type of cheese, although each type was offered at multiple tables. Here were the cheddars, there the Goudas, over farther the blues, and down the row the chèvres and flavored chèvres. Here were sheep cheeses; there were goat cheeses; over there were cow milk cheeses. Here were soft cheeses, farmer cheeses, cream cheeses, and yogurts. Butters and flavored butters also were available, and I had my first experience with sea salt butter — smooth, creamy richness with tiny specks of crunchable sea salt. Fruits and breads were offered alongside the cheeses to cleanse your palate between sampling binges. In the middle of the room a woman was sculpting a cow out of cheese, and another was carving the words "The American Cheese Society" into four big cheese bricks.

This was a showcase of cheeses. Volunteers had spent many hours over several days cutting the cheeses into sample-size pieces. We couldn't believe how much cheese we saw — and ate — dozens of varieties apiece. Warwick was no longer the measure.

I was already thinking ahead to the next year's conference in Chicago. I could not wait to sign up. The three of us went together again, and the sessions did not disappoint us. I went to a presentation on how medium and large chain supermarkets train their cheese specialists, a town hall meeting where cheesemakers and retailers debated vigorously about ensuring that consumers buy cheeses only when they (the cheeses, not the consumers) are at their peak, and panel discussions on selling cheese to chefs and creating a successful restaurant cheese program. I went to a session entitled "Wine Versus Beer Smackdown: Which Goes Better with Cheese?" I also went to "Coffee & Cheese Pairings: The Battle of the Terroirs." It seems in today's world that beer, wine, and coffee vie for face time with cheese.

The Festival of Cheeses was again an overwhelmingly delightful sensory voyage through the even-larger ballroom at the Chicago Hilton. This time the cheese sculpture was a four-foot-tall, ten-foot-long re-creation of the Chicago skyline. Again there were almost 1,200 types of cheeses to taste and hundreds of cheesemakers to meet. We estimate that among us we sampled close to two hundred cheeses and met close to one hundred cheesemakers. After Warwick and Burlington, we understood what the new American cheese looks like. Chicago presented us with another extravaganza of cheese and gave us our first opportunities to meet with and interview some of the new artisanal and farmstead cheesemakers.

A rendering of the Chicago skyline done entirely in cheese. *This spectacular display was featured at the 2008 American Cheese Society Annual Conference.*

American
Cheese Society
25TH ANNIVERSARY

B
2005 Kana
Dark Star

C
Père Jacques
Goose Island

1. Bandaged Cheddar
Bleu Mont Dairy Co

4. Ocooch Mountain
Hidden Springs
Creamery

2. Rogue River
Blue
Rogue Creamery

3. Winnimere
Jasper Hill Farm

A
2006 Yamill Valley
Vineyards Estate
Pinot Blanc

D
Alpha King
Three Floyds

American Cheese Society 25th Anniversary Conference -- 'Wine vs Beer Smackdown: Which Goes Better with Cheese
Saturday, July 26, 3:30 – 5:00

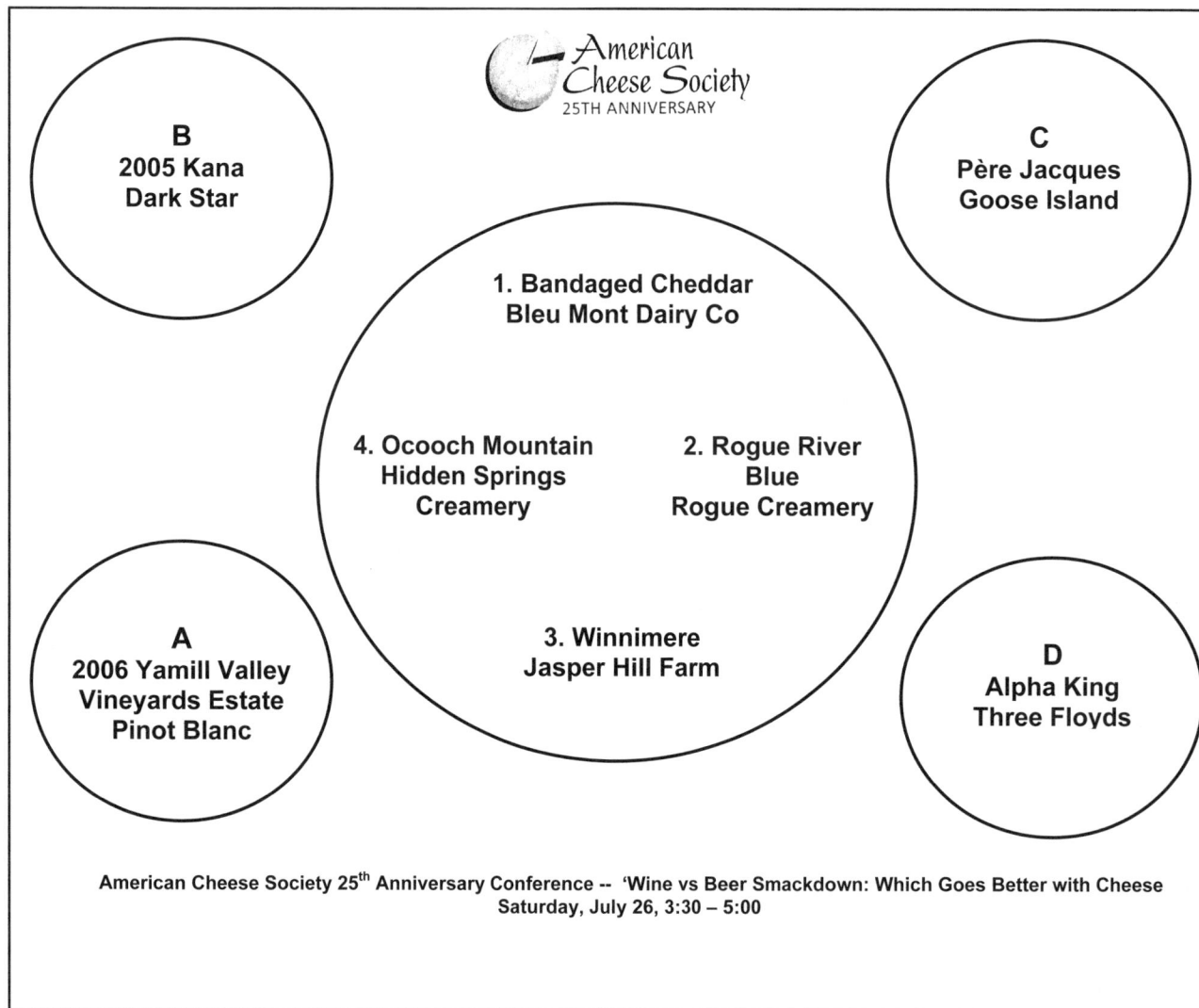

Beer versus wine smackdown. *We used this scheme at a 2008 American Cheese Society tasting session to discover the best pairings. We placed our wines on A and B, beers on C and D, and cheeses on the numbers 1 through 4. As we tasted each cheese with each beverage, a voice vote determined which pair best complemented the other.*

Short Take: Kitchen, to Cheese Room, to Factory

American cheesemaking has gone from the farm kitchen to huge factories capable of turning out hundreds of millions of pounds of cheese per year. In part this has been possible because certain aspects of cheesemaking are well-suited to scaling up—being made in ever larger batches.

Curd formation (renneting, cutting, cooking, and draining) used for most cheeses is one part of cheesemaking that can be scaled up relatively easily. The two-gallon stockpot we used for making cheese at home, the thirty-gallon vat of a farmstead cheesemaker, and the large vats in the factory in Cabot, Vermont, all do essentially the same thing. We were able to make one two-pound cheese with our vat, the farmstead cheesemaker could produce about 15 two-pound cheeses, and vats like we saw at Cabot might hold 3,000 gallons and produce 64 40-pound blocks of cheese.

Other processes used in production of certain kinds of cheeses are more difficult to scale up, however. The type of aging is critical. Surface-ripened cheeses, for example, must be small so that enzymes produced by bacteria or molds can penetrate to the center; some of them and some other cheeses must be treated frequently by careful turning, washing, or brushing, which are usually done by hand. We can imagine a warehouse-like aging cellar packed to the ceiling with 40-pound blocks of cheddar, but we can't envision a Brie or Munster being aged in such surroundings.

The scaling-up issue is one reason why so many more kinds of cheese are available now than when all our domestic varieties came from factories. Factory-made cheeses, for the most part, involve processes that are easily scaled up. Hand-made styles of cheese are difficult to industrialize, however, and thus include many varieties poorly suited for manufacture in factories.

Our home "cheese vat."

Small commercial vat. *A farmstead cheesemaker shows off his 30-gallon cheese vat.*

Cheese vat in a large factory. *We did not learn the size of this one, but know that vats of this type are available that hold up to 25,000 pounds of milk.*

Wintertime. *This image from the New York State Museum of Cheese was probably made in the early twentieth century. Obviously the iced-in canal boat pictured wouldn't be transporting cheese anytime soon. Contemporary farmstead cheesemakers don't have to worry about frozen canals, but they share a problem with cheesemakers of past centuries. Little cheese is made in the winter because the supply of milk decreases drastically when animals are preparing to give birth.*

Meeting the New American Cheesemakers

Our first indications of how farmstead cheesemakers—those who produce cheeses from milk produced by their own animals—see themselves and their profession came during three long interviews and several informal conversations at the Chicago ACS conference. Although we had met a number of cheesemakers the year before at the cheese festival in Warwick and the ACS conference in Burlington, we hadn't sat down and talked with them about their work. Awestruck by the sheer number of cheeses and cheesemakers at the earlier events, we were too distracted to engage in more than a few casual chats.

I can't put my finger on why the cheesemakers themselves intrigued us and why we felt others would want to know about their lives. But because they intrigued us, we thought the stories of the cheesemakers were probably part of why other people also are so enthusiastic about the new American cheeses. Each American artisan cheese seems intimately linked to the farm and the people who create it. Even the names of American cheeses we tried at festivals and tasting events— Humboldt Fog, Alderbrook, Holly Springs, Gore-Dawn Zola, Cave Aged Marisa—say more about where they come from and who made them than what they taste like.

An artisan cheesemaker's life appeared, from the distance of this cheese enthusiast's shopping basket, to be a return to the good old days of foods made by hand by people who care about their animals, their products, and those who eat what they make. In my mind's eye, artisan cheesemakers knew and controlled the source of everything they used to make the cheese. And the results of their labors were healthy, wholesome, and delicious foods. Whatever

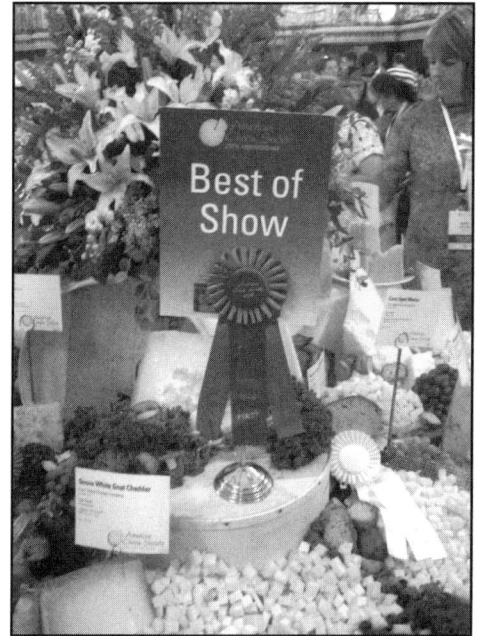

A coveted prize. This was the top award winner at the 2007 American Cheese Society annual judging.

our unconscious, intuitive reasons were for wanting to know about the cheesemakers—not just the cheeses—we knew they were going to be important to our understanding of the new American cheese.

At breakfast at the Chicago conference, we had joined a table of six strangers. Our tablemates were cheesemakers, and the discussion concerned regulations. An experienced cheesemaker regaled us with a story of having to get a milk-hauler's license for her car so she could drive small samples of milk to a neighbor's farm where they could be tested for antibiotics. Of course, she had not given any antibiotics to her goats so there could not possibly be antibiotics in the milk. Nevertheless the test was required of all milk used to make cheese. Not yet having the pricey instrument to test the milk herself, she drove to her neighbor's a few miles down the road and used his. The antibiotics test seemed reasonable since it is important to consumers to know if the milk is contaminated with them. But we laughed and laughed at the idea of regulators thinking a Pontiac Vibe driven by a cheesemaker to a neighboring farm ought to have a milk-hauler's license just like a refrigerated big rig driven by an over-the-road trucker.

One of the others at the table was a new cheesemaker in her inaugural season. She was glad that California, where she lived, did not have that antibiotics testing requirement. Silence fell. It seemed only three of us at the table did not know the requirement was federally imposed—me, Russ, and the new cheesemaker. Disheartening as it was to learn from her colleagues that she needed to test each batch of milk, and as hard as she tried to resist accepting what the other cheesemakers were saying, the message was clear: regulations may be funny, but they cannot be overlooked.

As we prepared to move to the first session of the day, I asked the milk-hauling cheesemaker if she would talk to us later about her farm and her operation. Willing and gracious, she was our first interview and our introduction to the story of life as a cheesemaker.

An early surprise in our conversations with cheesemakers was that there is no single model for "a cheesemaker's life." These people lived very different lives, on very different farms, pursuing very different goals. One couple described their sixty-eight-acre farm with one thousand milking goats fed primarily hay grown on the farm. We could picture a horizon of grain blowing in the humid southern breezes, a farm store and adjacent petting corral, employees (many from Mexico) making award-winning chèvre in forty-pound blocks as well as in family-size portions for farm visitors. The larger batches were frozen immediately for commercial customers, who would flavor, wrap, and prepare packages for marketing under their own brands. These cheesemakers made a lot of cheese. Commercial cheese operations were a profitable market for them. It was the first clue for us that farmstead cheesemakers were not all on small farms, making and selling under their own names.

Initially, this same couple said, they had sold exclusively to wholesale, commercial customers. But one day while he was working in the field a car pulled up and stopped. The driver asked if he made and sold cheese and wondered if his family could buy some cheese and see the farm. Russ and I were amazed that someone had been so bold, but the farmer said he was happy to call over to the cheese room on his cell phone and have some fresh chèvre brought out for purchase. He told the visitors to go ahead and look around. After a few more families happened by with similar requests, the farmer and his wife decided to turn an unused little building into a store. They built a corral and brought a couple of goats over so families could meet them. That started their retail operation.

That farmer's story was in contrast to the first we had heard, when we met with the milk-hauling cheesemaker and her husband. They had described a three-acre farm with fifteen named milking goats. She has two employees, a high-school boy and another neighbor, who help milk and care for the goats. The one-acre pasture used to be their herb garden. Her

Escape artists. *Goats seem more intelligent than most herding animals. They are naturally curious, and more than one goat farmer remarked about their inborn talent for escaping from fenced corrals.*

cheesemaking room is so tiny they can hardly turn around in it without bumping butts. In that room she turns out cheeses to supply local farmers markets and regional fine-dining restaurants. That description fit better what we'd thought farmstead cheesemaking would be like—bumping into each other in little cheese rooms and selling all the cheese locally.

When we met with the owner of a third farmstead and her head cheesemaker we got another version of the story. The owner painted for us a verbal image of the two thousand-acre rural resort that she and her husband had created. Lakes and timber cover the rolling land. Visitors dine on farmstead cheese made on site from the milk of resident Jersey cows. The head cheesemaker is a microbiologist by training and is recognized nationally for award-winning cheeses. Our idea of the makers of the new American cheese was expanding.

Granted, we knew that cheese is made by all kinds of artisans using milk they purchase, or milk from their own farms' animals, or some combination of these. But it was a surprise to hear stories about how some of the cheeses at the conference were made in cheese rooms as small as one hundred square feet by cheesemakers who had milked their named goats a few hours earlier. In contrast, others were made by cheesemaker-employees in commercial-grade buildings with milk from large on-site herds.

It was also surprising to learn that cheeses made by such different operations were entered into the same competition at the ACS conference. Two judges, one for technical qualities and another for aesthetic ones, evaluated each cheese against set criteria. It was no small accomplishment to come in first, second, or third in your class at the ACS judging. Each of the cheesemakers we interviewed had won a prize.

After the conference we continued our interviewing, visiting four cheesemaking farms on our subsequent trip to the Adirondacks. We picked them, as we had our cheesemakers in Chicago, on the basis of who was available and willing to spend time with us, rather than any cheese-based criteria.

In all our meetings with cheesemakers we asked how and why they had gotten into the business, expecting them to say it was because they loved cheese. But even more than a love of cheese, the appeal of farming and rural life was a strong draw for all of them. And whereas some had grown up on farms, others had not and had only fantasized about a farming lifestyle. Still others had turned to rural life and farming in reaction to their urban and corporate opposites. Love of cheese was not their first response.

One couple had always been farmers but had begun dairy farming only recently. Another cheesemaker told us that dairy farming was part of her family heritage. Her grandparents had cows. Their farm was one of her favorite places to be as a child and teen. She even liked the farm chores. Getting to live on a farm was one of the big appeals of becoming a cheesemaker. The family of the cheesemaker with a resort had owned timberland. She felt almost genetically linked to woods and rural landscapes. Cheesemaking was part of getting back to the land, but the land was the draw, not the cheese.

We also heard that you don't have to have grown up on a farm, come from a farm family, or lived in rural America to feel passionate about farming and the rural lifestyle to find yourself making the new American cheese. We talked to cheesemakers who had been professionals with intense and successful legal, financial, university, and health careers and no farming background. Nevertheless, they turned to farming as second careers. One family told us they had always talked about running away from their city life and starting a goat farm. Eventually they did.

Some cheesemakers told us the idea of the farming lifestyle was an early, persistent fantasy. One had wanted to be a farmer since she was a little girl although she had no family background or experience in farming. It was "just out there in my imagination,"

Farmstead cheese room. *We were permitted to make this photo from the doorway but were asked not to enter, in order to avoid possible contamination of the cheeses.*

she told us. When she and her husband bought a weekend home in a rural area near the city where they both worked, just being a part-time resident in a farm community brought back the dream, and they decided to try the real thing. The appeal of farming was enduring, and cheese was one of the ways to make farming work for her family financially.

It was a similarly long and convoluted journey for another. She had always secretly harbored the idea that farming might be a great way to live. The thought followed her from childhood, and eventually she bought a few goats—just because she liked the idea—and made soap from their milk. (It seems that people who like raising goats sooner or later have to address the problem of what to do with their output. Goats produce abundant milk, and readily produce more goats, who produce more milk. What starts as a hobby soon takes on the aspects of a business.) She also had a large garden. Vegetables and soap led her to help establish a farmers market in her town. But she remained a health professional who lived in the country. She was not yet a farmer.

Not unlike our daughter leading us on some of our initial forays into the world of cheese, it was actually this woman's children who introduced her to the rich array of new American artisanal cheeses. With two chefs in the family, one on each coast, she and her husband were introduced to many new cheeses when they went to visit. The cheeses were "wild cheeses," nothing like what was found near their home, she told us. She and her husband started wondering "Why don't we have local cheeses like that around here?" It got them interested in cheesemaking. She read. She went to Vermont and traveled the cheese trail—a network of cheesemakers who encourage visits by the public. After much thought and exploration she left her previous profession to become a cheesemaker and take on a real farming lifestyle.

She also was the first cheesemaker we talked to for whom the cheese itself was a driving force. For most, making cheese was initially a way to support living on a farm. Only when they started to make the cheese did they become passionate about the cheese itself.

More typical was a couple with a family farm. They want their children to be able to stay on the farm when they are grown. That means the farm needs to continually increase its profitability so it can support more families. Incomes from farms in their region have dwindled—no surprise—and they have to come up with new ideas to expand profitability. Cheesemaking is one of those ideas.

That couple talked about how farming has evolved, making it necessary for farmers to adapt and be creative. Decades ago, they said, dairy farmers could receive a price for their milk that was adequate to cover the cost of maintaining the animals and make a profit. They also could raise their own non-dairy animals on their own pastures and then sell them for meat. But government regulations and incentives, as well as changes in the agricultural economy, lowered the price of milk and caused shifts toward aggregation of farms. The process of raising the animals changed too. In the new process, the integrator process, one farmer raises the animal only until it is weaned. Another farmer then raises it to full-size. "You either have to adapt and become part of the integrator process, or get out of the business and go to work in town. We chose the farm life. It is what we want for us and our kids. We both grew up on farms; we plan to stay here. But it means constant change, and one of those changes has been goats, milk, and cheesemaking."

Until recently it did not make business sense to this farm couple to have goats because the price they could get for their milk was too low, they told us. The new interest in specialty cheeses had changed the equation. Although the price for fluid goat milk is still low, if the farmers turn the goat milk into farmstead cheese, it returns a quite good price. These farmers saw the growth of interest in the new American cheeses as a business opportunity and by adding cheesemaking to their farm's activities they created significant additional profits.

Holstein cattle. *These familiar black and white cattle are the overwhelming choice of most dairies in the United States because of the large volume of milk they produce. Cheesemakers often prefer other breeds that produce lesser volumes, but milks higher in butterfat content.*

Pigs and cheese? *Pigs can be part of an integrated cheesemaking operation, consuming whey, which otherwise might be a difficult waste product. Turning it into pork is far preferable to paying to have it hauled away.*

It might seem to you, as it did to us before we met farmstead cheesemakers, that cheese and pigs have little in common. But that is not true. The first time we heard about the pigs and cheese partnership was from this same family-farm couple. For a long time they have raised pigs. They used to raise them, grass fed, to full grown. Now with their farm as part of the integrated animal-raising process they only raise the piglets for a few months. After weaning the piglets move on, and another farmer feeds them to full size. The piglets and their sows live in a relatively small area and their manure needs to be dispersed. The farmers spread it on fields, nourishing production of hay, which in turn is good feed for goats. They bought the goats and built quite a large cheese factory. The decision to buy goats and produce cheese was a response to changes in the farming environment. Making cheese became a way to add to the productivity of their whole farm system.

Similarly for the large farm-resort invested in timber, recreation, and agri-tourism, cheesemaking was added because of its symbiosis with the other activities on their spread. Cows graze on the abundant pasture, making good use of the grasses and spreading manure the old-fashioned way. Guests and visitors dine on award-winning farmstead cheeses, adding to the reputation and tourist appeal of the farm. Experimenting with sustainable land-use models appeals to the owners for whom the viability of the agricultural economy in their region is important. Cheesemaking is part of their big picture but was not its starting point.

We began to understand that the possibility of making those rich, stinky, creamy, sharp, uniquely American cheeses was less the motivation for moving to or staying on farms and more the tool for sustaining the farms where the cheesemakers wanted to live.

On the other hand, we had not been totally off base in expecting that some people would turn to making cheese as an antidote to a fast-paced, high-pressure, urban lifestyle. "It was a midlife crisis," said one cheesemaker. She worked in the city but lived outside it, where she kept goats and made cheese for fun. She described herself as a lifelong animal lover who never had enough time at home with two-legged and four-legged family members. Serendipitously she spotted an ad for a goat farm and cheesemaking operation in the Adirondacks, much closer to her extended family than where she was living. She negotiated a telecommuting arrangement with her firm, bought the farm, packed up the family, animals and all, and headed for the Adirondacks.

Another, a healthcare professional, started making cheese because she was sick of fighting the third-party payers who stood between her and her patients.

The microbiologist-cheesemaker had grown up around his grandfather's several restaurants and had known when he was young that he wanted to continue to be involved with food. "I trained as a scientist and started working in laboratories," he told us. "Eventually I ended up as a brewer, then as a production scientist in a bakery. Then I went to Vietnam with a friend and saw all their wonderful 'rotten' fish products." Being from Wisconsin, he said he started to think about dairy products and what the fermented Vietnamese fish might have to teach him about other fermented food products. After a while he found his niche in fermented food, making artisanal and farmstead cheese.

We had a long conversation with one cheesemaker who does not live on a farm. His cheese is handmade but not farmstead since he has no animals of his own—and doesn't want any. "I really don't like large animals, except big dogs," he told us. "The cow is one of the most stupid animals. Goats are only a bit better." He got into the business because of the cheese itself. "I love making it. I love the smell of my hands when I'm making cheese," he said. He had been making cheese as a hobby for about ten years and gotten quite good at his favorite, a Camembert-style mold-ripened cheese. His second home, a historic early twentieth-century building, is located in a small city popular with tourists. He restored the exterior and renovated the kitchen into a cheese room, with stainless steel tables and chambers and presses.

He had a plan that after he retired he would make about a hundred and fifty pounds of cheese there each week and sell it to tourists. It would be a unique addition to the city's historic district and a nice way to spend time getting better and better at his cheesemaking.

As it turned out, he never opened his little business. The city had no zoning category for home industries, for people who wanted to make and sell pies or jams, for example. It required that he rezone as light industry, paying many thousands of dollars for a city review of his plans and registering with OSHA and the EPA. "I'll tell you," he said, "this dealing with the city was so hard. I felt completely flattened by it."

He had met other barriers along the way. He likes to use cow milk for his cheese and is perfectly content to have it be pasteurized. But "if it is homogenized, there is no way you'll ever make cheese out of it," he insisted. "The molecules are too uniform." He and his wife went to a farm to ask if they could buy a few hundred gallons of pasteurized milk before it is homogenized. "We nearly got bitten," she told us. "Yes, he set his dogs on us," the cheesemaker reported. "They chased us right off the farm." The farmer told them he could go to jail if he sold milk to them because of a state regulation against direct retail sales. In the end, the cheesemaker decided to buy skim milk and add cream to make his own non-homogenized milk. It was from him Russ got that idea and used it in his cheesemaking projects.

That cheesemaker mentioned that he thinks the increase in interest in cheese in America in recent years is part of a broader renaissance of interest in food—"the Slow Foodie thing," he called it. We heard similar ideas from others. Cheese seems to be a way of looking at the world. For example, another cheesemaker told us she and her husband are unhappy with the way food is produced and sold these days. "As a nation, we have gotten away from the traditions of growing our own food and being sustainable. Something is wrong when we import more food products than we produce, when food safety is a constant concern, and when energy must be invested to transport all the imported food." They want "to do something we feel is right for individual, national, and global reasons. It is a sort of mission to produce something we can be proud of ourselves and that we can contribute to the economy of our state," she said.

As appealing as is the image of living the pastoral life, with its beauty, peacefulness, happy and healthy animals, fresh country air, and no drives on a beltway to get to work, it didn't take us many visits to discover that life as a cheesemaker makes hard demands. No one we talked with complained, although it is easy to imagine former cheesemakers out there who couldn't find an acceptable balance between the work and its rewards. In addition to their discussions about why and how cheesemakers got into the business, they also told us about the work of setting up a cheesemaking operation, about the care of the animals and the farms, about learning to make the cheese itself and about their quite divergent ways of marketing their products. We had guessed correctly that meeting the cheesemakers would be integral to telling the story of cheese.

Cheesemaking woman. This image, from the New York State Museum of Cheese, shows a woman holding a cheese knife. With blades arranged like the strings on a guitar, the knife would be pulled through the curd, cutting it in small cubes in order to promote the expulsion of whey. The slightly slumped shoulders and blank expression on her face suggested fatigue to us. While none of the cheesemakers we met complained of long hours or grueling work, we became aware that being a cheesemaker is physically demanding and far from an easy life.

Short Take: Our First Surprise
Why People Go Into the Cheese Business

When we talked with people who were either cheesemakers or worked in retail or some other aspect of the business, we expected a certain amount of passion. Indeed, some of our cheese professionals were passionate. But contrary to our expectations, their passion was often not for the cheese itself. It was for the cheese business, the lifestyle afforded by being in the cheese business, or any of a large number of other things that motivated them. What we expected and failed to hear, was that most or all of them had an extraordinary and uncommon liking for cheese.

Part of our motivation for writing a cheese book was that the two of us really like cheese, and we had projected—wrongly as we learned—this motivation onto others. Maybe we are hopeless idealists, but we had blithely believed that people become coaches because they like sports, they become mechanics because they like engines, and they gravitate to the cheese business because of a love for cheese.

So on the facing page are some of the things we heard about that had motivated people to follow their career choices.

Some people gave multiple reasons, and most often they did not cite a single overwhelming reason. A typical answer might be: "We were tired of our old jobs, we saw an advertisement for this business, and we always thought we would enjoy running a shop." Note number 20. We include it because we believe that someone must have given us this reason, although it doesn't show up in our transcripts of interviews.

I first got into the cheese business because I…

1- wanted to escape from a high-pressure or unsatisfying profession

2- like animals and wanted to work around them

3- operate a successful farm and wanted to increase profit margins

4- operate a marginal farm and wanted to make it sustainable

5- have a background in farming and wanted to stay in touch with my roots

6- have no background in farming, but have a desire to live close to the land

7- felt drawn to retail sales and thought cheese would be an agreeable product

8- enjoy dealing with customers and colleagues at farmers markets

9- am naturally restless and want to try a variety of different careers

10-felt that cheese is a growing business and a good career move

11-had strong beliefs about foods and found cheese to be a natural

12-was interested in the technical complexities and challenges

13-was interested in keeping old traditions alive

14-needed a job and this was the best one available

15-was in some other aspect of food or agribusiness and got assigned to cheese

16-enjoy the opportunity to travel and see interesting people and places

17-felt it would be the best use of my university training

18-was recruited by spouse (significant other)

19-inherited the farm (factory, shop, etc.)

20-have a special liking for cheese

Canton, New York Cheese Plant.
Kraft Foods ceased most of its operations there in 2003, resulting in a net loss of 50 jobs and placing strains on the local economy.

Short Take: The New American Cheese and the Rural Renaissance

For more than a decade, people have been predicting a so-called rural renaissance. Russ came across the idea while doing research for another book. Since then, the idea seems to have expanded to take in a much wider range of understandings, depending on whether the emphasis is on material well-being or the quality of life. Not surprisingly, these different visions of a rural renaissance may clash seriously.

We understood that the common hope shared by all who envision the various versions of this renaissance. People will rediscover the virtues of life in the country, the historic migration from the countryside to the cities will be reversed, and chronically underpopulated and economically distressed rural areas will see vast improvements in the quality of life. More cash pumped into local economies, a wider range of job opportunities, better medical care, adequately supported schools, improved shopping choices, and cultural amenities will accompany the new prosperity. And the hope is that bucolic settings and the slow pace of life in rural areas will be unaffected by all the new people and new activity.

Surely many of the areas we visited looked to be in need of a rebirth. How do people here earn a living? We wondered. Do they all work for government agencies? They might survive by selling things to each other but we were at a loss as to where the money might come from. Even in what we believed was rich farmland, we saw little evidence of prosperity or growth. Disintegrating barns, rusting implements, and empty silos occupied landscapes no longer farmed.

We visited attractive towns, apparently quiet, comfortable places, the kind where almost anyone would like to live. Nevertheless, when soberly asking how it might be possible to migrate to one of these appealing places from some teeming urban center, the answers were few. Sure, a professor, social worker, or civil engineer might find a suitable job there once every decade or so when someone retired or died. But realistically, how were these areas to satisfy the economic requirements of more people?

It was clear to us, as to others, that a rural renaissance wouldn't be happening unless new opportunities were to materialize.

We first learned about the idea of a rural renaissance from reading *The Rise of the Creative Class* by Richard Florida. As is evident from the title, his focus is on creativity. Creative activities—the kinds of things propelling the new information economy—are increasingly freed from the constraints of location by advancing technology. Writing software programs or books, counseling clients on investments or college admissions, or marketing specialty products are activities changed by new technologies. Because of the Internet, effective transfer of information no longer requires physical proximity. And logistics have become highly effective, with almost no one more than a day away from a FedEx or UPS delivery. If your work can be performed using these services, why work from a dismal office hemmed in by a congested city? Instead you can sit in a quiet house in a quiet rural town and function as well as or better than in the old setting. And the community would also benefit.

Alas, we later stumbled on another cruder and almost antithetical vision of the rural renaissance on the World Wide Web. Its premise is that using farm products in the production of biofuels—specifically corn-based ethanol—will transform rural life by injecting prosperity into communities too long suffering volatile and often inadequate prices for agricultural commodities. Even the Adirondack Crescent might benefit if citizens could muster the political muscle to snag subsidies

Street scene in Canton, New York. *The village offers many attractions for those who appreciate small-town living, but it could benefit from more economic opportunities.*

A rural paradise? We found the village of Canton to be highly attractive on our many visits there, and we were distressed by evidence that the local economy, particularly the agricultural sector, seemed to be in decline. This appealing logo is shown on the web page of the Canton Chamber of Commerce.

for biofuels produced locally. Obviously, this agri-industrial production of commodity materials has little to do with the kind of creativity considered by Richard Florida.

A third, back-to-the-earth version of the renaissance asserts that the greatest value in rural life lies neither in twenty-first century creativity nor increased involvement in production of basic materials, but rather in a return to time-honored kinds of activities practiced by more or less traditional methods. Eschewing both participation in the global information economy and generation of significant new infusions of cash, all this has in common with the other versions of the renaissance is a generalized goal of revitalizing rural life.

We noted that the cheese business in America has elements of all three of these different visions. We saw in the biofuels vision much reminding us of the industrialization of mainstream cheesemaking—a resemblance that should counsel caution. By becoming commodity producers, mainstream cheesemakers tied their fortunes to a marketplace beyond their control or influence.

We thought some of the new cheesemakers exemplified both of the other visions of the rural renaissance. Some obviously were primarily motivated by the desire to be creative. They like the challenge of making cheese and inventing new methodologies and new kinds of cheeses.

Still others who are making cheese chose this pursuit because it gives them opportunities to live in the countryside, raise animals, heat with wood, and all the other accompaniments of rural life. Their vision of the renaissance seems rooted in a celebration of traditional values.

The question of whether the new American cheesemakers will bring about a renaissance broadly shared by the citizens of their rural communities remains open. Surely their presence in some communities has helped by bringing a measure of revitalization.

The Farm, The Animals, and Becoming a Cheesemaker

We learned a lot by talking to the cheesemakers and our farm visits added another dimension to our understanding of the animals, farms, barns, cheese rooms, and lives of cheesemakers.

Goats are curious and like to be petted. Sheep stay far afield, munching. Cows look at you as if they don't quite get why you are looking at them, and as if they would prefer you keep your distance. Barns are uniformly airy and clean while they smell of grass and warm animal bodies. The goat and sheep barns we were in did not smell of manure. We did not visit any cow barns.

We saw raised milking platforms and ramps the goats and sheep follow to their stations, where they munch on favorite grains while providing raw milk for the cheese. Predators, such as fishers (a large member of the weasel family of Canada and the northernmost parts of the United States), are more of a problem than we would have thought. The farms had guard animals—dogs, of course, but some had llamas and donkeys too—to keep the predators away. Used to thinking of farms as rolling expanses of growing grain, we found it odd when we learned that a goat farm might be only a few acres and feel a bit more like a country suburb than a rural outpost.

One of my favorite discoveries is that the animals themselves are the appeal of the cheesemaking life for some people. Goats are downright lovable—to these folks, at least. We visited a couple who never intended to make cheese. He wanted "show" goats. They needed to be really classy, he said, with all their papers. Initially he bought four beautiful goats, and he raised a collection from there. He sought out excellent bucks—the best buck he could find each time he bought one—paying $500 apiece for two of

Sheep far afield. *This was as close as we got to the sheep herd on a visit to one farmstead cheesemaker.*

them. Understandably these classy goats had some very nice kids. So they kept the does. Pretty soon, they had an excess of milk.

Solution? Get some calves to raise on goat milk and sell for veal. But the price to buy the calves went sky high and that idea didn't work out so well. They didn't want to pay the price for the calves, and the veal got to be worth less than the price of the new calves. "You can't make money doing that," they told us. Still all that milk. So they got some pigs to drink the milk. In fact, they still have pigs. We were really wrong that pigs and cheese have little in common!

The couple started to wonder if they might be able to sell the goat milk. The milk selling led to the cheesemaking. But it all started because they wanted to have show goats. Even now, years later, they still say they couldn't bear the thought of giving up their goats—"no matter what."

Animals are the heart of these cheesemaking operations. One family with more than a hundred goats had named them all. "How can you remember all their names?" I asked. As we walked through the barns, the goats trotted over when called by name and nuzzled up against the farmers. "How could we not remember them?" They answered.

Other farmers we met, even without naming their goats or sheep or cows, clearly valued what the animals bring to the farm's viability. They admired the animals as producers and as resources.

By studying the history of animal husbandry in the region where her farm is located, one cheesemaker learned that farmers had raised sheep there, long before cows were brought in. The cows were sold off when the consolidation of farms in the 1960s changed the farm and dairy landscape. Her family is returning sheep to the region where they had thrived in earlier times. The animals are a regional legacy as well as the core of her thriving business.

We saw a second way to match animals to the land.

"Many of our goats are crossbred with thoroughbred Boers," an Adirondack farmer told us. Boers are not dairy goats; they are a hardy breed of meat goat. "We also have some thoroughbred Alpines, LaManchas, Oberhaslis, and a few Toggenburgs. We have Saanens, the kind of great white Alpines. We have one Nubian and lots of Nubian crosses. We have Pygmies, Nigerian Dwarf goats—I think we have eight different breeds now." It is really cold in the Adirondacks in winter, and this farmer believes

Farmstead infrastructure. *Outbuildings on a farmstead producing goat cheese. Goats must be provided with warm shelter in cold climates, and some breeds are more sensitive than others.*

the crossbred goats are best adapted to the climate. "Sure, mostly we have mutts; at least half of ours are crossbred," she told us. "Many farmers try to create purebred goats, which have a resale value somewhere else. We are really breeding for hardiness."

In an e-mail we received months after our visit, a farmer told us that "Starting the middle of December we have had snow and cold. At the lowest, it was minus 30 here last week, and it's been below zero for most of two weeks. The barn is cold but the critters have winter coats and deep bedding. They are not out in wind and sub-zero temperatures like a lot of animals. It still bothers me to see cattle left in the woods—that surely is a poor excuse for a shelter." Her e-mail made us think that hardy breeds are a good idea in the Adirondack Crescent—both the farmers and their animals.

We spent a delightful early August evening on a farm in the Adirondack region feasting on roast chicken raised on site. The farmer couple was wonderfully cordial and welcoming—the aromas from their country kitchen equally so. The woman had started making cheese in a tiny, perhaps seven by nine foot, cheese room in their village home before they moved out to the farm. She got all her milk from local farmers and they eventually found this farm to buy. They wanted to have their own animals and experiment with building a cheese cave into the earth. They moved into the house on the former tenant farm during a November blizzard. The house had been abandoned for two years and "needed some work." The goat herd would arrive in December, and there was no barn. While living in the house and upgrading it to "livable," they poured the concrete floor for the barn—twice—the first time, it was too cold to set properly.

They are a hardy pair. He mentioned how consistently demanding the work is. In past jobs, he would put in a 40- or 50-hour week, but he only worked Saturdays or Sundays when he wanted extra money. Goats honor no weekends, he pointed out. Happily the goats do take a break from milk-making from about November until spring when they give birth, which for some reason that must be related to reverse psychology is called "freshening." During those more relaxed months, the farmers also could take a vacation if they could find someone to feed the goats and the woodstove twice a day. That had not happened yet, which, engagingly, made them laugh.

Their impression of the growing interest in the new American cheese is that it is part of the broader change in attention to how food is produced. They sell cheese at two farmers markets each week. The woman impressed me with her comment that the community of buyers is so cordial that if she didn't have cheese to sell, she'd want to sell something else just to work with these customers. The general philosophy of food at the two markets embraces the idea that buying locally is important for global reasons.

The customers talk about how foolish they think it is to burn fuel to move food from other countries to the Adirondacks so people can have "fresh" fruits and vegetables there in winter. They remembered customers talking about Michael Pollan's *Omnivore's Dilemma*. Theirs is not an artsy place or a college town, just a regular working-class community populated with people who want to know where their food comes from and who produces it.

After dinner, we met the goats as they climbed the ramp to their milking parlor. We chatted with the farmers as the husband prepared for the milking. The wife brought us outside when it was time for him to start because the noise from the vacuum pumps is very loud.

She took us to see the then under-construction cheese cave, which had not yet produced quite the right conditions for aging the cheese. From her cooler, we bought cheeses to take back to Star Lake—a fresh goat cheese, a feta, and a nutty tasting Gruyère type of cow milk cheese.

Having these lovable, productive animals totally dependent on you means it is really hard to get away for activities such as the ACS conferences or to pick up awards your cheeses win. A farmer told us she received a phone call from the head of the state cheese competition one year, urging her and her husband to come to the awards ceremony. They really didn't want to go, but it became clear their aged feta was going to receive the best-in-show award. So, they got up at three in the morning to have breakfast and do the milking, drove four hours to the event in time to receive their award, which was a piece of paper printed on someone's computer, and hightailed it home in time for the evening milking. The homemade certificate has a kind of grassroots charm. They framed

Farmstead cheese cave. *The owners who built this one told us that further development would be needed before it met their expectations.*

it, and it hangs on the wall in the cheese room. They clearly love telling the story because it so typifies the constraints their beloved goats place on them.

Our interviews convinced us even more that the phenomenon we are trying to understand is not just about cheese. Making the new American cheese is a way for the people to be close to the land, to raise healthy animals, to enrich their lands by using byproducts of good farming practices, to supply a consumer market that is growing with a new consciousness about food in America. We know we like the new cheeses in part because of how they are made by hand by people who care, but we had not supposed that the cheesemakers would like it in part for the same reasons.

We learned that the startup path is steep. You need money—lots of money—and you need to be certain before you begin that your expenditures will create profits, or at least break even. A farmer told us that cheese is only one source of his income and that although he didn't really have to make much money on it, he certainly couldn't afford to lose money. Unlike him most of the people we met needed real profits from their cheese enterprise.

Feeding time. *Herds kept by farmstead cheesemakers may feed in pastures, but most seem to rely to some degree on commercially prepared feed.*

We also learned that you need to know how to take care of the animals properly. "We've met people at the ACS conference who are thinking about starting and they don't know anything about making cheese or taking care of goats. We didn't know about making cheese when we decided to get into the business, but we knew the livestock part," said one of our interviewees. The cheesemaker who was already well experienced in managing and harvesting her land before she started with dairy animals and cheesemaking said that, even with all the research and careful planning they had done, when their first cows arrived she and her husband had a brief moment of panic: "Oh my gosh, now what do we do?" She made us laugh when she said, "Then the cows started having babies, and we knew we had to get expert help."

In addition to knowing how to care for the animals, there are regulations and safety requirements to know, equipment to purchase and set up, and marketing skills to learn. The getting-started stories wove all these threads together.

When we made cheese at home to see how it was done, Russ used our soup pot for a cooking vat and inverted our cast-iron kettle over a big can of tuna to jury-rig our original cheese press. Real cheesemakers need to invest in much more. They told us that it not only takes a lot of money to start the operation but more and more as time goes by. "A lot of people are going into this who are never going to make it," guessed one.

Everyone had cost- and revenue-related stories. One farmer told us that in trying to decide when and whether to start making cheese, the main question had to be, "Will I be able to get my money back?" He and his wife wanted to add dairying to their other farming endeavors: "But it didn't work on paper. If it didn't work on paper, it wasn't going to work actually." They looked for a viable dairy farming business plan for at least two years before buying a goat. "Finally," he said, "we had a model we thought would work. You crunch the numbers and crunch the numbers. I knew how much it was going to take, and how much a pound it was going to cost. We had a so-many-pounds-of-cheese-per-goat-per-year analysis. You have to know what it actually costs to produce a pound of cheese."

Costs must be kept down and revenues up. "Costs pushed us to be more grass fed," said another cheesemaker. "It was a very good thing. Our cheese is better for it, even though we started it with a cost-saving motivation."

"We can't charge top dollar here where we live," another said. "Living so far from a major market limits our ability to charge more. We need to understand what we really can get per pound, and it is not what we could get in a big city."

Milking time. Walking up a ramp to the milking station and eager to be milked, these goats were nevertheless curious enough about the arrival of strangers to turn around to look back at us.

Equipment needs. *This custom made pasteurizer, fashioned from a hospital soup kettle, took more than a year to fabricate while the would-be cheesemaker waited for the only available certified welder to finish the project.*

It took one farm couple we visited more than a year to get their equipment in place. And that was two years after they had begun to sell milk and get everything lined up so they could pass inspection to produce cheese. For starters, they told us, the "small" vats and the pasteurizers available at the time they started held 500 gallons. They wanted to deal with no more than 50 gallons at a time. To satisfy themselves and their dairy inspector, they had to have a certified welder build for them what they came to think of as a "designer pasteurizer." In their rural area, there was only one certified welder for miles around. He had bigger jobs in line that paid more. Theirs kept being delayed. "We decided to start with a 35-gallon soup kettle, like they use in a hospital kitchen," the farmer said. "The welder cut the bottom right out. Every week or two, I'd drive over to see how it was coming along—for a year!" Later when they had their similarly small cheese vat built, they found a metal shop in a city about a hundred miles away and had it done there. "It was the first vat they'd ever made."

The delays might have been intolerable if they hadn't been, at the same time, getting their act together in other ways—like renovating a garage into a cheesemaking room and building a convenient and comfortable milking parlor in the barn.

Another family had cashed in on the real estate market at exactly the right time, providing a mountain of capital to buy a so-called turnkey farmstead cheese operation. But it takes "an amazing amount of capital, for fixing up barns and replacing worn equipment that would negatively impact your quality of life," they said.

"We had earlier professions," said another. "We purchased the farm and built much of our infrastructure in those days, while we were employed by other people. Earlier we had a different house that we'd fixed up. We sold it to buy this farm that had more commercial potential. We started fixing this one up—the barns, the fences." She explained that they did not make cheese in the beginning. They sold other farm products. "Infrastructure—building a cheese room and putting the equipment in it—is tough. That wasn't part of the initial farm purchase, and we financed what we needed for cheesemaking through sales of our milk, meat, and other products," she said. "We had the luxury of having income from our professions, and using our sales to build our cheesemaking infrastructure. We started really slowly."

Capitalization is the key. Having adequate capitalization is a critical first step. One couple gave us an example. "A girl came by recently to ask us about our place. She lives way out here in the Adirondack region far from any cities, like us. She's already milking quite a few goats. She'd like an operation like ours eventually," they explained. "We told her it takes a lot of money to get into it." They felt it was their most important message to her. "She and her husband are young. They've got truck payments and all that kind of stuff," the couple told us. "We're always going to be small. This is never going to be our only income. A 35-gallon pasteurizer and a 35-gallon cheese vat are fine for us," they went on. "But I told her if she would wait and get herself a 50-gallon, and were a little bit older with the bills paid off and without three or four vehicles, kids running around or off to college—probably they could live on that. Of course, you're going to work an 80-hour week, I'll tell you. But if it is something you like, you'll make it work," said the cheesemaker encouragingly.

A herd of sheep. We found them less attuned to our presence than goats, which seem to seek out interactions with people.

We heard many stories about learning the regulations and meeting your own personal requirements for safety of your animals, equipment, and cheeses. One of our favorites was from the farmer who wanted show goats. "First we had goats, because I loved

French farmers market. We saw this booth at a market in France where cheeses, sausages, and pâtés are displayed together. An American cheesemaker we met found it remarkable that in Europe these kinds of products can be produced in a single facility, something that would never be permitted in the United States for fear of cross-contamination.

them. Then we had more goats; I still loved them. Then we had an awful lot of milk. We sold some but after a while I thought, 'Well maybe we need to make cheese.' The inspector came down and told us what we needed to do and what he expected of us. I thought, 'Gee, I don't know.' It seemed like quite a lot of work just to get ready to begin."

Cheesemakers and retailers are all in the same boat when it comes to not wanting to have problems with spoiled or tainted food. At a factory we heard that "Once you have an active culture in the cheese, you've got the safest food in the world. But it is a matter of fear for a retailer. Big name firms have gone ka-phlattt, out the window, because they've had a problem. Stockholders and everyone says the company needs to do everything it can to be sure everything the consumer buys is perfectly safe. It is not just about government regulation; the bigger retailers have more strict regulations and accounting requirements than the government."

A small producer told us, "Regulations are discouraging at first. Once we got into it though, looking back on it, it wasn't that bad. Our inspector is really strict, but he is a good guy."

The inspectors often are not accustomed to small operations, such as many farmstead cheesemakers have, the farmers told us. Often inspectors think of farms as having only big animals, big herds, big barns, large pastures and large output to commercial outlets. Learning to work with inspectors and regulators whose thinking does not really match your own small operation reality is challenging for both the farmers and the inspectors, said the couple. "The first day our inspector came to us," said the woman, "I had all our cheeses out that we'd made in the house to learn how to do it well. I had ice cream, too." The inspector told them theirs was "the first goat cheese I've had that doesn't taste bucky." They laughed at the memory. The inspector had been dealing with "people who don't take care of their milk, or they let the bucks run with the does. We know you can't do that," said the man. Russ and

I didn't know that. I felt as if we had captured a piece of absolute insider information: Keep the buck far away from the does, except when he is "on duty."

Many cheesemakers commented on the usefulness of regulations. "There is a barn inspector and a milk inspector. I'm not saying there would otherwise be bad milk out there, but you don't need anything more to worry about," a farmer told us. Another said, "It is good that well water is tested and that an antibiotic test is required on every batch of milk. But it is sometimes a funny scene when these regulations written for the large cheesemakers play out with the small producers," he said. It reminded us of the Pontiac Vibe story at the breakfast table in Chicago.

One cheesemaker was familiar with European farmsteading because her family had lived in France for several years. She said that regulation is good but that it does inhibit what we do in the United States, and some of it doesn't make sense. "The French can produce wonderful cheese on such small farms because they are more heavily subsidized and less heavily regulated. It is a combination of the two," she said. "Also the farms in Europe tend to have been in the families for years and the farmers are not paying off mortgages. And, they can sell practically anything they can produce. Heck, they can make their own sausage!"

Regulation did shut down some cheese producers when it first became stringent, we heard. "In the days when we were coming up, there was a cheese factory in every town," said one cheesemaker. "The farmers milked in barns with dirt floors. They put the milk in cans and hauled it to the town factory. Then regulation came along. You couldn't do this, and you couldn't do that. The farmers all needed to put concrete floors in the barns. With the price they were getting for the milk, they couldn't afford it, and they all went out of business. The cheese factories had to shut down." The regulations just did not match the reality of small farm ability to take on new costs. Nor, in the opinion of that farmer, did the regulators understand that on a small farm near to its milk factory the farmer

Farm building. *This one was converted to serve as a combination cheesemaking facility and owner's residence.*

Young buck. On this farmstead as on others where quality goat cheeses are made, the male goats are kept separate from lactating does to avoid imparting a "goaty" flavor to the milk.

can produce clean, good milk without the sterile environment needed by a large farm that will send the milk long distances before it is processed.

A thought-provoking discussion emerged around the kitchen table at one farm we were visiting. The ideas touched on several of the topics we heard in many places: costs, revenue, capitalization, regulation, taking care of the animals. Neighbors dropped by midmorning at this farm—an apparent daily routine.

Because we were there, or possibly just because they had this conversation often, they started talking about the sustainability of small farms. The cheesemaker was the optimist. She said she thinks small farms are going to make a comeback. "People will start growing things again and making stuff at home."

The rest thought mega-farms had killed any chance for small farms to return and be sustainable. "Farms are industry now, no longer family," said one neighbor. "Dairy farms will never come back," said another. "They sold the property to a big farmer who didn't want the buildings, just the land. The big farmer sold the house to somebody and the barns to somebody else. You will never reunite that piece of property. It's gone." "If the family in the house wants to have a couple of cows, they have to drive twenty-five miles to get hay for them. And then they have to buy the hay from the person who owns the land that used to be the farm that the house is on. Something's wrong!" Said a third. "I can't see how you could make money—even before fuel cost so much."

"Well, look at New York City," said the cheesemaker. "They say every flower box has something more than a geranium in it. Maybe it's a left-handed cigarette, but more likely it's some herbs or something. People are thinking back to the old victory gardens and stuff like that. I think small farming can and is coming back."

Every farmstead cheesemaker we talked to had ideas for additional products they could sell to make their farms more sustainable. Surprisingly, most had more demand for their cheese than they could meet. "We produce, and what we produce we sell it all, without advertising. It is all word of mouth," said a cheesemaker. The limit on their sales had as much to do with their ability and willingness to increase the size of their animal herds and to process more milk as on the willingness of customers to buy the relatively expensive specialty cheeses.

They were almost all thinking about non-cheese products too. "There are a lot of spinoffs from goats and the dairy that we could do, with stuff we have to deal with anyway. We could actually do bagging of the goat nuggets. Fertilize your flowers," said one. Others we met were already bagging and selling the "nuggets."

We got the impression that financial sustainability of the cheese farmsteads is in the eye of the beholder because the cheesemakers have such differing goals. Among those we talked with, the goals ranged from supplementing the family's income so they could live on a productive farm, to increasing the farm's profitability so it could support the families of the now-grown children as well as the parents, to creating a model of diversified farming that helps make a whole region—not just a single farm family—be at least minimally self-reliant.

What was definitely not just in the eye of the beholder was how these farmers work to have healthy, happy animals giving naturally nutritious milk, to have healthy well-run cheese rooms and meet all the regulations, to make good cheese and sometimes to age it, and to get the new American cheeses into the hands of those who want to buy it.

Short Take: Difficult Choices for the Cheesemaker

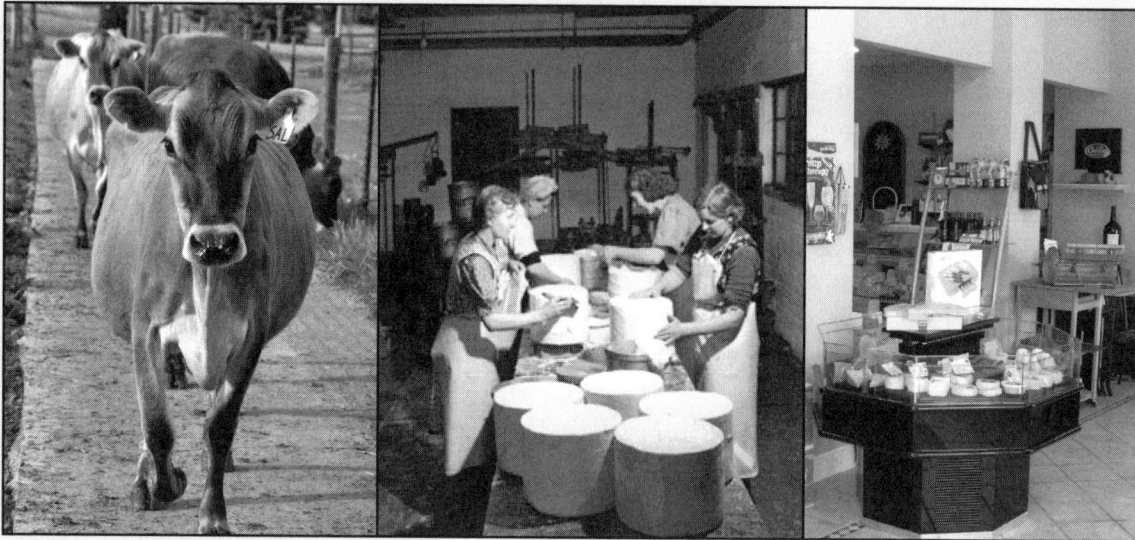

Depending on the model employed, aspects of a cheesemaking operation may include (left to right above) dairy farming, making cheese, and marketing. Each of these can be a major preoccupation.

If all three are included in a small or family-run operation, number of animals and kinds of cheeses produced are likely to be small, cheeses made may be of less demanding styles, and their availability to customers is apt to be limited.

If a small or family run operation handles the farming and cheesemaking aspects, but leaves marketing to a distributor, production volume, variety of cheeses, and availability to customers can be greater, but profits must be shared with distributors.

Rarely a small operation might do both cheesemaking and marketing, leaving the farming to others. This would help to increase production volume and preserve some of the profits from sales, but the cheesemaker would lose control of the supply and quality of milk available.

The cheesemakers enjoying the greatest financial success might focus on the making of cheeses, while developing a network of suppliers to ensure that milks are of high quality and available as needed. Likewise, they could exercise a measure of control over marketing by developing home markets in addition to using outside distributors. Ideally, they would be able to make several kinds of high value-added cheeses.

Choice of strategies might be difficult for beginning cheesemakers. In the end, tradeoffs between financial goals and personal preferences may need to be made.

Short Take: For the Love of Animals

We knew from our interviews that some people get into the business of making cheese because they are fond of animals. We also suspected those who may have gotten involved for other reasons might become fond of their dairy animals after dealing with them on a daily basis and coming to see them as partners in earning their respective livelihoods. We wondered if the *business* of cheesemaking did not frequently clash with the sentiments of those who found themselves liking their animals. What if one of your faithful servants—perhaps a goat you have milked for many years—stops giving milk? Do you establish a retirement home for her and other worn out goats and resolve to care for these wards for the duration? Or do you turn excess livestock into goatburger, knowing that you must seize every possible advantage if your business is to thrive?

The very thought of facing the need to offload animals no longer meeting the needs of your business made us uncomfortable. We had been through the wrenching experience of putting down aged and infirm pets, and any raising of the subject was certain to fire off irritable nerves. Based on this background, we avoided asking any farmsteaders what we thought might be an overly personal and perhaps painful question about the disposal problem. Nevertheless, we saw and heard things that helped us identify who among our farmsteaders might fall in among the sentimental and some others whose inclinations would clearly be toward the business side.

One farmstead we visited in addition to making cheese, was proudly operating a retirement home for goats, as well as for several other kinds of animals brought there by people seeking homes for homeless beasts. No question there; when the issue arose, the sentimental would always win out over the practical.

At the other extreme, we sensed there was no way the farmer we interviewed who had more than 1,000 goats was likely to get sentimental about any of them. Nor did we detect any strong sentimental bent in the sheep farmer who told us that her dairy could be sustainable only if she found markets and received adequate remuneration for all the products of her farm. These included not only cheese, wool, and manure, but also meat and hides.

It was the people in the middle who we found most interesting—those who we believed were often faced with dueling sentimental and business interests.

One story brought the inner conflict home to us. A cheesemaker told us how she and her husband had gotten their newest acquisition, a Jersey cow. Searching far and wide, they had finally found the cow they wanted downstate. They were planning to begin milking right away, but the timing wasn't what they had hoped for—her calf wasn't due until April. The milking season would be late, but she seemed just right otherwise and they had purchased her anyway.

While the story was told to us, the cow who was one of its central characters looked at us with curiosity, from perhaps 25 yards away in a small pasture. When we remarked about her apparent interest in us and suggested that we might approach her more closely, the owner told us it would do no good. The cow was gentle and friendly to the owner and her husband, she said, but was suspicious of strangers. If we got close, she would turn her tail to us and look the other way.

They had purchased the cow in the late winter, April had rolled around and, unfortunately, the calf she delivered was a bull. This was a problem. Nobody wants a bull calf, the owner told us. They looked into selling him, but no one was willing to pay a decent price for him. He was a fine animal, she said, and husband and wife had debated for days about what to do with him. In the end they reluctantly decided to "veal" him, even though they were not in the practice of eating beef, and she had never cooked with veal. They fed him nothing but milk, she told us, and he dressed out at a surprising 150 pounds (underscoring, we believed, her earlier statement about what a fine animal he was).

All of this was said dry-eyed and with a level, business-like tone. Nevertheless, the regret in the words she spoke and the barely discernible hesitation in the way she said them was unmistakable. The saga, in this farmer's view, was far from a happy one. And six months later the regret was still there.

We were moved by her story, and also inspired. Those who love animals so much that they want to work with them as a lifetime occupation, we began to understand, must buy the whole package, which surely involves decisions at odds with their preferences. We probably read too much into the episode, but we even thought we detected something akin to a belief often attributed to Native Americans. We had heard they felt that hunting, killing, and reaping the bounty offered by animals was a solemn experience—a way of commingling with and thereby honoring the spirits of these fellow beings.

We can accept all humane and reasonable views of how people and animals should interact. We felt some sympathy for the animal lovers who refused to dispose of animals, and a bit less for those who find raising animals more akin to raising cucumbers than to a holy mission. But we found the greatest liking for those in the middle—those who knew and accepted, often with regret, what they had to do—but did so soberly, with a sense of responsibility, and ultimately with a full measure of humanity.

Making friends. Peg gets acquainted with the classy goats on a cheesemaker's farm in the Adirondack Crescent.

Short Take: Artisanal Cheese in Florida

Clearly the new American cheese is a phenomenon sweeping the nation, and we expected to find new cheesemakers in Florida, our home state for more than a decade. At first we searched in vain. We heard of someone near Fort Lauderdale making cheeses primarily for family and friends. And we met a would-be entrepreneur who had hoped to make cheeses for sale in a historic downtown, but was discouraged by a maze of urban regulations.

Luck favored us just as this book was nearing completion when we learned of a new cheesemaking family near us making pasteurized cow milk cheeses. They alerted us to another, the Winter Park Dairy, a new cheesemaker producing a raw-milk blue-veined cheese. We later learned that the Winter Park Dairy was the first, and so-far only facility in the state, certified to make and sell raw-milk cheeses.

Winter Park family farmers with twin daughters and some of their small herd of Jersey cows.

We found the farm nestled in the sprawl surrounding Orlando. Gracious owners David Green and Dawn Taylor-Green, joined by daughters Eugenia and Eleanor, showed us around their eight acre mini-farm. A handful of Jersey cows, including milkers Molly and Bessie, look through fences into suburban yards, a busy highway, and one of the many picturesque local lakes.

A lesson in simplicity and appropriate technology, the facility is a marvel of thoughtful planning. Engineering accomplishments pale, however, compared to the delightful cheeses issuing from them. We sampled and brought away a complex, creamy blue-veined cheese with a surprising edible white-mold rind. Their Sunshine Bleu, is certain to convert cheese agnostics into true believers. Attending a national conference nearby and plying attendees with the Winter Park Dairy cheese, we became one of the conference's major attractions (some might say distractions.)

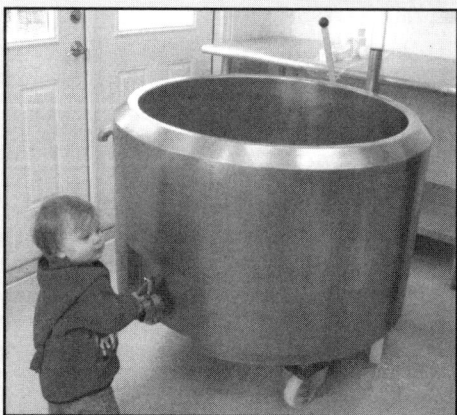

Future cheesemaker Eleanor examines the Winter Park Dairy cheese vat.

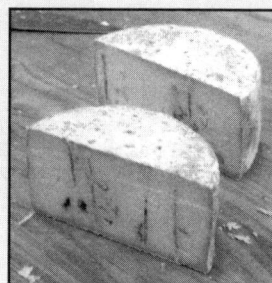

Making and Selling Cheese

Desire for a rural lifestyle, acquisition of farm and animals, understanding of agricultural economics, accumulation of startup capitalization, meeting regulation and licensing requirements—these are the precursors to finally making and selling cheese.

Making cheese is a skill, a science, and an art. It involves multiple upfront decisions, multiple precise moves during the process, and for many cheeses extraordinary attention after you are "finished." Despite the fact that people have been making cheese since pre-historic times, each cheesemaker we met seemed to be self-taught in an artistic sense. Although they might have sought out old recipes, taken a short course, apprenticed with an experienced cheesemaker, or read everything they could find, the final step in their learning was to practice, develop their own taste and style, and become unforgivingly discerning about the quality of their cheese.

Some early American artisan cheesemakers, such as Laura Chenel, Mary Keehn, and Allison Hopper, traveled to Europe and picked up cheesemaking know-how there. But even after learning the ways of French experts, the new American cheesemakers seemed to grow their cheeses with a lot of grassroots experimentation.

Many cheesemakers seek formal and informal education and then participate in regional associations such as the New York State Farm & Artisan Cheesemakers Guild and national organizations like ACS to keep up with or ahead of peers and experts.

"We learned cheesemaking from the folks we bought the farm from," a cheesemaker said. "They taught us their process. Then we streamlined it to make it more

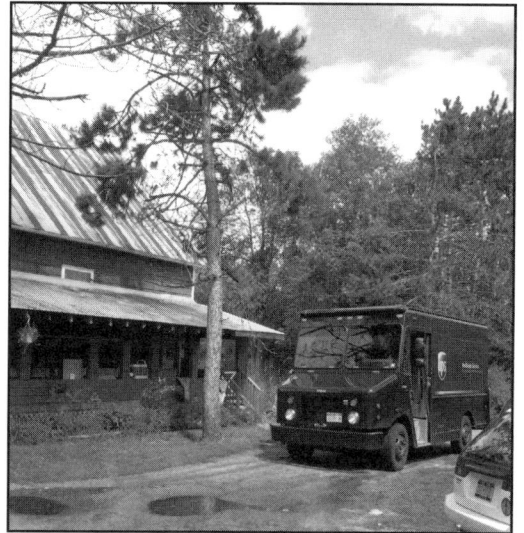

Modern farmstead logistics. *Despite the overall back-to-nature aspects of farmstead cheesemaking, the success of these enterprises often requires rapid and efficient transport to markets.*

dependable. People love the artiness of artisan cheese, but they also want a consistent, predictable quality each time they buy it. Through experimentation, we improved on the predictability of the processes we learned from the former owners."

Old cheese recipes gleaned from books, from friends, and from family launched some of the people we met onto the learning curve but they were not enough. "We had a few family recipes," said one. "Right," said her husband. "My mother made cheese up at the house. But you and I kind of taught ourselves, don't you think?"

One farmsteader said she and her husband had started by experimenting. Her recollection was that "It was such fun, so interesting, and very difficult. But we soon decided it was best to find some real expertise."

The experiments Russ did in our Florida kitchen convinced us of two truths: that making cheese is not difficult and that making good cheese consistently is not easy. "We started making cheese with a few Nigerian Dwarf goats," said a farmsteader. "It was a hobby. The cheese tasted really good, and we thought we had it down. Later we learned that Nigerian Dwarfs have very high butterfat and it is hard to make cheese from their milk that doesn't taste great."

Another said that "It was a long learning curve—years, really. In the beginning, we just milked. We didn't have a background in agriculture. There were few models out there for an operation like we envisioned. We sold the milk, but it was not economically feasible to get by on those sales. I experimented in the kitchen with cheesemaking until I had a pretty good knowledge of it. Then it was like diving off the high board: You just have to do it."

"Learning to make cheese?" Echoed one woman. "What a long road! I made it at home. The chèvre was okay; it is hard to really screw up chèvre. But, the cheddar—it was terrible."

Coursework doesn't always help. A couple told us about their experience. "We took a two-day class. But I didn't get anything out of it," said the woman. "I didn't either because the teacher would do four or five kinds of cheese at once and expect us to keep up with what he was doing," added her husband. "It was very technical. It was the way you're 'supposed' to do it," he said. "We've had people ask if we have the pH meter that we learned about in the class. We have one, but I never use it. I really can tell if the cheese is ready by the look of it. We've done the same thing right along, and it comes out fine." "I tell him," said his wife, "I hold my breath every time I put the rennet in." "Nah, I don't even think about it," he responded.

In contrast, formal education better fit the learning styles of other cheesemakers. One took courses at a university and, of course, one was a microbiologist. Others took short courses from individual artisanal cheesemakers or state guilds and cooperatives. One talked about learning by visiting others' farmsteads to observe their processes. Another brought someone in for a few days to guide her through the transition from small-scale, kitchen-based cheesemaking to the large scale of her commercial cheese room. "I knew how to make the cheese, but it really helped to get guidance with the logistics of managing on the larger scale."

Process is crucial because it creates safe, good-tasting, quality cheese. One couple explained their thinking about safety. "We pasteurize," the husband said. "Someone could get sick on a hot dog and blame it on our cheese if we used raw milk. We don't want that risk. We pasteurize at a low temperature and hold it for a-half hour. This way we don't get a cooked taste. You need to keep some of the bacteria, or you don't get a good cheese." "A visitor tried our cheese," said his wife. "It didn't taste like what she thought cheese from pasteurized milk was going to taste like—cooked or burned. Anyway, she was quite happy to learn what we do." We had tried their milk too, while sitting around their kitchen table with the neighbors solving the farm problems of the world

Cooler in a farmstead cheese room. *Fresh goat milk is placed in the cans seen here, and then into this cooler. When the doors are closed, the cans are bathed with chilled water. This produces more rapid cooling than a household refrigerator, in which cooling is accomplished by contact with air.*

and wondering what people grow in the flower boxes in New York City. It certainly didn't taste burned to us.

Our very first cheese interview was not with a cheesemaker or cheese vendor but rather with an "enthusiast." I asked her, "Where did your cheese interest begin? Have you always been a cheese lover?" She told me that she must have been born loving cheese. "When I was not happy," she remembered with a smile, "my mother would always give me cheese." But we heard about many people who, unlike this enthusiast, were highly resistant to trying unfamiliar cheeses. Public acceptance of, and demand for, the new American cheese was no slam dunk. Having not started out as a cheese lover myself, I found it quite easy to empathize with the "bad guys" in stories we heard from our cheesemakers. I was slow to develop a taste for my father's favorite sharp, white New York cheddars, but having once found those taste buds I was eager to feed them more and more exotic and sophisticated cheeses. Apparently many people came more slowly than I did to the now widespread appeal of the new American cheese.

When cheesemakers began trying to market their artisan cheeses, they met some funny (in retrospect) reactions. At their local farmers market, their neighbors and friends went far out of their way to avoid one cheesemaker couple. Their friends really did not want to eat goat cheese. They would walk all the way around the outside of the market to get past their cheese stand, so as not to have to reject a sample. Eventually, one brave or kind-hearted soul came over, tried it, and liked it. He encouraged the skeptics; they started trying it too. Later a major discussion ensued about the difference between this cheese and the "goaty" cheese they had eaten as children on their farms.

Restaurants are a primary market for some farmstead cheeses. On the menu in August 2009 at the Windfall Restaurant near Star Lake we found a salad special that included County Meadows chèvre, an Adirondack Crescent farmstead cheese. The move to fresh and local cheese in restaurants probably started with Alice Waters using Laura Chenel chèvre in the 1980s to top her locally grown baby greens at Chez Panisse in Berkeley, California. Okay, it took twenty-five years or so to get from Berkeley to the Adirondacks, but there is no denying the market is now widespread. Gradually or instantly, in restaurants, at farmers markets, and in grocery stores, in cities and outside them, people stopped backing away from goat cheese. Laura Chenel is quoted in the *United States of Arugula* as saying that "Nooooooo!" was the customer response when she first offered samples of her goat cheese.

The growing popularity of the new American cheese in restaurants, stores, and farmers markets is a key influence on farmers who are looking for ways to increase the profitability of their farms. Said one farmer, "We could see this evolution of cheeses and that goat cheese was getting to be very popular. We felt there would be a demand for it if we started making quality goat cheese. Initially we sold one hundred percent wholesale, sold only to other cheese plants. They would take our cheese, add herbs or other flavoring, vacuum pack it, and sell it. Every place we shipped, they also made their own cheese, but they couldn't produce enough themselves for the market demand. Now we do some retail sales as well, but if we tried to sell all our cheese to local retail markets, we'd starve to death." We were glad to have met him because he helped us understand the importance of the wholesale side of the new American cheese phenomenon.

Retail sales are the primary focus of most other cheesemakers we met. Some sell through distributors and to restaurants, some to retail stores, and others sell directly to consumers. The reasons for choosing how to get their cheese to the markets relate to location, how much cheese they make, and the individual farmers' priorities. For a big farm, remote from a city market, producing a lot of cheese, and wanting to maximize cheese income, we now understood that wholesale makes the most sense.

Aging cellar. *Existing cellars of houses in the northern states often provide ideal conditions for aging cheeses.*

It does not for others. "Probably 80% of our gross sales are to retail customers, with restaurants and a couple of small cheese shops making up the rest. That's how we intend to stay," said one. She has access to a high-end farmers market where, in a couple of day-long visits a week, she sells all they produce on her farmstead. She is unwilling to have a distributor or even many specialty shops market her cheeses. By having a distributor handle the sales of the cheese, she would save herself the long days at the farmers market and free up time to make more cheese. However, a major portion of the price the cheese brings would go to the distributor. Also, she would have to relinquish control of the product before the consumer buys it, creating the risk of the cheese not being handled optimally. She would rather spend her time at the market, selling directly to the consumer, ensuring that the cheese is handled the way she wants all the way from farm to sale, and gleaning the full revenue from each sale for the farm rather than paying part of it to the distributor. "We'd have to take care of the pastures and take care of the animals and go through the birthing season and milk them and make the cheese and wrap the cheese and get it to the distributors. Then the distributors and retailers would get the lion's share of the value. That's not our model," she emphasized.

Another family said they had reluctantly started using a distributor after they decided they were too far from sufficiently large retail markets. The time and energy spent getting their product to retail consumers was better used to increase production so they could maintain their revenue without long trips to distant markets. They still deliver to local restaurants and shops, their longtime reliable customers who cannot meet the minimum orders required by the distributors. Leaving most of their distribution to third parties and limiting their personal distribution efforts to these relatively few, nearby, high-quality retailers and restaurants, they also have made more time to focus on the on-site sales to visitors who come, sometimes bring their kids, and return regularly to stock up on favorites.

These same cheesemakers said, though, that as happy as they are to have given up the unproductive, exhausting, dangerous hours of driving to markets (we cringed hearing about a serious accident they had returning on icy roads from a much-too-long day at a distant farmers market), they are still very concerned about giving up control of their product before it reaches customers. "We have very solid distributors. But we liked it when we sold it ourselves at farmers markets or knew every retailer who sold our cheese."

Competition came up in our discussions. Competition from within the domestic cheese market does not worry the cheesemakers, except that they don't want people producing bad-tasting cheese. One remembered people commenting, "Goat cheese? Yuck," when she offered samples at a tasting event. One woman told her that she "only eats yellow cheese." Any bad-tasting cheese that makes it to market claiming to be artisan or farmstead is bound to damage the growth of the still young and possibly tentative consumer base. "But there is plenty of room for more good cheesemakers," one claimed. Another told us that he had taken over a cheese operation from people who really didn't have the expertise they needed. That is a disaster for all cheesemaking—bad cheese hurts all the good cheesemakers.

A third said, "I believe you can give away knowledge and not have any less of it. We all need to do that to avoid having bad cheese out there." She had counseled a new neighboring cheesemaker that her cheese was "really pretty awful—and here's what to do about it." She wasn't at all worried that the new cheesemaker would cut into her business when she improved. In fact she said, "I absolutely know we can sell more in our region. We sold all of our cheese last year, and we will this year. We're trying to find a way to make a little more." If more people have access to good cheese, at least in her opinion, the market will just keep growing for everyone.

Even though domestic competition is not a concern, competition from European cheesemakers, who

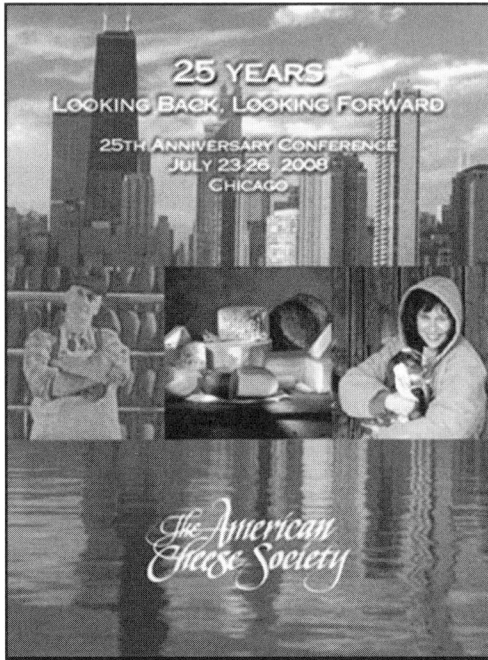

Poster announcing the American Cheese Society 2008 Conference.

have better subsidies and fewer regulations than Americans, is. The 2008 strength of the euro over the dollar helped level the market. As the high-priced euro brought the cost of European cheeses into line with the cost of American ones, people discovered the American ones—a bit of a silver lining to the global recession.

Competition worries are related to cheesemaker concern about sustainability of their farmsteads. Financially, if the farm is well capitalized without a big mortgage or big debts for infrastructure costs, the ongoing operations seem to sustain themselves quite well. But the limits are clear. "Every bit of milk I have goes into fresh cheese to meet my commitments to local restaurants," said a cheesemaker. "I cannot make more cheese, even though I could sell it."

"I don't have enough milk," said another. "I can't fill my orders if I use any of my milk for any aged cheeses. I need it all for the fresh cheeses that can be to the customers quickly." Another told us, "There are only so many animals that we want to keep—only so much time that my husband wants to spend milking. We are limited by what we think is the right way to raise the animals. Our animals need to be on pasture. It makes for better milk and better cheese. We believe in traditional techniques. There are shortcuts we could take, but we're not going to take them."

"How long can you do this?" Asked one. "At what age does it no longer make sense to heft up these five-gallon cans? I mean, its fifty or sixty pounds at a time. Can we do this at age 60? Can we do it at 65?" Even as quite robust retirees who have trekked as much as two hundred miles just for the joy of it, we were happy her question was rhetorical. Neither of us would want to lift those cans. And it seemed likely to us that not all the cheesemakers we met will have been able to build an adequate retirement income by the time hefting milk cans no longer makes sense.

The idea of retiring from the cheese farmstead circled us back to why we had started down this trail of interviews. We had guessed that the farm life of cheesemakers entwined with the taste of the cheeses to create the appeal of the new American cheeses. People want to buy cheese from producers closer to home and, as with other foods, to have the chance to meet the people who produce their food.

For consumers as well as some of the cheesemakers, the appeal is in having a unique product to place in competition with all the global players in the cheese world and to out compete them in a global market. For others, the appeal is to produce only as much as the animals you want to care for can supply and you can sell with your own hands. The unique products of one kind of farmsteader will swell the types of cheeses available to us in our cheese shops and supermarkets. The products of the other type of farmsteader will always be available only in their local regions, thus renewing the days when experiencing unique or regional foods was one of the expected treats of traveling around the country.

I have fond memories of the infrequent road trips my family took when I was young. Stopping to eat at restaurants that sold food foreign to Rochester, like grits and sweet tea, was one of the best parts. I want cheese to be like that. I do not hope for a day when I can get every farmstead cheese I like delivered to my supermarket near home in Florida. I'll be happier knowing there are some in the Adirondacks that I have to drive all the way there to eat, like cheese curds.

On National Public Radio's "All Things Considered" in January 2009, we heard an interview with an artist who said that he spent 50 percent of his time making his art and the other 50 percent marketing it. That fit with much of what we heard from cheesemakers. Moreover, there are not enough 50 percents in a day for the major categories of work: the farm, the cheese, and the marketing.

Taking care of the animals includes not just the milkers themselves but also those not being milked because they are still too young or already too old. For goat farmers there are the bucks that need to be

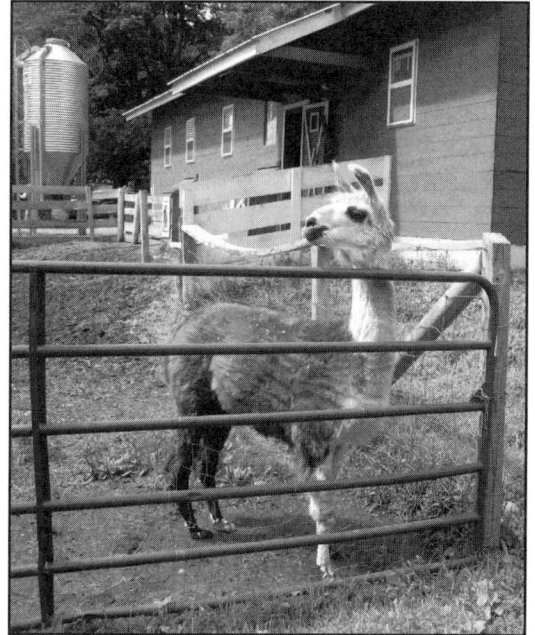

On guard. *Some farmstead cheesemakers use llamas or donkeys as guard animals. They are said to be effective in driving off certain predators that might attack goats.*

Farmstead goat barn. *Facilities once used for small herds of dairy cattle are often converted to house dairy goats.*

cared for and kept separate from the does. There are guard animals, including dogs and cats, and maybe llamas and donkeys. Helping the cows, goats, or sheep during birthing is clearly no small task. Then there is maintenance of the barns, the pastures, and the fences, the milking rooms and equipment, the farm tractors and other big and small farm tools, and possibly even farm roads. The cheesemakers we talked to who had many animals also had some farmhands to supervise.

Looking only at the cheesemaking itself, tasks are also abundant. Maintaining equipment and keeping records for the inspectors are both time-consuming. The cheesemaking processes are long with unforgiving, inflexible schedules. Since milk differs depending on what the animals are eating, if the animals are pastured the cheesemaker needs to adapt the processes to fit the milk as the seasons and pasture grasses change. Even after cheeses are made they demand time-consuming attention. Aging cheeses require turning and rubbing for weeks, months, or years, and in the beginning it can be more than once a day.

Marketing has its own challenges. The cheeses must be sold when they are mature, not too young and not overly ripe. Cheeses that age until they are hard are in no danger of becoming too ripe, but semi-soft and soft cheeses have a smaller window of peak flavor. If they are distributed to distant markets, transportation time uses up shelf life. Both the cheese retailer and the cheesemaker want them to arrive on the customer's table in perfect shape. All the facets need to align or it doesn't happen. Therefore makers of fresh, soft cheeses are more likely to sell them locally, which means we consumers are less likely to find fresh, soft cheese in our stores than we are to find aged hard cheese. This marketing challenge led in part to the establishment of the processed cheese industry. It produces a consistently-the-same "cheese product" with a long shelf life rather than a seasonally different, milk-dependent cheese with a short shelf life. When it comes to fresh, soft cheese, cheesemakers either have to sell locally, directly (online, for example) to customers who share the cost of temperature-controlled fast delivery, or through specialty distributors who can manage the transportation challenges. Making fresh, soft cheese brings revenues back to the cheesemaker more quickly but presents greater challenges for getting the product to the customer in the best condition. Aging cheese lowers the risks related to distribution but increases the work for the cheesemaker and lengthens the time before there is a return on the investment.

Some of the cheesemakers we interviewed were successfully managing it all: the farm, the cheese, and the marketing. They kept their operations small. Others had chosen to do either the farm part and sell their milk to the cheesemakers or the cheese part and buy their milk from trusted farmers. The marketing component also split, with some cheesemakers selling all their cheese themselves, and others selling at least some of it through distributors. Understanding the complexity of the farming, cheesemaking, and marketing components of the story led us to pay more attention to the people who neither care for farms nor make cheese but are retail cheese experts. These are often the people who sell us our cheeses and they are the topic of the next section of our book.

Short-take: Chef-Owned Restaurants Often Feature New American Cheeses

Restaurants are a primary market for some farmstead cheeses. On the menu in August 2009 at the Windfall Restaurant was a salad special that included County Meadows chèvre, an Adirondack Crescent farmstead cheese. If you have the impression that only hotsy-totsy urban restaurants serve farmstead cheese, The Windfall is the antidote to that image.

The place, Windfall, is a crossroads with a handful of houses three miles off Route 3 in New York's Adirondack Park. It is named for a huge blowdown of trees by a tornado in 1845. The restaurant, Windfall, is a chef-owned establishment located at Windfall and featuring local foods…to the degree possible in this region where the growing season is really short. It is at the crossroads of the Tooley Pond Road, 12 unpaved miles with hiking trails to six waterfalls, and the road to Newton Falls, a town of about 400 residents where the paper mill that was closed for seven years recently reopened hiring back about 100 workers, not all from Newton Falls obviously.

Despite hikers and workers, Windfall is quite ghosty. It is an unlikely location for a successful restaurant, proving that reality can beat likeliness in the Adirondacks. In the Windfall's bar folks play darts and jam sessions are a regular weekend feature. A frosty mug of Stella or IPA costs $2.25. Better yet, we got "premium mystery beer" for $1. What you get is "bartender's choice." The first round turned out to be a bottle of Red Stripe and a bottle of lemonade-flavored beer (not quite as bad as it sounds, sort of like a wheat beer.) The next round included Sam Adams and Yuengling. Good fresh local food too, with farmstead cheese as a featured item. Go Chef!

Part Five:

Selling and Buying the

New American Cheeses

as told by Peg

Farmers market. *Dairyman selling raw goat milk and raw-milk cheese at a farmers market. Farmers markets provide an easy-entry way for beginning cheesemakers to get started in retail sales.*

Independent cheese shops, farmers markets, restaurants, and specialty supermarkets play a major role in the story of artisanal and farmstead cheese. The shops I visited on the retail tour that was a pre-conference option in Chicago were beyond anything we have in our hometown, even though we have three shops that provide cut-to-order cheeses and a fresh food market with a nice selection of cheeses that are not processed cheese food varieties. We wanted to know more about such boutique cheese shops and the people who own them.

We also wanted to learn more about cheese at farmers markets. Cheesemakers had told us about selling their cheeses at local farmers markets. There was no cheese at the farmers markets in our town until spring 2009. We had heard that in our area farmers markets tended to be quite limiting about what could be sold—only food the farmers produced themselves, only food grown within a certain radius from the market, and often only produce. We were not thinking about cheese as a farmers market product when our exploration of cheese was getting underway. It apparently appeared much earlier at farmers markets in places other than our town. What was that story? And what about the supermarkets?

How were cheeses finding their way to those counters? Where did they come from, and were the new American cheeses among them?

Equally fascinating to us were questions about who the new cheese customers and enthusiasts are. The story of the new American cheese seemed, in addition to being about the cheese itself and the people who make it, also to be about the people who sell it, and very much about all of us, the people who buy it.

Cheese shop in León, Spain. *Despite its size, this shop carried relatively few kinds of cheeses, most made in the region.*

Meeting the People Who Sell the New American Cheeses

Behind me on a bus full of people I didn't know, a couple got a call on their cell phone. It was clearly not good news—lots of "Oh no!" and "You have to be kidding." We were on our way to the first stop on an American Cheese Society (ACS) pre-conference tour of cheese shops in Chicago. Although most of us on the bus were strangers, we were all cheese people. The couple's phone conversation pulled us into an empathetic little cluster of eavesdroppers.

It turned out that the contractor for the cheese shop the couple was building (actually the driver of the contractor's Ditch Witch) had discovered that the sewer line their shop needed to hook into was to be found no place close to where the city maps said it would be. The Ditch Witch was digging up more and more of the city street with no luck finding the sewer. When the call ended, the flurry of sympathetic "Yeah, its always something" stories introduced me to this second batch of people who are part of the phenomenon that is the new American cheese. While Russ was bussing to Wisconsin to visit cheese factories on the other pre-conference option, I was glimpsing the world of the people who sell cheese to us.

Although many cheesemakers sell directly to consumers, most do not sell all their cheese that way, and some do not sell any of it that way. As much as we might like to buy our cheese directly from the people who make it, most of us don't. We need stores. But stores are not quite enough because—just as Russ and I initially fled cheese-less from our first attempts to shop at a specialty cheese counter—many of the other

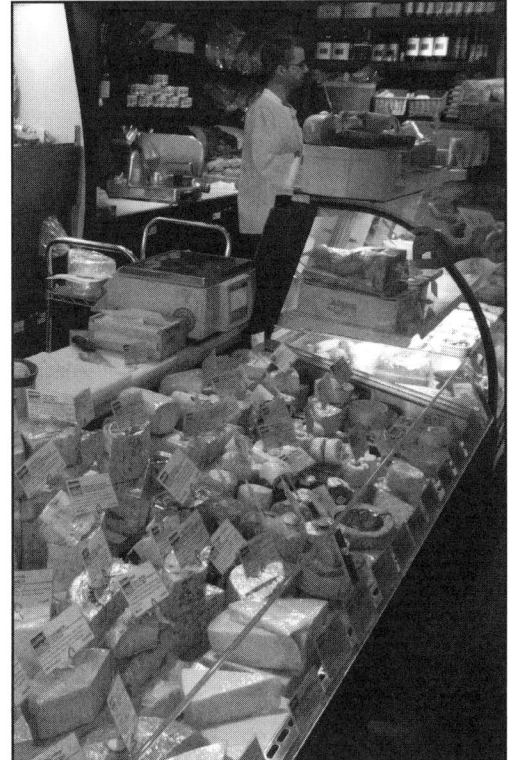

Counter in a cheese shop. *Customers can request special cuts from the bulk cheeses at this counter.*

cheese enthusiasts we have met said they too were at a loss for knowing how to get started exploring all these new cheeses. Not only do we want stores, but often we want people in the stores who know cheese really well and can help us select something without being embarrassed by our naïveté or feeling like we just fell off a turnip truck, as my grandmother used to say.

We talked at length at the conference with several cheese retailers who were my bus buddies on that pre-conference tour. And when we traveled during the next year, we set up interviews at cheese shops and farmers markets. By sheer serendipity, when I walked into one of those interviews, who should be the owners? You guessed it: the couple with the cell phone and the hard-to-find, but eventually hooked-up, sewer line.

Part of the fun of the new American cheese is shopping for it, which makes the retailers part of the phenomenon. Had we assumed the cheese retailers would have chosen to sell cheese because they loved it, we would have been no more correct than when we assumed people got into the business of making cheese primarily for that reason. Whereas with cheesemaking the appeal was often with the pastoral or agricultural life, the animals, and the additional profit that cheesemaking could bring to the farm, with cheese selling the appeal also hinged on business and lifestyle as much as the cheese itself. With cheesemakers, a love of the cheese itself was inevitable regardless of what brought them to start making cheese. Both a love of cheese and a passion for knowing everything about all kinds of cheese were inevitable and invaluable for cheese retailers, regardless of what brought them to begin selling it.

The cheese retailers we met had broadly differing former careers. Among them were a former financial advisor, chef, massage therapist, food-industry marketing and management professional, film and video producer, and military officer. None knew the new American cheese well before getting interested in the business.

After he got his MBA and served with the navy, a shop owner told us, he'd decided: "I don't want to work for anybody. I'm tired of working for other people. I'm going to start a cheese shop." The idea did not pop up from nowhere. While he was serving in Vietnam, he had kept in touch with a graduate school friend who had opened one of the earliest successful cheese specialty shops. The friend was willing to mentor him. Using the friend's business model and advice from another shop owner, he opened a cheese store in a small city. His initial passion was not the cheese; rather, it was to be his own boss.

When he started in the 1980s, even good, mainstream, factory-made cheese was not easily available in the supermarkets of his town. "People came to my shop from a hundred miles around to get cheese in those days," he told me. Later, when cheese was less of a draw because it was more available in supermarkets, he added wine to his inventory. Now with competition from both traditional and fresh-food supermarkets, he is selective and price sensitive with his cheese offerings. He said, "I focus on our customers' tastes and the degree to which they are willing to pay the premium price for American artisanal cheese. I don't carry cheeses that I cannot sell while they are still at their prime." Decades after opening the shop, cheese and wine are still the main products, the shop is a mainstay of the community, and he is one of the city's recognized cheese experts.

In a not dissimilar story, a man told us that he was looking for a new job in mid-career after his company was acquired. He decided that buying a business would be more appealing than "interviewing new potential bosses." He and his wife already had business savvy from her years in a designer-product retail business and his in the food industry. They found an independent wine and cheese store for sale by its longtime owner-operator who was ready to retire. Located in an upscale community, it had a solid customer base and reasonable profitability. They bought the standing business. Although they always had an interest in wine and cheese, they bought the

Cut-to-order cheese shops. *These allow customers to buy as much or as little as they want and be assured that their cheeses have not spent months encased in shrink-wrap.*

shop with an eye toward its potential as a successful retail business more than because of what it sold.

Another shop owner got into the cheese business when she was ready to escape from a harried, hectic, successful, intense financial-industry career. She decided that it would "not be a bad idea" to give up her crazy pace, own a little shop, and be surrounded by cheese all day. More so than the other two, cheese itself was a magnet. She comes from a family where "the Food Network played all day, the cellar held a collection of fine wines, and cheese was the dessert of choice." She partnered with the owner of an established wine shop to acquire a store big enough for both wine and cheese in a prime location in a booming resort and retirement area. She cashed in some of a 401(k) and put it into getting the cheese shop started in the summer of 2007. She talked about it being hard for her to take that risk. We later thought, given the stock market behavior in the second half of that year and in 2008, that the risk actually might not have been nearly as extreme as it seemed when she took it. She probably capitalized the shop with money that would have evaporated if she'd not cashed it out when she did. Nevertheless, the gamble was a big one and she recognized she was being impulsive rather than deliberate. "I ignored the sharp-pencil planning that I knew I shouldn't ignore," she said.

Another owner told me that food was always his first love, although his profession was in film and video production. His grandfather had defied the stereotype that a real man can only cook at a grill; he was a superior in-the-kitchen cook. Following in those footsteps, the shop owner had always liked to cook large multi-course meals for friends and family.

"I fell head over heels for cheese a few years ago," he told me. "I probably knew that I was really in love with cheese over a piece of Beaufort, a true Alpage-style Beaufort. The finish was incredible. It just knocked my socks off. From there I just wanted to find out more, to learn more. I read a bunch of books. I tasted whenever I could. That was my start."

The cheese shop can be a consumer delight. One in particular gave me almost the same feeling as that first cheese festival we attended in Warwick: an overwhelming sense of awe that I could choose from so many cheeses. As in Warwick, it felt good, not intimidating. The open, long counter welcomed me with its bright display and colorful signs describing each cheese. That shop's owner wanted to replicate the European experience of going to a specialty store operated by someone expert in what he sold and being surrounded by all the sights and aromas of that food—bread, or cheese, or meat, or fish, or vegetables. He decided he would specialize in cheese because his city didn't have a cheese shop and because he liked the idea of becoming a cheese expert.

Like the cheesemakers we met, retailers with their own cheese businesses have entrepreneurial courage. They add sweat equity and financial risk taking to the growing appeal of the new American cheese. Also like the cheesemakers, cheese retailers have a learning curve, both on the business side and the cheese side.

Having discovered 1,200 varieties of cheese to sample at the ACS conferences, Russ and I were beginning to realize how much cheese shop owners would have to learn about cheese. They sell such a wide variety: artisanal, farmstead, domestic, and foreign. It impressed us that unlike cheesemakers who sell only the work of their own labor, the shop owner must select from among many hundreds of choices. Retailers need to know all cheeses well. They must be able to talk about all of them to help customers experience the abundance and variety, the similarities and differences, and to help consumers find unusual and new cheeses to try or familiar favorites to take home again.

Retailers learn to know cheeses by reading about them and tasting them. One owner told me she reads every book she finds and after one ACS conference had to buy another suitcase to get all her new books home. Another shop owner said she and her husband read many books to get background, but they need to

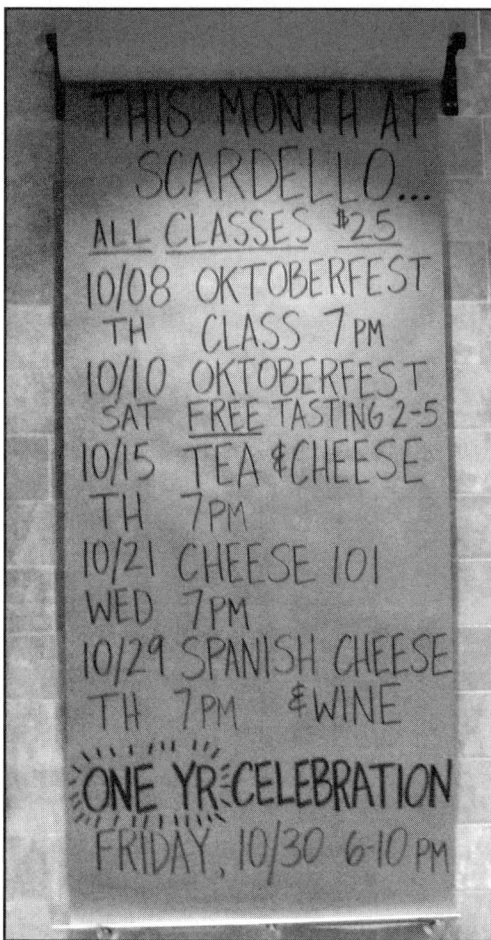

Educating consumers. Sign in a cheese shop listing upcoming events intended to inform the public about cheese.

taste the cheeses before they buy them to sell. They go to food shows and conferences. They visit cheese shops in other cities to taste and buy different cheeses. They explore regional cheeses when they travel, and they seek out cheesemakers to discuss the possibility of adding their cheeses to the store's offerings. "We pretty much had very little knowledge in a way, about what real cheese was, before we decided this was the store we wanted to buy," one said. "Becoming experts on cheese was one of the appeals of the business. There are always new cheeses to learn."

Another told us, "I had not known American artisanal cheeses well before I started the business. Off the top of my head, I could not, for example, say 'Oh, that's cow milk cheese and that's goat milk." For her too, learning to be more of a cheese expert was part of the appeal. After hearing about, tasting, and taking lots of notes on cheeses she liked at conferences and food shows, she went to the books and researched them all to learn everything she could about the people who made them, how and where they were made, and whether she could get them to sell in her part of the country. She spent an extended period of time visiting cheesemakers and cheese shops in other regions to hone her knowledge.

At ACS conference sessions panelists sometimes described cheeses the way wine experts describe wines: where in your mouth you get the taste, whether the cheese is pungent or creamy, if it has an herby taste, and so on. A shop owner said she was initially frustrated at not being able to segment the taste of the cheeses and provide those wine-like analyses. But after a year or so of studying cheeses and working on developing the tasting pathways between her mouth and her brain, the descriptions became second nature.

Russ and I, having both been teachers at various points in our careers, are aware that one way to master a subject is to explain it to someone else. Therefore, we were not surprised to hear shop owners say that the classes they offer with titles such as Cheese 101, Pairing Cheese and Wine, and Cooking with Cheese help them get different cheeses well fixed in their own heads, while they help their customers. They also told us that it helps them to write fact sheets about the cheeses for customers. Grouping their cheeses in display cases by region of origin, cheesemaker, type of cheese, or some other category and designing the signage for their stores also consolidates their knowledge. "Keeping the descriptions short enough to fit on a sign is a sure way to force yourself to choose words that give the key differences among the cheeses," according to one. It reminded us of selecting words for PowerPoint presentations.

Vermont Cheesemakers Festival. One of the barns at Shelburne Farms was the scene of the August 2009 festival. Only 1,000 tickets were available for the sold-out event, and the crowds nearly overwhelmed the facility.

Consumers can't always shop at independent cheese shops with knowledgeable owners like those we interviewed. That made us curious to interview some managers of cheese departments at bigger stores. At a Central Market, I met a manager who had previously been a cheesemaker supplying cheese to the store where I met her. Her love and knowledge of the cheeses overflowed to her customers. No shortage of care for the cheese or the cheese consumer was evident in that store, although we often heard that the supermarket cheese departments were less careful with their cheeses than the boutique stores were.

We also talked to cheese counter managers of other larger stores -- a suburban wine and cheese discount store, an independent grocery store, another fresh foods supermarket. One disappointed us by not knowing if a cheese I asked about was a raw milk cheese or if it was from America or Europe. We decided he probably couldn't help anybody make a good choice. The other two were more interesting.

They took their jobs with no particular passion for or background in cheese. But they loved what they were doing. They raved about their work. "It is really nice to have a job with benefits and stuff like that," said one who was formerly self-employed. The job is "the best I've ever had, with really nice colleagues and managers," he said. They each mentioned having always been interested in food and cooking and said that working with cheese retailing was a wonderful career. "Even the history of cheese is part of the appeal to work with it," one commented. "Learning things like that Roquefort was a mistake and that cheese has been around forever and ever make this an awesome way to make a living," he added. For both these young people, learning about cheese was a serious bonus to having a job that was good in other ways.

"How did you learn the cheeses?" I asked. One said her bosses taught her to describe them and to help customers pair them well with wines. She also learned how to cut the cheeses. Her store has a certified kitchen, which is required if you provide the cheese cut-to-order rather than as pre-cut and packaged. I was glad to know that retailers can't cut cheese on the employee lunch table, in the back room, or some other place like that.

When the other manager was starting out, the company sent a corporate trainer. His store's general manager gave him books and videos about cheese to study. He was able to attend an annual training conference for the cheese managers of all the company's stores. He said he keeps looking for new cheeses because he enjoys the informal rivalry among the cheese counter managers to find a cheese that sells well and recommend it to peers before they find it on their own. The company makes sales data available to all the cheese managers, and he likes seeing how different cheeses appeal to customers in different parts of the country. The parent company encourages its cheese distributors to visit each store's cheese department and provide training programs, which the manager said was very helpful to him. He also tended to order more of the products that he'd tasted and liked in the training programs. He convinced me that if I ever work for a grocery store, I'd want it to be in the cheese department of his chain.

We heard less about learning to manage the business challenges than learning about the cheeses themselves, but a few points intrigued us. Growing the number of return customers is important to becoming successful. Every store we visited offered classes about cheese. The classes attract new customers and help establish a personal and loyal relationship from the start.

Especially during the 2009 economic downturn, it seemed possible that there would not be enough customers in some areas to make any cheese shop viable. But an owner-couple told me their store, in a rural, resort area, draws on only about 2,000 to 5,000 potential customers and has about 200 regulars. For stores like theirs in non-urban areas, they believe the location must have affluent, sophisticated, traveled, worldly gourmets. Their few hundred regulars are reliable cheese buyers. If they weren't, their population base would not be big enough to maintain the shop.

Russ and I noted their point when we were preparing to go to interview a cheesemaker in another part of Florida. I surfed the Web and found a newly opened cheese shop in that region. We planned to stop in and look for new cheeses, but when we got there it seemed to have closed, quite possibly a casualty of the recession.

People who buy specialty cheeses are still a relatively small market niche. Said one owner, "Handmade, wonderful artisanal cheese is never going to replace Kraft singles in a total market. It is not going to

Thoroughly cheesy. *Customers at a counter sit on stools fashioned from milk cans. Dimitri Petropolis snapped this photo at Beecher's Handmade Cheese at the Pike Place Market in Seattle and shared it with us.*

happen." That fit with another who talked about people trying expensive American cheeses once but not buying them consistently week after week. But the small market seems to still be growing and, as we heard, it is big enough even now if you have regular, returning customers. "Ninety percent of the people who walk into our store buy something," one couple said. "We are pretty much a destination shop."

Learning about cheese and about business issues are big challenges. Getting the cheeses to sell presents another one. Cheese shops sell specialty cheeses, some handmade and some made in factories, ordering them either directly from the cheesemakers or acquiring them through cheese distributors. "At conferences and shows, you learn, you taste, you meet the cheesemakers, you decide what cheeses you want," said a shop owner. "But, knowing what you want to sell does not mean you can get it into your shop."

Acquiring the cheeses a shop owner would like to have may be difficult because, as we learned from talking to cheesemakers, many of them sell everything they make in their own region. "Lots of cheesemakers don't make enough to ship any, or they just don't want to ship," said one shop owner. "They are so into their cheese, they don't want to risk the integrity of their name and their product by having their cheese sitting on a UPS bus for two days. And, they don't know me as a retailer, and how I'll treat their cheeses," he pointed out." Cheeses that are sold only in one locale often become the small-cheesemaker gems that we consumers tend to consider a "catch" when we get to the region and buy them. We find them in cheese shops only near where they are made, if at all.

But many other cheesemakers sell their cheese beyond their local region both retail (directly to consumers through the Internet, for example), wholesale (directly to cheese stores that then sell it retail to consumers), and through distributors who then manage the interface with the retailers.

We talked to shop owners who prefer to buy directly

from the cheesemakers, and others who prefer to work through distributors. The reasons for choosing one over the other gave insight into the complexity of the artisan cheese business.

Explaining why he prefers to work with distributors instead of ordering directly from the cheesemakers, a shop owner told us that when he orders directly from the cheesemakers he generally needs to ship via next-day air to get the cheese in its freshest condition. "So," he said, "where I'd be paying a distributor maybe twenty or twenty-five cents a pound for shipping, when you talk about shipping direct from the cheesemaker you are talking about shipping costs of well over a dollar a pound, often two dollars."

He said that he used to buy direct from one cheesemaker because she did not use any distributors and he really wanted to carry her cheese. It cost him almost four dollars a pound for shipping, which had to be added to the price of the cheese. Recently that cheesemaker has begun to make her cheeses available through a distributor that the shop owner already uses for other cheeses. He gets about 400 pounds of cheese biweekly from the distributor but must pay shipping for the minimum order, a full pallet, which is 1,000 pounds. So when he adds this cheesemaker to his biweekly order it will essentially be free of shipping cost since he was already paying to ship 1,000 pounds. He will now save four dollars per pound on the cheese from that cheesemaker. No wonder he thinks, "There really is no alternative to using distributors."

Another shop owner said it was easier to use a distributor than to deal with many cheesemakers with different shipping and ordering processes. However, as a relatively small shop he had trouble selling enough to deal with distributors' minimums. He can order large amounts of aged cheeses, because they can be stored well for long periods of time. However fresher, softer cheeses do not store well. He needs to sell them within a few weeks, so he must order smaller quantities at a time and usually cannot meet the minimum order size.

Also, shop owners mentioned that problems frequently popped up with distributors. "I buy direct if I can," said an owner, "even if I am paying a bit more. I didn't always get the best product from the distributors." Another said, "Sometimes I get cheese in from the distributor, and I ship it right back because it is squished, just from being on a commercial delivery truck under thirty pounds of whatever. So I prefer to get it direct, even though it is easier to use a distributor."

A different owner said that he prefers to buy direct from the cheesemakers when they are in his part of the country. Those cheeses will arrive overnight without assessment of a premium-shipping fee, so he always buys those direct. Others he buys direct only when he has had a problem with their distributor. "It is frustrating," he told us, "when I go through a distributor and get someone's cheese and I know it is not what it is supposed to be. Somehow distributors can get me the European standard cheeses in good shape, but certain American cheeses just don't come in the way they should from the distributor." When he has trouble with a distributor he calls the cheesemaker and says, "Hey, I'm not getting what I want from the distributor, the way I know you want it." He said the cheesemakers are generally happy to work with him to get the cheeses to him direct, without the price being prohibitive.

Russ and I went to a one-day Vermont Cheesemakers Festival in summer 2009. As we sampled the cheeses, beers, and ciders, I talked with several cheesemakers about their interest in working with independent retail cheese shops. Some said they were eager to work with retailers, and talk with them about shipping options and logistics. Others specifically said they would be happy to talk about shipping aged cheeses but not their soft cheeses, because of transportation issues. Some cheesemakers said they work only through distributors. Not surprisingly, several said they already were selling all they could make and did not have any cheese to make available through retail stores. All their comments affirmed what we'd heard earlier.

Both supermarket cheese counter managers we interviewed said they worked primarily with distributors. One was not allowed by the company to buy cheese except through the approved distributors. The other, however, could buy direct and did, when her distributors did not have an item requested by her customers.

We interviewed and I later went to visit a retailer who does not have a shop and sells only at farmers markets and to chefs. She started as a chef herself and knew she wanted to specialize in selling local, handmade, artisan cheeses. She had spent a lot of time in Europe observing and interning in cheese retailing. Her booth at the farmers markets creates a place similar in feel to my favorite cheese shops, welcoming and comfortable for the beginning cheese buyer, as well as brimming with choices for the consumers who know what they want.

It is part of the appeal of her model that the cheesemakers she buys from can rely on regular sales to her, freeing them from marketing tasks and providing more time to make more cheese. Some of the cheesemakers she buys from are too small to sell through a distributor because they do not produce enough cheese for a distributor to carry them. Some are too distant from a good farmers market to go and do the marketing themselves.

I watched the retailer interact with customers at the farmers market. She talked not just about the cheese but also about the cheesemakers. She offered samples to all passersby, and most stopped to try her cheeses. Most also bought. Many clearly were repeat customers; they asked for specific cheeses they'd tried earlier and were attuned to seasonal issues. It was March, and I remember a few asking if a certain goat cheese would become available soon. Some of the smaller farms stop production in winter when they don't milk their goats. The regular customers knew they'd be back soon and were waiting eagerly for old favorites.

Aging cheeses. *Cheesemakers producing aged cheeses have a waiting period between the times cheeses are made and can be sold. This has the potential for causing cash-flow problems, particularly for small operations.*

Other passersby were trying the cheeses for the first time. The retailer listened to their reactions and offered types of cheeses she thought they would enjoy tasting. She had storyboards with pictures of the cheesemakers, the animals, the cheese rooms, and the farms. She talked about the history of the cheeses. Customers seemed at ease with her, even when they were a bit uneasy about trying new cheeses. A cheesemaker selling her goat milk cheeses at the same farmers market told me she thinks this model is really important to the success of cheesemakers who are remote from farmers markets and population centers. Having a steady buyer for their cheeses is essential, especially as they are starting up. She also told me that people think of the retailer as a third-party endorser. Being selected by the retailer gives credibility to new and less well-known cheesemakers.

The farmers market where I visited her was a meeting ground for natural and local food enthusiasts. The retailer told me she believes her customers expect to meet and talk to the producers of the food, or at least to people who know them and their farms. Her business model works because the cheeses are fresh and local and because she is regularly in touch with the cheesemakers themselves and knows what is happening on their farms. Using the farmers market instead of having a store keeps her overhead lower. The fast growth in the farmers market movement would seem to provide opportunities for increasingly robust sales over the next few years.

Although some supermarkets also are beginning to carry new American cheeses along with their mainstream cheeses, like one-off art pieces, which are more likely to be sold in galleries than alongside mass-produced pieces in department stores, handmade and artisanal cheeses do not fit easily, comfortably, or well into outlets where mainstream cheeses sell. Mainstream supermarkets seem not to be a strong venue for the new cheeses.

Artisanal cheeses are best when handled by experts. Humidity, temperature, display, packaging, and age are all crucial to the quality of the product we consumers purchase. The specialty retail venues create for us consumers the wonderful world where we can find, see, smell, and taste our new cheeses. Without them, the cheese world would be less beguiling and rich.

Farmers market near our Florida home.
Nationally the numbers and popularity of farmers markets have been increasing dramatically.

Short Take: The Role of Farmers Markets

We didn't expect farmers markets to be a big part of the story of the new American cheese. But we were wrong. Certain cheesemakers sell mainly or exclusively through them. They also are important for cheesemakers who are just starting out and are not ready for other distribution networks. They are a meeting ground for people who like natural and local food and therefore a place where new cheesemakers can test and sell their products. People at farmers markets expect to meet and talk to the producers of the food they buy.

One cheesemaker we met had helped establish her town's farmers market before she got into cheesemaking full-time. She hires someone to sell there for her now because the need to show up weekly interferes with her other duties.

A retailer we met sells at farmers markets instead of having a shop. Her model is to buy farmstead cheeses from several cheesemakers in the region and sell them at several farmers markets. She selects cheeses she feels will appeal to her customers and takes care to ensure that her suppliers are not competing head to head with each other. She told us that she talks with customers at the markets, not just about her cheeses but also about the cheesemakers. She displays storyboards with pictures and the history of each cheese. She sees herself as a direct connection between the cheesemakers and her customers. She has fresh, local products and less overhead than if she were renting a shop. She expects to ride on the coattails of the burgeoning farmers market movement in her state and build her business quickly over the next few years.

When he first began making goat cheese in a region where dairying was traditionally based on cattle, one cheesemaker took his cheese to the local farmers market. The shoppers were all his neighbors—people he'd known all his life. He said it was actually scary to go. For his neighbors, goats, their milk, and cheese made from it all had a disreputable, foreign flavor. He said that eople would walk way out and around so they didn't have to see them or buy from them when they knew they didn't want goat milk cheese. Finally, a few did take some samples, but they took them way over to the park to try them. Then they'd come back and buy. "We don't go to the farmers market any more because we don't have enough milk to do all the things we used to. But we still have customers from there that come here to the farm to buy."

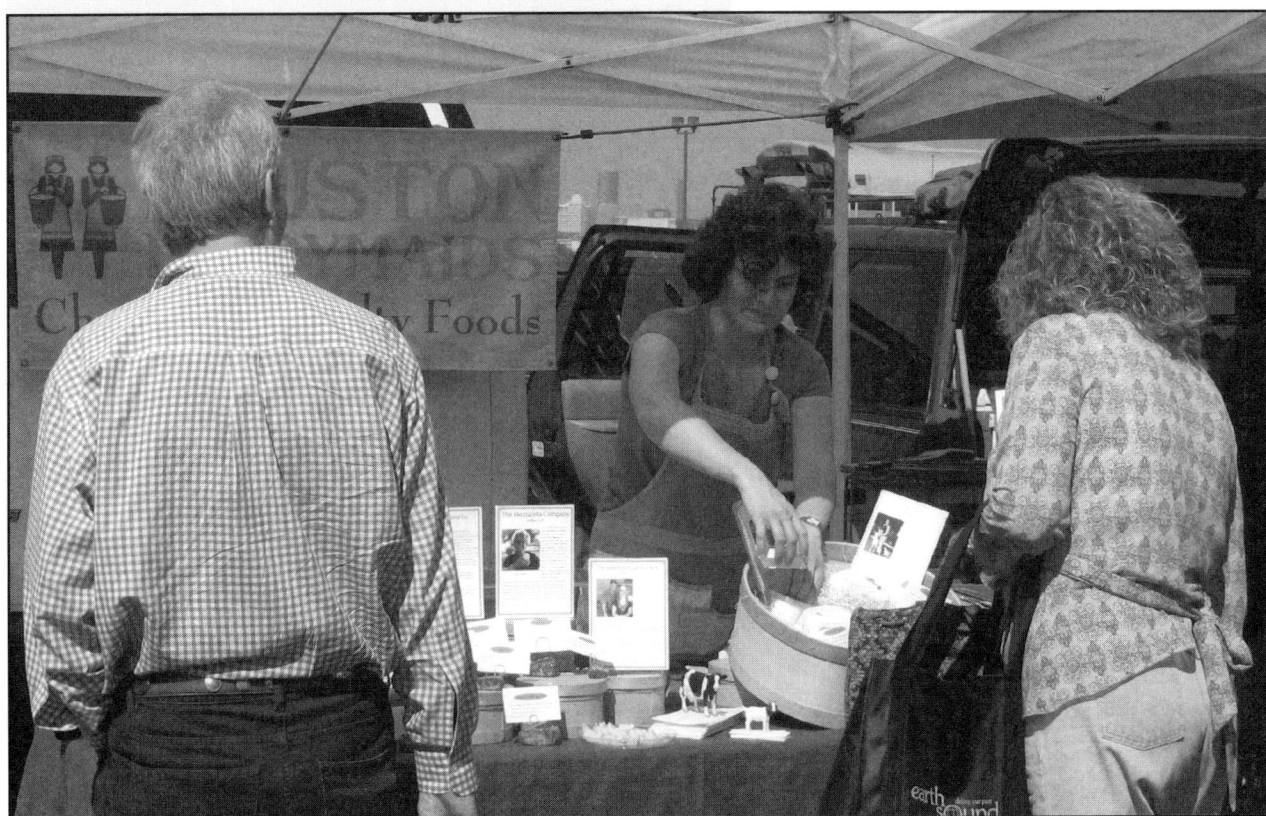

The allure of the farmers market is strong for some. One cheesemaker family said they do not use distributors and they do not have drive-in sales at home. They sell at three farmers markets. "We love going to the farmers markets so much that we would have to sell something else if we didn't have cheese to sell. It is a welcoming community, very supportive of the artisans who make the food and other products."

Cheese vendor at a farmers market in Texas. She is not herself a cheesemaker but instead retails the products of several farmstead cheesemakers in the local area. This frees the cheesemakers from the need to engage in retail sales and provides greater exposure for their cheeses than they could get otherwise.

Short Take: New Business Models

Order a Holiday Cheese Board

Give the perfect host gift

Gift Subscriptions: One, Two or
Three Months of Cheese

Cheese to You

**Bringing Cheeses from
the Farm to our
Community**

Cheese to You

637C Waddell Street

Lexington, VA 24450

mycheesetoyou@yahoo.com

**MeganMary Hall,
Cheesemonger**

Business opportunities. *The new American taste for cheese has created opportunities for nontraditional retailers. This brochure describes a business in which the proprietor, a food professional, selects cheeses and orders them in bulk, filling orders placed by local customers, supplying local restaurants, and offering occasional sales at the warehouse and aging facility. Some foreign cheeses are offered, but the emphasis is on new American varieties. As with many cheese retailers, this one provides the additional benefits of sponsoring tastings and educating customers about cheese.*

Short Take: A Cheese Hierarchy

The supermarket where we usually shop has four separate cheese counters, reflecting a hierarchy.

At one end, seen here in the top photo, are the highly processed varieties, including Velveeta, Cheese Whiz, and grated cheeses.

> *In the town where I grew up, Velveeta is found in the gourmet section of the supermarket.*
>
> Oft-heard statement reflecting on the status of culture in small-town America.

One step up is the counter, shown in the middle image, featuring everyday cheeses, including cut and wrapped chunks of cheddar, Monterey jack, mozzarella, and feta. It also includes a variety of sliced and grated cheeses.

The ultimate is the gourmet counter, shown at the bottom. Its has mostly European and a few higher-priced American cheeses, all factory packaged.

Not shown is yet another place to buy cheeses in this store—the deli section—where prepackaged or in-store sliced-to-order cheeses are provided by Boar's Head, an independent supplier. Only a few kinds of cheeses are available in this department.

A more upscale market where we sometimes shop has a greater variety of foreign and American cheeses. Cheeses are cut and packaged in the store but are not normally cut to order for customers. A nearby cheese shop has fewer kinds, but all are in wheels or other forms in which they were made, and customers may purchase large or small quantities as they wish. Surprisingly, its cheeses are often less expensive than in the grocery stores.

Romanticizing the rural life? One colleague and friend, unlike most of our countrymen, has first-hand experience living in farming communities. He cautions us to avoid excessive romanticism in describing rural living, which he notes, has seldom been idyllic. "Farming," he says, "always was a business, not a romantic style of life." Commenting also on our enthusiasm for the revival of home gardening, he notes, "When I was a boy we had a large garden not because we were involved in a back-to-basics movement, but because my dad didn't work steadily and we needed the food." Aunts and uncles who were farmers had also helped them by donating food. We believe our friend's perspective is important. Coaxing needed quantities of food out of the land is unforgiving work, and nostalgic longings for past centuries are mostly naïve. Few Americans would want a return to times when home gardens and the help of relatives were necessary to put enough food on the table. However, many of us are now fortunate in being able to enjoy some of the pleasures of the lives of those who came before us without enduring the grueling hardships they suffered.

Who Are the Consumers?

At first we thought the phenomenon of the new American cheese was all about the abundance we saw at the *Festival des Fromages de Warwick* and the ACS Festival of Cheeses, and even the appearance of hand-smoked cheeses in a tiny Port St. Joe supermarket. We thought it was all about how many new cheeses were joining the few good celebration cheeses we grew up with and how they were so different from the same-old sameness of our childhood everyday cheeses.

When we began to meet cheesemakers, we had a new thought. The new American cheese was about more than just abundance. It was about who created the abundance. We met cheesemakers on their farms with their animals, at conferences and festivals, and at farmers markets. And it was not only farm-based cheesemakers making the new cheeses. Factory cheesemakers were creating the new American cheese, often from local milk, even sometimes from milk from pastured, hormone-free animals. Factory cheesemakers were not all making the old standardized cheeses. More than a few were making cheese in small batches, using techniques similar to farmstead cheesemakers, even carrying out some of the processes by hand.

Then we came to see the people who serve the new cheeses in their restaurants and those who sell them in cheese shops, at farmers markets, and at the cheese counters in wine stores and fresh-food markets as another part of the story. Their knowledge, expertise, and willingness to bring this handcrafted, highly perishable food to our neighborhoods is what makes the new cheese accessible.

But in the end we came to believe that what makes the new American cheese a phenomenon and not just a new product is all of us. The many consumers who have taken an interest in new American cheeses propel the phenomenon. Now we see the new

Information sharing. *A group of cheese conference participants, many of whom are themselves cheese retailers, visit a cheese and wine shop in Chicago.*

American cheese encompassing cheesemakers of all varieties (except the factories that still just crank out their same-old, always exactly like yesterday's, you-can-count-on-it-to-never-taste-a-bit-different cheeses), retailers, and chefs. But primarily we see the phenomenon as the story of those consumers among us who have begun to think of it as our new "everyday" cheese.

What are we like? Much of what we learned about consumers we learned from the people who sell cheese. But we also learned from discussions with people at conferences and festivals, from our reading, and from participants at the new American cheese presentations we have given for community organizations. Small details as well as characteristics that are more philosophical describe us.

Chefs, it turns out, are a very important consumer category for the new American cheese. One of the first cheesemakers we met with said that as comfortable as she was with the care of her goats, and as good as she became at making cheese, she was equally uncomfortable with and felt she would be horrible at "hawking" her cheese. She said she would have no idea how to market it and had no inclination to do so. Serendipitously, before she was in cheese production full-time, she met a chef who told her he'd like to buy fresh cheese from her when she had good cheese to sell. When she was ready, he liked the product and she has been able to sell essentially all her cheese to him and others he has sent to her.

Ethnic consumer groups also have contributed to artisanal cheese growth. For example, the Vella Cheese Company in California began in the 1930s to meet the cheese tastes of Italian immigrants. It continues to make artisan cheeses and never became a producer of standardized processed everyday cheeses as so many other factories did. Now that more people are seeking out artisan cheeses, Vella Cheese has become even more popular, but it hasn't really changed—the consumers did.

Chefs, immigrant groups, and other clusters of

consumers aside, we heard mostly about individual consumers. For them, age and health factors were mentioned. One retailer told us that his younger customers were not so willing to try different new cheeses. "But the older age group?" I asked. He replied, "I see them as getting into different kinds of cheese and being accepting of change. They are adventuresome." Another owner said that younger customers were more concerned about cheese making them fat and affecting their health negatively. But a third said that students, professors, mothers with little kids, and the "sort of middle-aged couples in their twenties and thirties" bought regularly from her. The idea of twenty-year-olds as "middle-aged" we found more than a tad alarming as well as a bit amusing.

We heard too that some of us find the new American cheese while we are being agri-tourists. People bring their kids and grandkids on mountain drives into the Adirondacks and the Green Mountains not just to look at autumn leaves but to tour goat farms. They leave with cheeses made from the milk of the goats they just met, having shopped for the cheeses not in a store but in the coolers on the farmhouse porch or in a side room. We heard similar stories from cheesemakers in other parts of the country. People boldly stop their cars when out for a drive in the countryside of the South and ask a farmer working in his field if he'll sell them some of his cheese. People spend vacation time at resorts that are sustainable farms with active dairies and farmstead cheeses.

Popular culture is a factor, we were told by several people. We did not welcome this news because Russ and I do not watch much television and are not very knowledgeable at all about popular culture. In fact, we had first heard of chef Rachel Ray when a teenager we know had a crush on her. Hearing that pop culture had embraced cheese, I was lured into watching some food shows while working out at the fitness center. Now I can say that I have been "Down Home with the Neelys" and also visited "Giada at Home" on the Food Network. But I am sure that

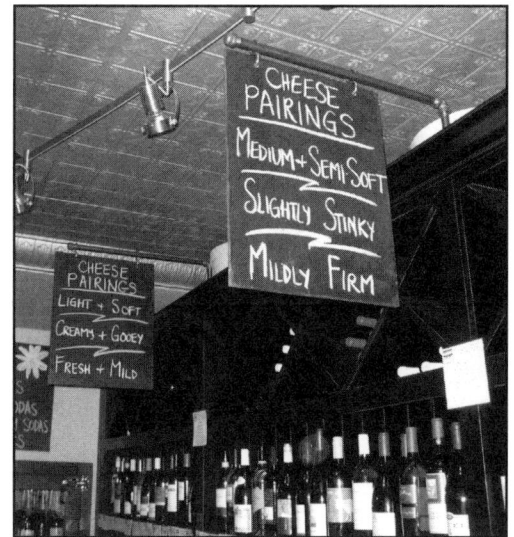

Cheese and wine shop. *Cheese shops often also sell wines, both to help with cash flow and for the convenience of the many customers who are attracted both to cheeses and fine wines.*

Price list. *Posted by a cheese vendor at a farmers market, such lists can make shopping for cheeses less intimidating to new customers. Also farmers markets with good cheese vendors can provide an accessible way to learn about the new American cheeses.*

doesn't bring us up to speed, so we are relying on what we learned in our interviews.

One shop owner said, "There is now so much food on television, in the cable area, whether it be the Food Channel, the Top Chef reality program on Bravo, the restaurant series on Reality, or Gordon Ramsey and other celebrity chefs—those shows are getting good ratings, big numbers. People are becoming more attuned to food, more attuned to entertaining at home, more attuned to eating fine foods."

Similarly when we asked a shop owner why she thought consumers were interested in American cheeses, she said, "I think it is all part of the movement of natural, organic, sustainable foods. I also think it is the popularity that food is gaining in our culture, the momentum. It is not just the Food Network anymore. A&E has food shows. Bravo has food shows. The Travel Channel has food shows. In your own home, you're flipping through the stations, you're seeing all these chefs. Chefs are now celebrities."

"I also give credit to food TV," volunteered a cheese enthusiast when we asked why he thinks more people are enjoying more kinds of cheeses these days. "In the last ten years it has opened people up to the potential that they can get. I saw a Martha Stewart show probably ten years ago where she went to Artisanal, the cheese shop in New York City, and that made me connect to the place. But there are so many shows. Rachel Ray will talk about a specialty-aged Gouda. Or a show will bring in Manchego and talk about Spanish sheep milk cheese. Obviously Giada, because she's Italian, often brings in some cheese to what she is cooking. And I think that really does expose people to the potential cheese offers them."

From rural cheesemakers who live in traditional dairy regions like the Adirondack Crescent we heard that despite their initially strong resistance to new styles of cheese, consumers have changed. Maybe television helped overcome some of that early consumer resistance. In the beginning, said one cheesemaker, "It was hard to introduce new things in an area like this. Asking them to try goat cheese was like asking if they'd like a case of leprosy." Another said that, "In rural areas, people grew up around a few goats. They know bucks, and they know they reek. Goat milk smells terrible when the does have been near the buck, or when the milk has been sitting around for a while. I remember from when I was a boy. I know why they resisted the very idea of goat milk cheese when we first made it."

We heard from some shop owners that in addition to initially preferring more traditional cheeses because of their comfortable familiarity, consumers also have been skittish about paying the price for trying the new American cheeses. One said, "The American artisanal cheeses usually live up to their hype, are good and tasty. But they're three times as expensive as good, tasty, traditionally made foreign cheeses. Customers buy it once, but two times, or three? No. They don't. Can I routinely, day in and day out, sell a cheese that is twice as expensive or even three times as expensive as another very good, mainstream or large-dairy produced product? It hasn't seemed like I can. If you buy a five-pound wheel, and you sell one pound, your markup is not going to cover that. Cheese at twenty dollars and thirty dollars per pound is pie–in–the–sky, at least in my town," he said.

But as the factors influencing their thinking have changed, consumers have apparently become less price sensitive. At one shop the owners said they have experienced double-digit increases in sales volume for each of five years in operation. They have increased the number of cheeses available at any time from about 50 to about 100. Their focus is on American specialty cheeses, and they have sold many more than the 100 kinds that are available at any one time because they continually add new ones and drop others as seasons, or consumer interests, change.

Consumers like the personal connection they develop with shop owners and cheese vendors. They like the ambiance of cheese shops, the cheese classes, and the fact that they can taste the cheeses. Customers and

Self service. Customers can get cheeses from some farmsteads by selecting them from coolers on a porch or entryway. One cheesemaker we know has a can for "cold cash" inside a cooler, so customers can leave money behind on the honor system.

shopkeepers know each others' names or at least they know their customers "by sight and by their favorite cheeses," said one shopkeeper. We heard that "Cheese looks good, tastes good, smells good. It pulls you in, like a bakery." A retailer told us that "The way a specialty cheese or wine store can survive and compete against large stores is to give hands-on service. A lot of people want that. Our business would be half of what it is if we were not a cut-to-order cheese store."

Shop owners told us their customers seem to greatly enjoy being able to talk about all the cheeses in the shop – whether they know they like them or are not yet familiar with them. They expect the shop owners to introduce them to other cheeses based on what they already like. A retailer mentioned how much fun it was to introduce American cheeses when the value of the euro was high, bringing the prices of European cheeses into line with American ones. It was a perfect time to introduce his customers to American cheeses that were similar to their favorite European types because the costs were about the same.

Real cheese enthusiasts who love finding a new American cheese are also a factor in the growth of interest. They write books. They blog. They establish Websites. They belong to the ACS. They buy lots of cheese. One enthusiast said he thinks cheese enthusiasts "collect" cheeses, like they would "collect vinyl records or vintage books." "It is like bird-watching," another told me. "Finding a cheese on a small farm in a remote corner of your state is like spotting the ivory-billed woodpecker in an Alabama woods. Among other collectors, it gives you credibility, even fame." They put a finger on that little swell of pride I feel when I introduce a cheese-novice friend to a raw goat milk cheddar or better yet a perfectly aged bloomy-rind.

Russ and I also learned about the factors influencing the growth in interest in the new American cheese from the participants in our community presentations. They tended to be curious about cheese but not real enthusiasts and not yet aware of the growth in new

American cheeses. One of the presentations was part of a continuing education program at a community college. The audience members had no particular focus on food topics. As we were setting up, people chatted with us about their impression that there now are many more kinds of cheese in supermarkets, especially the fresh-food supermarkets. A few talked about particular favorite cheeses they buy, almost all of which were European. One impression we got from people in the audience is that American cheese still fits their idea of standard cheese and the special-cheese niche is more likely occupied by European cheeses. This made a wonderful background for our presentation because so much of what we said surprised them.

Another presentation we gave was to our local Slow Food chapter. Everyone in the audience was interested in food issues, but few were cheese enthusiasts. Again we noted that many thought of European cheeses as the special cheeses and were unaware of the many new American cheeses that would fit their idea of special and local. Both examples illustrate what we also see as good news for the new American cheese because these audience members foreshadow the coming wave of consumers for domestic cheese wonders. These are people who know they enjoy cheese, who see good cheese as good food. They want to eat it more often than they have in the past. They are not particularly put off by the higher price tag. They take pride in knowing that American innovators are making these wonderful new cheeses.

More important, the participants in these events reflect what we heard and observed in other situations: consumers of the new American cheese see it as part of a philosophy of food that values local, fresh, and seasonal. The growth in interest in the new American cheese seems to us to be part of a big-picture shift in thinking about food. Consumer desire for clean, fresh, nutritious foods, including artisanal cheeses, is growing. This has helped the growth of farmers markets. The online Farmers Market Directory maintained by the U.S. Department of Agriculture showed a 13% increase in the number of farmers

Cheese label. This popular original bloomy-rind cheese is made in the Adirondacks.

markets -- from 4,685 in 2008 to 5,282 in 2009. One cheesemaker told us she thinks farmers markets build a sense of community among consumers and vendors. The customers are eager to talk about cheese, local foods, and sustainability of the agricultural life of the region.

Generally we American consumers are accustomed to getting any food product, anywhere, at any time of the year. Artisanal and farmstead cheeses defy the modern expectation of year-round food availability and immutable taste. Cheeses, like strawberries and tomatoes, are seasonal. Cheese made from milk from different farms will have unique tastes because what the goats or cows or sheep eat is unique to those farms or regions. Some cheese consumers will go hunting, like life-list birders, for a unique cheese sold only on site by the farmstead cheesemaker. These cheese enthusiasts want not only to experience the cheese but also the bragging rights for having had the experience. That's what some of us are like. We want to find a cheese handcrafted by a couple of members of a family working in a small cheese room on their small farm using the milk of their own cows made healthy by walking from their pasture to the barn at milking time rather than by being dosed with antibiotics.

As Russ mentioned, Liz Thorpe, in her entertaining, intelligent, and approachable 2009 book *The Cheese Chronicles*, proposes that we use the word "artisanal" to refer to cheesemakers who adapt their processes to the milk the animals are producing at that moment, rather than adapting the milk to the cheesemaker's standard processes. It is a grand idea. What we get with the new American cheese is the taste of the milk, more grassy if the animals are pasturing, more herby if they graze in an old herb garden. If milks are pooled and standardized to ensure that the end product will always taste exactly the same, cheeses made from them will not be artisanal even if they are handmade.

The Vella Cheese Company understands artisanal the way Liz describes it. The Vella Website claimed in October 2009, "Quality starts in the pasture. Every cow is not the same. Every day is not sunny; every blade of grass is not green and lush. But, if you insist on the finest breeding of herds, the finest feeds, the greatest care in milking and transporting the top grade milk, so that you have the best possible natural raw material, you have set the stage for super cheese."

One enthusiast gave us a similar description of how he understands the meaning of artisanal. "It rocked my world to figure out that the spring versus the autumn Parmesans were different because the cows were eating different grass. Of course they're different and they're producing different milk! I figured out that I could see it in the color of the Parmesan and in the texture of its grain. That's like vintage wine. It's produce. For me, Parmesan just doesn't come out of that green can any more. Now I understand it: grass—cows—cheese!"

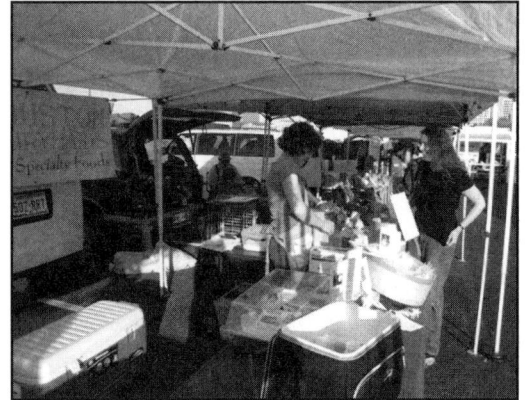

Cheese vendor at a farmers market. Such markets bring a variety of cheeses to customers who do not have nearby specialty retail stores.

Most of us get our artisanal cheese relatively close to home and relatively conveniently from local stores and cheese shops. Because the product is seasonal, retailers who sell American artisanal and farmstead cheeses will not always be able to give us the cheese we have in mind to buy. That is in part why we feel so lucky if we have a local cheese shop. We expect the shop owner to know what is available and to help us select something like what we thought we wanted. How nice to have to wait for a cheese until it is ready. We learned our lesson with strawberries and tomatoes. Having them available year-round is not worth the loss of quality inevitable in making it happen.

The new American cheese consumer is willing to let a cheese be out of stock when it is out of season. Something is wholesome and comforting about having less milk available when the animals are freshening. It is good that our cheesemakers may have the luxury of taking a vacation while their milk-producing animals are pregnant. Artisanal cheese gives us back the seasons and the taste of nature that disappeared into the global food industry. We like having it back.

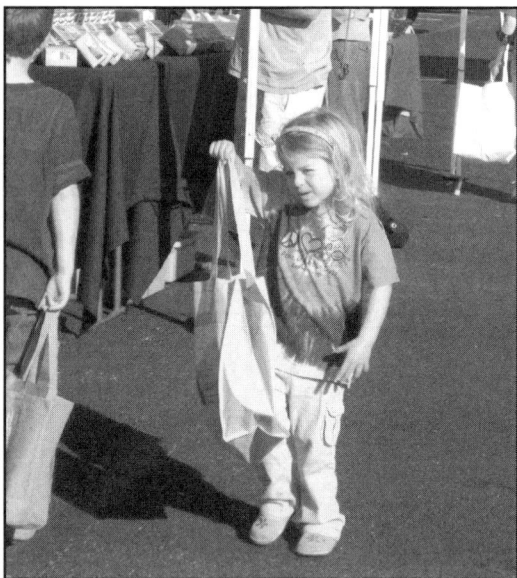

*A **satisfied customer.** This girl happily carries the bounty of cheese her mother found at a farmers market.*

A cheese enthusiast told us, "With this economy, with our reassessment of agribusiness, is it really so affordable to get stuff from Chile all the time? Really, isn't there somewhere local where we can get good quality and feel that even if it costs more than when it is agribusiness-produced, we prefer it because it is local and more nutritious? I am happy to see that we've got a victory garden at the White House. It encourages all of us to rethink what we can do at a lower level."

At Heritage Cheese House the retail manager told us "We run out of cheese sometimes. We always feel bad when that happens. We're happy that we sold out, sold all we had, but we feel bad that people made a trip to come over here and we're sold out." Her customers tend to be local people and regional tourists; they are drop-in customers. The store does not have a Website or accept online orders, so they do not run out because of shipping the cheese to far corners of the state and country. Often they cannot even respond to phone call requests because everything they produce has already been bought by people who came into the store. Why don't they make more? Because, she said, their milk comes from local farmers and there are only so many of them.

Later Russ and I talked about what she had said. Arising from somewhere in our subconscious, we both had the thought that it is a violation of the American way of business to fail to make more when you could sell more, that if there is more demand, you ought to find a way to meet it. But the Heritage Cheese House manager was telling us that the farmers are happy because they sell all their milk, the people who work there are happy because they have good jobs doing interesting work that makes their tiny town more prosperous. Consumers are disappointed when the cheese is not available, but it does not make them stop coming to shop. Is anything wrong with this picture? We had to admit there probably is not. In this case, what brings people to this factory store is the cheese, especially the cheese curds, and the story of the Amish farmers who supply the milk. The consumers apparently would not want there to be more cheese if it meant that the milk was not from the local Amish farms. The consumers are willing to live with the scarcity, and perhaps cherish it a little, like the absence of sweet corn in December that makes it taste more wonderful in July.

There is little doubt that increasing numbers of consumers have come to artisanal cheeses over the past decades. Even in regions not seen as progressive about foods, they have come. A rural cheesemaker told us that he is not surprised when "In the cities, restaurants put on their menus that they are serving local produce and supporting local farmers. Lots of people are real foodies, and artisan cheese is hot. People like to seem knowledgeable. But to see it up here, in the boonies, in an area not known for having eclectic and high-profile interests in food, this is impressive."

The interest in the new American cheese is still emerging, despite how fast it has grown already. It is tied to both small-picture interests in finding fun new foods and big-picture interests in turning away from the global food industry toward building sustainable local, healthy, trustworthy food systems. It is about looking the producer of your food in the eye and becoming partners in the promise that good food will be there when you need it.

USDA food pyramid. *Recommendations on what constitutes a healthy diet have been evolving. This 1996 version of the USDA pyramid was replaced in 2005 by a less intuitive one. Many consumers have tended to leapfrog recommendations provided by such organizations in opting for diets containing greater proportions of natural and unprocessed ingredients.*

Short Take: Cheese and Healthy Living

An item in our local newspaper carried some tips emanating from the American Dietetic Association under the banner *Consider Healthy Cheese Options*. The options presented were designed to limit the damage to health caused by the high butterfat content in cheese. Despite appearing to provide some tips allowing people to eat more cheese without worrying about their health, in fact the piece encouraged people to eat less cheese. The options provided (select lowfat mozzarella; choose sharp cheese to provide more flavor with less fat; buy shredded cheese in order to use less; and grate or crumble cheeses to extend flavor and get by with less) basically appeared to buy into the notion that eating cheese is an inherently unhealthy habit that, if not avoided, at least should be minimized.

The attitudes expressed in this article reveal one side of a major fault line in debates over food and health: they ignore a growing body of evidence that incorporation of foods like cheese into the diet is a sensible and successful way to improve one's health. They fail to take into account statistics revealing that French people and other nationalities consuming cheese with nearly every meal are on the whole healthier (particularly with respect to diseases popularly associated with excessive fat consumption) than are Americans.

Real cheese is a natural product with no chemical preservatives, processed ingredients, dietary supplements, emulsifiers, or flavor enhancers. It incorporates all the qualities that a growing number of food experts would regard as an uncommonly healthful food.

While we applaud well-intended efforts of groups such as the American Dietetic Association to improve our eating habits, we are likely to keep our own counsel when it comes to cheese.

Part 6:

Discoveries

as told by Russ

We now find ourselves at the end of our first journey along the cheese trails—through the new world of American cheese. We know much more is to be seen, but we at least have visited diverse parts of it. Our tour took us from childhood to the present, and from the dairy farms of the early nineteenth century to that first factory in Rome on the southern edge of the Adirondack Crescent, to the ever-larger factories of the twentieth and twenty-first centuries, to the leading edges of twenty-first century cheesemaking. We have seen destruction in the form of idle cheese factories, and we have met unemployed workers. And we have seen creation—a sea of creation—giving rise to what we and others have dubbed the new American cheese. Some would call the transitions underway creative destruction, although we find the term is far too analytical. Some changes we have seen are the result of sweeping, impersonal forces, but in the end we have found the really interesting ones to have more to do with people than with science and economics.

Before examining these changes, we want to highlight some of our real discoveries—the things first we set out to discover: the new American cheeses. And while our searches have taken us to some of the rarer nooks and crannies of the cheese world and given us the opportunity to sample some really remarkable cheeses, in the first section of Part 6 we will confine ourselves to describing the kinds of discoveries we hope you will be able to make at home.

Too many choices? *A selection of new American cheeses offered by a vendor at a fresh food market in Virginia.*

The second section concerns that other kind of discovery: not cheeses we have discovered but rather our discoveries about the world of cheese. Ours was to have been a voyage of learning, and having completed our travels it is appropriate to ask what conclusions and generalizations we have reached. We not only need to reprise what we learned on our journey, but we also need to consider what it means in larger contexts and what lessons it might possibly have that extend into the future — first and foremost as it relates to cheese, but perhaps even beyond the realm of cheese.

Cheese Discoveries

We originally wanted to highlight some cheeses in this book but weren't quite sure how to do it. After sampling hundreds, we hardly knew where to start. In the end we decided to keep it simple. We wouldn't try to include only our favorites—for one thing, just deciding which ones were favorites would be a daunting task. Nor would we tantalize anyone by focusing on hard-to-get cheeses, like those sold only from farms or at certain farmers markets or sampled only in venues like American Cheese Society conferences. We would include only those we were able to find close to home, in our local cheese shops, upscale supermarkets, and stores specializing in natural foods. We did visit friends in Texas and sampled the wares of a couple of well-stocked cheese shops there, but we did not make special out-of-town trips in search of rare cheeses and did not order over the Internet. This strategy constrained the view of all the new American cheeses available, but it had the advantage of ensuring that at least some of those mentioned here would be accessible to our readers.

The cheeses mentioned in the following pages are all good, but we made no effort to pick out the very best of their kind. For a list of those judged to be the best, a good reference is the American Cheese Society Website (www.cheesesociety.org), which annually posts the results of competitions.

The issue of perishability is something to keep in mind if you live in a small town or remote area where specialty food stores are not available and transport may be a problem. Many new American cheesemakers who produce excellent cheeses protect the quality of their products by controlling the conditions under which they are shipped, stored, and offered to customers. Some cheeses are produced in small quantities and supply only local retailers or restaurants. Particularly with fresher, soft cheeses with limited shelf lives, cheesemakers may decide not to entrust their products to shippers who, for example, might leave them out on a loading dock in extreme temperatures or retailers who might store them in less than optimal conditions and sell them after their quality has begun to deteriorate. As a result, some of the best cheeses may have extremely limited availability. Conversely they may be the best precisely because of the extreme care with which they are handed. Young, soft cheeses are less robust than hard cheeses, and so the former — good ones at least — may be relatively harder to find.

Keep in mind also that tasting cheeses is a skill that one acquires through experience, but it is also one that can be improved by coaching. We found at first that we liked almost all the cheeses we sampled. We liked some better than others, but we were often at a loss in trying to describe what qualities contributed to our preferences. As we progressed, we found that sampling a number of different cheeses of similar kinds was helpful. And reading helps also. Liz Thorpe's *The Cheese Chronicles*, while not strictly about tasting, nevertheless helped us to learn to distinguish desirable and less desirable qualities in certain cheeses.

There are good cheeses, okay cheeses, and bad cheeses, and there are also imponderables. Dimensions of quality may be overcome by personal preferences, the roots of which are obscure. I liked all the cheddars, and Peg took no real fancy to any of them. She actually thought that one of my favorites was unremarkable. I liked the blue-veined cheeses but was less taken with them than she, who gravitates more to salty foods. I think I was more enthusiastic about the washed-rind cheeses than she was, and she seemed to like the fresh goat cheeses more than I did. Neither of us could find any explanation for our preferences. I suppose that if our tastes were all alike, a group of expert tasters could rank every cheese as if cheeses were college football teams. We would never have to sample any of them but could just look at the rankings and choose ones from the top ten.

So here is our list, arranged alphabetically by style, and by name within each style group. Some people will question whether all of them are artisanal, and surely some of the cheeses hardly qualify as "new." Nevertheless, they may provide a starting point for anyone wanting to get a sense of the diversity of American cheeses available.

BLOOMY-RIND CHEESES

The edible rind of these soft cheeses is a white mold, *Penicillium candidum*, applied to the surface of the cheese and causing it to ripen from the surface to the interior during the aging process.

Champlain Triple. This triple cream is a bloomy-rind cheese produced by Vermont's Champlain Valley Creamery using cow milk. True to its kind, it includes abundant cream, has a yellowish tint in the body and a soft, oozy interior. We liked its salty, sweet flavor and its melt-in-the-mouth quality. We got this at a cheese shop in Texas.

Humboldt Fog Cypress Grove Chèvre. One of the larger and more celebrated of the new American cheesemakers, Cypress Grove products are more widely available than most artisanal cheeses. Humboldt Fog is a delectable, creamy, tangy goat milk cheese with a distinctive layer of ash running through the center of the cheese. It may be the most widely available mold-ripened cheese made in America. Purple Haze and Truffle Tremor are other unique Cypress Grove cheeses made in Arcata, California.

Sainte Maure. Its namesake is the famous French cheese Sainte-Maure de Touraine, but this one is made in Texas by Pure Luck Dairy. Our sample was starkly white in its interior, while the bloomy rind showed tinges of gray owing to the ash mixed with the ripening culture. It was firm in body and less creamy than other bloomy-rind cheeses. People seem to vary in preferences, and several of our testers found this to be their favorite, based primarily on its texture but also on its subtle flavor.

Seal Cove Pearl. Seal Cove Farm has been producing goat cheeses in Maine since 1976. Pearl is a Brie-type cheese made from a blend of cow and goat milks. Typical of a goat milk cheese, the color was pure white. The body of the cheese was oozy. Some tasting this detected what they described as a slight note of bitterness, while others found this note to be very pleasant.

BLUE-VEINED CHEESES

These cheeses are veined with the blue or green edible mold *Penicillium roqueforti* that is innoculated into the cheese milk and grows into crevices in the interior to produce their unique flavor.

Amagorg. This surprise was the only already-crumbled blue-veined cheese we sampled. But first the surprise: blue cheeses have been made in Minnesota and aged in local caves since as long ago as 1936, and in 2002 the Faribault Dairy revived its manufacture, producing Amablu and Amagorg cheeses. So although this is indeed a new American cheese, it is one with a long history. Our cheese had a pleasant milky flavor, moderate saltiness, a firm but creamy texture, and the most pervasive *Penicillium* flavor of any of the blues sampled—this effect was less later when we tried a wedge of Amagorg. As would be expected of gorgonzola-type cheeses, this was less acidic than the other blue cheeses we tried, seeming to add a leavening mildness to its otherwise intense flavor.

Maytag Blue. Having been made since 1941, this widely available cheese hardly qualifies as a "new" addition to American cheeses. Nevertheless as a boutique product begun more or less as a hobby by the heir to an appliance fortune, it is far from the mainstream. The cheese has a firm, slightly crumbly texture that nevertheless melts in the mouth when tasted. We found it to be the saltiest of the blue-veined cheeses listed here. On the whole, we found consuming it to be a pleasant experience that keeps us coming back for more.

Point Reyes Blue. Of four (there are more) made in America blue-veined cheeses we obtained at our local retailers, this had the least amount of veining, and the least characteristic taste attributable to the *Penicillium roqueforti* mold. Its taste was strongly of milk, with a tangy, sourish finish. Its texture was creamy and somewhat moister than the others sampled. We have found Point Reyes in more than one retail outlet and suspect that it is widely available.

Roth Käse Buttermilk Blue. We wanted to try one of the many specialty cheeses produced by Roth Käse, and found Buttermilk Blue to be available in a local upscale supermarket. This one was creamy and milder than any of the other blue cheeses tasted. We particularly liked its texture. Having sampled six blues within a short period, we were struck with the wide variation we found in the relative amounts of *Penicillium* mold. This one had less blue mold than any of the others, with the possible exception of Point Reyes, and perhaps this accounts for its mild flavor.

Rogue Creamery Smokey Blue. One of several blue cheeses offered by the Rogue Creamery, this one is billed as "the first blue ever smoked." We liked its yellowish color, its crumbly texture, and its deep palate of flavors. We could not detect a distinct smoky flavor and suspect that the smoke (from hazelnut shells, according to the creamery) blends with the typical *Penicillium* compounds, softening them and perhaps helping them to diffuse throughout the body of the cheese. Of the blues sampled, this was the only one not prepackaged, although we later learned it is also available in individually wrapped wedges.

CHEDDAR-TYPE CHEESES

Cheddar cheeses are ripened by the bacteria introduced early in the cheesemaking process. The curds are "cheddared," which is a process of pressing them into slabs and turning them to expel the whey. They are then milled into small pieces and pressed while they age and the bacteria work their magic.

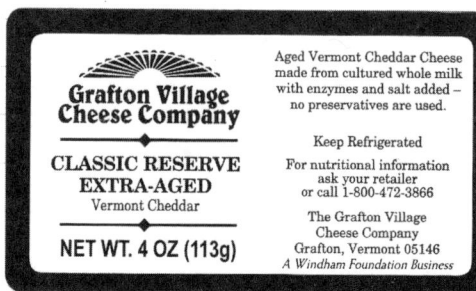

1000 Islands River Rat Extra Sharp Cheddar. We bought a two-pound wax-covered wheel when visiting northern New York. It comes from Gold Cup Farms of Clayton, New York, a company that traces its involvement in the local cheese business to 1885. This cheddar was white, moderately smooth, and flavorful. We liked its hint of acidity and aftertaste and considered it a bargain at less than $10 per pound. We wish we could get it near home.

Beecher's Flagship Cheese. Made by Beecher's Handmade Cheese, this one-year aged cheddar-like cheese has a smooth texture and a smooth, sharp, salty taste. We aren't sure, but we think its flavor is what experienced tasters call minerality. We detected none of the defects such as excessive acidity or aftertaste said to affect sharp cheddars, and found sampling this cheese to be an altogether highly pleasurable experience. We are expecting to see Beecher's cheesemakers in action at Pike Place Market when we visit Seattle for the 2010 American Cheese Society Conference.

Black Diamond Aged 6 Year Cheddar Cheese. At first we didn't know if this qualifies as an artisanal cheese because Black Diamond is a Canadian company owned by the Italian multinational Parmalat, known for its wide range of food products. However, we couldn't find it in the list of products given on the Black Diamond Website. We finally tracked its origin down to an Ontario cheese factory known for its line of aged cheddars. The cheese was delightful in texture and flavor, neither acidic nor overly crumbly, with a pleasant sharpness, subtle undertones, and a smooth, melting quality on the tongue.

Carr Valley 6 Year Cheddar. Another surprise, this long-aged cheddar was neither sharp nor crumbly — qualities we naïvely thought to be common to all long-aged cheddars. Smooth in taste and in texture, it had deep memorable tones that seemed to capture the essence of cheddar cheese — it did not taste like grass or have a mineral quality — nor did it have any of the qualities in cheddars usually regarded as defects. Like an aged Gouda that little resembles its immature stages, this cheese resembled common, imperfect cheddars only in the most subtle ways.

Grafton Village Classic Reserve Extra Aged Vermont Cheddar. Only moderately crumbly and with a creamy texture, this distinctive cheese had layers of tastes. Piquant, but not sour, we could not agree whether we were detecting intense flavors of grass. In subsequent samplings our ability to distinguish flavors in different cheeses had improved, and it was clear that it was grass we had been tasting. We later concluded that the black wax coating of the tiny (2 x 2 x 3-inch) cheese was applied after the cheese was cut and was not used as a coating during the aging process.

Mt. Sterling Co-Op Creamery Raw Goat Milk Mild Cheddar Cheese. After sampling this cheese, we had little doubt about the provenance of the Shiloh Farms goat cheddar (see the following entry). Other than their front labels, the packages were nearly identical, and we concluded at once that the Shiloh product comes from Wisconsin's Mt. Sterling Creamery. Remaining doubts were swept away by the tasting. The flavors of this mild cheddar were identical to those of the Shiloh Farms Sharp, only slightly less intense. This was the most flavorful mild cheddar we have tasted, and it's a delightful product.

Shiloh Farms Raw Goat Milk Sharp Cheddar Cheese. The label indicated this cheese was "packaged for Shiloh Farms." We learned this is a business operated by a Christian community founded in western New York but now located in New Holland, Pennsylvania. They offer a wide range of natural foods for wholesale and Internet sales. At first we wondered whether the cheese we sampled could be artisanal or even farmstead, but there was no way to know from the label. However, after tasting the Mt. Sterling cheese (see the previous entry), we thought we had solved the mystery, and the Mt. Sterling, Wisconsin creamery was the likely source of this cheese. The Shiloh Farms product was an excellent cheese, and we much enjoyed it. It differed from the cow milk cheddars we sampled in its subtle sharpness and undertones of intriguing flavors.

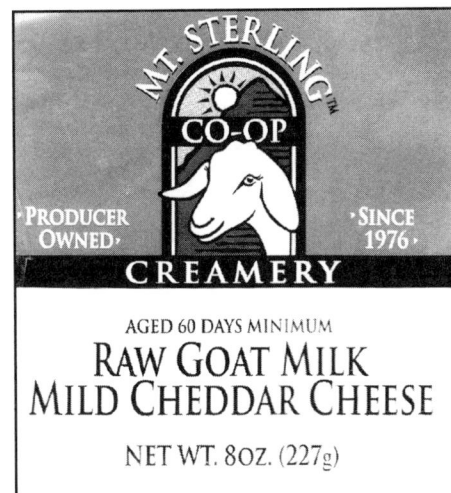

MT. STERLING CO-OP

·PRODUCER OWNED·   ·SINCE 1976·

CREAMERY

AGED 60 DAYS MINIMUM
RAW GOAT MILK
MILD CHEDDAR CHEESE

NET WT. 8 OZ. (227g)

Since 1942   Gen 49:10

SHILOH FARMS

Raw Goat Milk
SHARP CHEDDAR
CHEESE
Net Wt. 8 oz. (227g)

Packaged for Shiloh Farms, Sulphur Springs, AR

FRESH GOAT CHEESES

These cheeses are aged very little and are soft, fresh, and the simplest of the cheeses we tried.

Crottin Montchèvre. A simple chèvre, this differs in small ways from the others sampled and included in this list. It was the whitest of the three, seemed to be the driest, and nevertheless had a creamy melt-in-the-mouth quality when tasted. Its flavor was piquant, with hints of milk, sour cream, and buttermilk. A Wisconsin product, we suspect it is widely available. We got it in a tiny 3.5-ounce pill-shaped package, and learned that the Crottin name refers to cheeses made in this shape.

Laura Chenel Chabis. We got a 5-ounce pillow-shaped package of this cheese. We believed the name refers to the packaging and that the cheese is identical with Chenel's famous Chèvre, the cheese credited by many with signaling the birth of the new American cheese. Later we bought the traditional log and confirmed our first impression. Softer and smoother, and not quite as white as the others, it has faint hints of goat flavor. To us, the texture was its most noticeable and most alluring quality.

Vermont Butter & Cheese Chèvre. Smooth with a hint of fresh milk, this slightly astringent melt-in-your-mouth cheese delivered all you would expect from a fresh, well-made chèvre. Faint hints of citrus are said to occur in good chèvres, and we detected them in this one. Chèvres are the most basic goat cheeses and sometimes are sold or specified in recipes simply as "goat cheese." This was not a recognized style of cheese in the United States until the pioneering Laura Chenel used the term "chèvre" (the French word for goat) to describe the cheese she introduced to Californians in 1979.

WASHED-RIND CHEESES

These cheeses are ripened from the surface to the interior by bacteria that are washed over the rind during the aging process. They are characteristically aromatic.

Brother Laurent. Made in Vermont by the Boucher family, this washed-rind cow milk cheese follows the style of the famous Munster cheeses of France. In color our cheese was tan, and the texture we described as a dry paste was neither gummy nor rubbery. Pungent and flavorful, some especially liked its sharpness, while others preferred milder cheeses. We have found that many well-seasoned cheese enthusiasts prefer washed-rind cheeses above all others, while beginners usually prefer less aromatic kinds.

Timberdoodle. Taking its name from an alternative name for the American woodcock, this cheese is produced by Vermont's Woodcock Farm. This delightful washed-rind cheese is made from a mixture of cow and sheep milks in the style of a Havarti. Creamier and milder than Brother Laurent, it also was darker in color. Some tasters were particularly fond of its texture. Like Brother Laurent, this cheese made its way from Vermont to Texas, and it is potentially available in cheese shops nationwide.

OTHER STYLES

Cantaré Ciligine Mozzarella. Quite different from the goat mozzarella (see the Woolwich description below), this fresh cheese was closer to what we had come to expect of mozzarellas, only far better than the familiar plastic-wrapped kinds. Its mild, milky flavor and resilient and ropy texture are pleasant. It is the perfect accompaniment for olive oil, black pepper, and tomatoes. Cantaré Foods of San Diego represents the modern fusion of high-technology factory methods and careful fidelity to traditional products and methods. We bought this in the grocery section of a big box retailer. According to the Website, it should be available in many supermarkets.

Vella Bear Flag Brand Dry Monterey Jack. This was another surprise when we first tasted it, little resembling the bland but likeable Monterey jack with which we were familiar. Instead, this aged version,

an American original, reminded our unsophisticated palates of nothing so much as a Spanish Manchego. Mild and flavorful, it had us coming back for more, even when other delightful cheeses remained to be sampled. The Vellas, surely pioneers of the artisanal cheese movement, have been making distinctive cheeses since 1931.

Woolwich Dairies Goat Mozzarella. We had never tried a goat mozzarella and were curious to try this offering from Ontario, Canada. We first noticed that it lacked the springy elasticity of the familiar mozzarellas, and we wondered if it had undergone the typical stretching of *pasta filata* cheeses. The aroma and taste were a pleasant surprise. We noticed a piquant quality quite unlike other mozzarellas. Finally pinning it down, we identified a faint "goaty" flavor — not at all unpleasant and adding an element of interest to the cheese.

———————

We decided that 24 cheeses would be an appropriate number for our little hometown sampling but regretted reaching that number and having to quit. Now that we had achieved our arbitrary limit, we could no longer use professional duty as an excuse to go out and prowl the cheese counters.

Taking Stock

Having followed many trails in the world of the new American cheese, we found ourselves at a waypoint. More discovery lay ahead, and we were not ready to end the adventure. However, already much had changed for us in large and small ways, and it was time to take stock. We had tasted great cheeses, met many interesting people, visited places we otherwise would never have seen, and learned a great deal—about cheese, about other people, and about ourselves.

Following are some of the things we wanted to remember and to share.

#1: The new American cheese is bigger, more inclusive, and more complex than we initially understood.

We have related how surprised we were to encounter the crowds at the cheese festival in Warwick, Quebec, how astounded we were to see the variety of cheeses and the number of participants at American Cheese Society conferences, and how buoyed we were to discover the strong and growing interest in cheese, not just in people like us but increasingly in people who did not fit our demographic and socioeconomic profiles. The new American cheese is indeed bigger than we expected.

Moreover, the new American cheese encompasses far more variation than expected, and getting a handle on the whole thing is difficult. We found that the new American cheese has no sharp boundaries. It includes the farmstead cheesemaker we met who is milking six goats and selling one or two kinds of cheese in his hometown. At the same time it includes a company like Roth Käse, firmly planted in a large modern factory on American soil and producing many kinds of cheeses to meet the needs of increasingly sophisticated American tastes. It is the upstart farmer-entrepreneurs who are just now planning to release their first cheeses on the market. And it is also venerable cheesemakers like the Vellas who for decades have been producing cheeses for ethnic markets and have maintained and built upon traditions with roots in the Old World. It is cheeses made in tiny rooms in converted farm buildings and those coming from ultramodern factories specially designed to make artisanal cheeses. It includes cheeses treasured because the consumer can look the cheesemaker in the eye and those valued because their tastes reflect the changing of the seasons. It is cheeses made in styles that are hundreds of years old, as well as those in new, imaginative, and even revolutionary styles.

"Behind every cheese there is a pasture of a different green under a different sky: meadows caked with salt that the tides of Normandy deposit every evening; meadows scented with aromas in the windy sunlight of Provence; there are different flocks, with their stablings and their transhumances; there are secret processes handed down over the centuries." [Italo Calvino, *Mr. Palomar*]

The new American cheese is not a simple thing, and in confronting its complexity we, like others, at first fell back on how cheeses are made, coming up with more or less adequate definitions for terms like "artisanal" and "farmstead." In the end, however, we found this approach to fall short. We have come to believe that the real essence of the new American cheese has mostly to do with the interactions between cheeses and customers that are lost when things become industrialized and commoditized. The new American cheese is really about the complex of relationships with infinite variations in which the qualities of the cheeses—what they are, where and how they are made, and how they taste—interact with the unique sensitivities and values of customers. The new American cheese is real, but it is something quite different to each of us.

#2: Cheese has deep (and often obscure) roots in many people.

We recognized early on that we were attracted to cheese, not just as a food and a fascinating subject of study. There was more—something elusive. Along with this recognition came the surprising revelation that we were not alone; many other people seemed to be afflicted with a similar attraction.

When we found the new American cheese it was a discovery of something wholly unexpected.

Nevertheless, for the two of us, connecting with cheese helped us to connect with our own roots. We realized that many things in our pasts had led to, or at least contributed to our attraction to cheese. The first precursors of that attraction could go back as far as our first memories of events at our respective dinner tables, or even farther back in the experiences our parents and grandparents shared with us. And surely some strong roots were taking hold in the growing awareness about food that propelled many of our activities in the 1970s and 1980s and continued through later decades in various forms. Somehow cheese helped us to bring together these old experiences with our new ones and let us live them again.

Appreciating cheese is not only a way of connecting with the past, but also of connecting with the present and with other people. In conversations we discovered many others who shared at least a measure of our interest. The presentations on the cheese project we gave for groups were well attended and enthusiastically received. And who could fail to be impressed by those hoards of people showing up at cheese festivals and conferences?

Surprisingly, most of the people we talked with who were already cheese fanciers or interested in experiencing and learning more were inarticulate and imprecise in their expressions of enthusiasm. Reactions became almost predictable. "Oh, you're doing a cheese project. That's really cool," someone might say, never offering a reason for what was so cool about it. Perhaps, like us, they could not simply and concisely identify the source of the attraction. And as with us, perhaps the connections it enabled were too deep and too diffuse to be clearly seen or easily put into words.

#3: Satisfaction lies close to the source.

As we expected, the experience of making cheese would help us understand the process and the product, but it also provided other, unexpected benefits. Our cheesemaking caught us up again in the

> "I don't know much about it and wish I knew more, because I have always liked cheese." [Enthusiastic attendee at one of our presentations]

kind of spirit we had experienced decades before in first growing our own vegetables, cooking unfamiliar foods such as Jerusalem artichokes, making sauerkraut, and engaging in other homespun crafts. These had made us feel good by giving us a sense of accomplishment, self-sufficiency, and connectedness with our forebears.

> "I think more and more of my connection to my food is about my connection to the people who produce it. And I get so excited when I sit down to a meal and I can name where everything on my plate came from and who made it." [Cheese enthusiast]

Simultanously, making cheese gave us a better feeling for what it must have been like for the farm wives of centuries past who toiled endlessly, slaving over hot stoves to turn milk into cheese, and providing the farm's one and only cash crop. It gave us fuller insights into the lives of the new cheesemakers by taking us through the demanding and sometimes tedious chores they must undertake daily. And it even enriched our visits to modern, mechanized, and automated cheese factories by giving us a benchmark against which to contrast their production with what we and others had done by hand.

Much of what we learned about cheese was academic and dry, but our hands-on experiences led us to other visceral and almost kinesthetic kinds of understanding.

Not everyone will take up cheesemaking as a hobby, and we think that few of those who might like to try will ever get around to it. Nevertheless, in most cultures food is about sharing, and people can vicariously enrich their experiences by coming close to the source of cheeses and other foods. Knowing the source of cheeses will help them to better appreciate the skill, care, and labor invested in their products by the new American cheesemakers.

#4: Trends in mainstream cheese echo global changes in agriculture and business.

We found that when we were looking at the history of cheese in America we were also seeing the kinds of sweeping changes that have affected many other aspects of our lives. Everything we learned about the transition begun in the mid-nineteenth century—the farm to factory transition—we came to recognize as a series of events not entirely unique to cheese. The movement of cheesemaking from the farm to the crossroads cheese factory, and then to ever larger and fewer factories, paralleled changes going on in many other areas. The substitution of capital, technology, and fossil energy for human creativity and effort, and the emphasis on greater quantity and efficiency at the expense of the pursuit of quality and variety in cheesemaking might well serve as a metaphor for many of the pervasive kinds of changes occurring contemporaneously. Those other changes gave us Super WalMarts, thick-skinned grapefruits, tasteless strawberries, processed foods with too many calories and too much salt, and ground beef of unknowable provenance, all of which are now becoming recognized as examples of progress achieving limited benefits in some areas while incurring steep, often unrecognized, and usually unaccounted for costs in others.

These changes not only degraded the quality of products available to people, but also often visited hardships on individuals and communities. Stories we heard of human costs when farms were abandoned or cheese factories closed were little different from those we knew happened in towns with closed iron mines, paper mills, or automobile plants.

#5: Trends in the new American cheese echo broader changes in food production.

We recognized recent trends in American cheese that have taken it from the factory back to the farm as something far from unique. In other areas of food production, developments that have continued for decades have spawned opposite reactions in recent years. Surely the rise of farmers markets, share farming, food cooperatives, and the renewed popularity of home and urban community vegetable gardening attest to the current trends in the business of food production. These trends reflect the public reaction to mass-produced, highly processed, often unhealthful foods that have given rise to Whole Foods markets and many imitators.

"How and why did northern society move so rapidly toward a new social order in which national markets, urban centers, and large-scale production and consumption assumed central importance? … Dairying offers a window on these dramatic shifts." Sally McMurry, in *Transforming Rural Life*

"Well look at New York City. They say every flower box has something more than a geranium in it. Maybe it's a left-handed cigarette, but more likely some herbs or something. People are thinking back to the old victory gardens and stuff like that." [Farmstead cheesemaker—we chuckle to ourselves every time we recall this comment.]

"When you come here, really anywhere you go, if you buy an artisan cheese it will be a little bit more expensive, but it is going to be a lot more satisfying." [Cheese manager in a cut-to-order shop]

The rebirth of the new American cheese is even more striking than most of these other countertrends because the original handmade American cheese had all but disappeared. Some people continued to grow vegetables, seek out fresh vegetables and meats in local markets, and burn wood even as industrial agriculture and nationwide chains supplied most of the nation's food and power plants and pipelines provided energy for homes. On the other hand, the original American cheese—hand-made on farms in the early nineteenth century—for the most part had died out more than a century ago. These traditions faded farther into the past when ever-larger factories run by multinational corporations dominated the landscape. While some Europeans have been successful in maintaining the old traditions, on the whole the new American cheesemakers are less involved in maintaining old traditions and more engaged in using them as a base on which to build new ones.

#6: Quality and value are priceless.

In the past we had been confirmed bargain hunters, almost invariably selecting lower-cost goods— including foods—whenever given the choice. Our cheese experiences convinced us that—particularly in the selection of foods—well informed people will opt for quality and value over adequacy and low price. The cheesemakers we saw during our travels who were succeeding—selling everything they could produce—did not see low prices as their competitive advantage. Instead they were well supported by customers who sought quality and recognized value. This set them apart from commodity producers who were relying on ever-increasing scale and capital investment to keep down costs and remain competitive with each other. In pursuing that course, the factory producers were turning out unremarkable products, closing factories, laying off workers, and dealing with the constant threat of out-of-control inventories. Any attention to quality would inevitably be at the mercy of the primary imperatives, which were all about money. Most of the new American cheesemakers we met and those operating factories who have concerns about paying bills and making payrolls had to worry about money too. However, although they spoke without complaining about long hours, tedious chores, and the strict demands of their professions, none lamented they had too few customers or inadequate demand for their cheeses.

#7: The new American cheese adds value to rural life.

Before we began traveling along our cheese trails, we had thought little about rural America. Having been city dwellers for three decades, we took for granted that the countryside remained and would continue to remain much as it had always been. It didn't look that different to us, but we know now that we hadn't been looking closely enough. Oh, we had surely heard of continuing migrations of people to the cities, and we learned from years of news stories of the troubled economics and relentless industrialization of American agriculture. These things did not become realities for us, however, until we began learning more about cheese and the milk, cattle, farmsteads, and other things that go into its making. We had heard talk of a rural renaissance and expected to see it, but when we looked closely we saw instead a rural America facing very difficult times.

The new cheesemakers we met gave a wide range of reasons for choosing their professions. Nevertheless, all seemed to be on a mission to achieve what they as individuals regarded as quality, both in their lifestyles and in the products of their labors. We believe the cheesemakers and their customers are not the sole beneficiaries of the new American cheese, however. All across the nation, a scattering of neglected farmsteads are again becoming active, overgrown or ill-tended pastures are being rehabilitated, and small pockets of vitality are showing up again in communities that have long known nothing but decline. The new American cheese is unlikely to reverse all the unfavorable trends affecting rural life, but it is adding value in small ways and perhaps can help show the way to others who can bring about innovative changes.

"As we look back at the change in our economy and our concerns today, as we look at the European countries, you have to ask, How did we get so far away from the economic model that has worked well here and in Europe for centuries?"
[Farmstead cheesemaker]

#8: The new American cheese adds value to the food movement.

Having practically grown up with the food movement, we knew about the value of fresh vegetables, whole grains, hormone-free meats, free-range poultry, wild-caught fish, pesticide-free products, and many more kinds of foods that are healthy for us and for the environment on which we depend. Strangely, cheese did not become part of our continuing education about food until very late. Perhaps for most of the history of the food movement, cheese was regarded almost as a pariah because of the purported negative health effects of dairy products, based at least in part on their fat content.

The new American cheesemakers changed all that. People could eat their cheeses and know what was in them. They could know who made them. They could find out where the milk that went into the cheese came from and, in many cases, what the dairy animals giving the milk had been eating. They would know that they were consuming butterfat but could be confident they were not consuming preservatives and stabilizers. A wonderful new class of foods was added to the choices available to concerned and discerning people.

Consumers seek to add quality to their lives with the cheeses they buy. But they also find rewards in the knowledge that they are helping to enable the lifestyles of the cheesemakers, to preserve rural landscapes, to overcome a pervasive imposition of sameness, and to foster a more humane and sustainable economy.

#9: The new American cheese is novel.

The new American cheese did not evolve from the old American cheese, nor was it transplanted whole from the Old World.

If before our discovery of the new American cheese someone had asked us to link the terms "food" and "creativity," we might have thought of the many

"I started to realize that really our number-one impact on the planet is in relationship to our diet. I started to make those real connections and tie it all together. I realized that that was my calling—it's my passion calling." [Cheese enthusiast explaining her interest in food]

great chefs who produce wonderful meals from simple ingredients. Maybe if we had thought about it long enough, we could also have grudgingly cited the engineers who are working in corporate laboratories to develop even more ways of turning corn into new biochemicals for manufacturing synthetic foods. Had we not met the new American cheesemakers, we would have been unaware of the great creative energies they are unleashing.

Many new American cheesemakers have been inspired by traditional European cheesemakers, but for the most part they have begun independently and have broken ground not yet tilled by others. The term "renaissance" is often used to describe what is happening in American cheese and is perhaps on the verge of overuse. Nevertheless, it is apt in that it is not a revival of American or Old World cheesemaking traditions that is underway but rather a rebirth.

#10: If you make it, they will come.

When we first began to discover the new American cheese, we felt as if we were part of a trickle of pioneers, striking out boldly, far ahead of the crowds. It soon became clear, however, that we were instead in the midst of large and still growing crowds—a groundswell of people pursuing, luxuriating, and rejoycing in the new American cheese.

The number of people attracted to the new American cheese and their enthusiasm continued to surprise us. In the spring of 2009 we received the announcement of a Vermont Cheesemakers Festival to be held in Shelburne on August 23. Cheesemakers from Vermont would be displaying and selling their wares, and seminars and demonstrations on cooking and cheesemaking would be offered. Since we would be in the Adirondacks for most of August and, realizing that we could take in the festival as a day trip, we decided to attend. We bought three $20 tickets, planning to bring a friend along, but decided to forgo the instructions and demonstrations, each of which carried a hefty additional fee. We expected a relatively small event in which we would be able to

"Farmstead cheesemaking became a casualty of the transformation and virtually disappeared from the American scene by the end of the 19th century. Industrial cheesemaking was here to stay." [Paul Kindstedt, *American Farmstead Cheese*]

have some leisurely chats with cheesemakers.

A few days before the festival, we were visiting with some cheesemaker friends and discovered that they also planned to attend. Indeed, when we visited they were making cheese curd to sell at the event. We left expecting to see them again shortly, at the festival. That was not to be, however. Our cell phone rang as we traveled through the mountains on our way back to our camp. Cell phone service is spotty in the area, and we expected this call to be from our daughter, who would be picking up on an interrupted conversation. Instead it was one of the friends we had just left, calling to tell us they would not be attending the festival. She had learned they needed tickets, that registration was capped at 1,000 attendees, and that tickets had long been sold out.

Once more we were surprised by another bit of evidence of what a really big thing the new American cheese had become. One thousand people were purchasing $20 tickets and traveling long distances just for the chance to meet cheesemakers and sample and purchase their cheeses. Others were being turned away.

Nor was it only would-be ticket buyers who were being turned away. When we arrived at the festival, young employees at the gate were turning away significant numbers of drop-ins. The parking area was full, and the exhibit barn was packed with throngs of enthusiastic attendees.

Like writing books, stirring curds in a cheese room can be a lonely occupation. But in both pursuits, if you can make something really good then perhaps the rewards will be abundant.

"If a man can write a better book, preach a better sermon, or make a better mousetrap, than his neighbor, though he build his house in the woods, the world will make a beaten path to his door." [Ralph Waldo Emerson]

Short Take: Third-Party Endorsements

We have heard one knows an apparent trend is a real phenomenon when third parties have gotten onto the bandwagon. Suppose, for example, you buy a little sports car on a whim and then start finding unsolicited catalogs in your mailbox from companies wanting to sell you specially made accessories for your new vehicle. You then have pretty good evidence the model is a success. Others — at least some of whom are canny business people — believe there are plenty more buyers like you, that all of you are enthusiastic, and that enough of you will buy their products that they can make money.

The remarkable growth of interest in cheese is attested to by the recent launch of two magazines, *Cheese Connoisseur* and *Culture*. Both are glossy and expensive. The founder of neither is involved directly in the making or selling of cheese, but both publications are aimed at the broad spectrum of people making, selling, and eating cheese. Packed with informative articles about cheeses, cheese-making regions, and tips on ways of serving cheeses, they provide a forum in which producers, consumers, and everyone in the middle can communicate. And for readers, the magazines provide virtual pleasures of savoring cheeses, if only in photographs and descriptions. They are fun to read.

Although not exclusively devoted to American cheese, they signify the coming of age of the new American enthusiasm for cheese, not only as a vibrant market where producers and consumers meet, but also as a significant economic force.

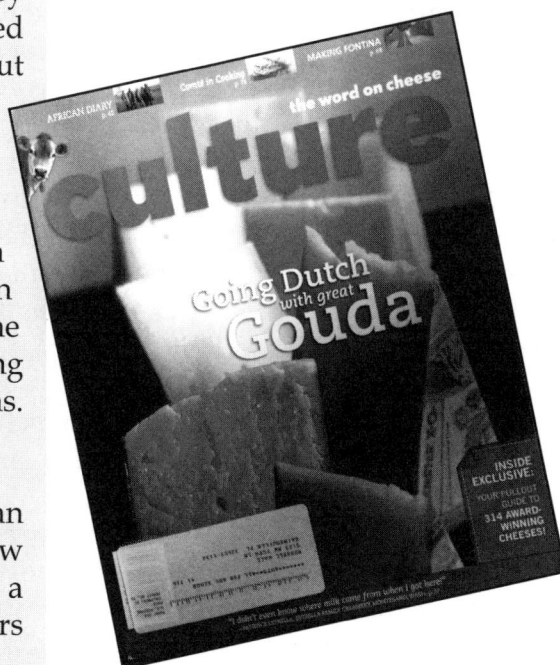

Short Take: Meeting of the Old and the New

We expected a lively competition and perhaps a serious rivalry between the old and the new cheesemakers, but we saw few signs of it. Some corporate cheesemakers seemed to be more active in the American Cheese Society than others, and one low-profile participant from a very large but poorly represented company joked that he was attending the conference as a spy. And there were rumors, never really substantiated to us, that industrial cheesemakers were lobbying regulators to make it more difficult to make cheese from unpasteurized milk, thereby hobbling many artisanal cheesemakers. Despite all this, we observed no overt rancor.

We might have predicted that the desire of the old and new to connect would be asymmetrical, with one side interested and little reciprocation on the part of the other. This prediction proved to be more or less true. Some mainstream cheesemakers seemed fascinated by the renaissance, perhaps because many were professionals with long histories of being interesting in everything to do with cheese. Artisanal cheesemakers seemed less interested in the mainstream, either because they tended in general to have the opposite of corporate temperaments or because they saw themselves as pioneers with little to learn from their mainstream counterparts. Nevertheless, we saw much that led us to the conclusion that both the old and new could often benefit from collaboration.

In some instances, the old and new see themselves as allies and have developed fruitful partnerships. This is exemplified by Cabot, the largest mainstream cheese company we visited. Despite its size, Cabot displayed an evident interest in achieving quality and distinctiveness of products by supporting the artisanal aspects of cheese production. The company is a founding member of the Vermont Cheese Council, an organization providing many services to the state's vibrant group of old and new cheesemakers. Moreover, Cabot developed a partnership with Jasper Hill Farm, a small family-owned cheesemaking operation with a cellar where cheeses made on the farm or those made by others can be custom aged, by artisanal methods. Small runs of select cheeses from Cabot's production have been aged in this cellar.

Jed Davis, Cabot director and former president of the Vermont Cheese Council, acknowledged the benefits of the partnership:

> "The Cabot and Jasper Hill partnership has been very rewarding in so many ways. It is also emblematic of the Vermont reality that collaboration among cheesemakers isn't the exception, but the rule. When Cabot Clothbound Cheddar won Best of Show at the 2006 American Cheese Society competition, it was more than just an impressive honor for one of the Green Mountain State's tasty dairy products. It was an industry-wide salute to Vermont cheesemakers' unparalleled recipe for success: take a healthy dose of camaraderie, add in opportunistic cooperation, and enjoy the resulting high-quality, innovative cheeses. The newly unveiled Cellars at Jasper Hill now takes this collective-

gains-through-collaboration approach to an even higher level. Vermont's brand and the prospects for increased sales of Vermont specialty and artisan cheese should both benefit handsomely."

We did not hear from Roth Käse about its collaborations, but we were led to believe it also had developed partnerships with artisanal cheesemakers in its Wisconsin neighborhood. Products of Crave Brothers, a small factory producing artisanal cheeses, are sold in Roth Käse's factory store and on its Website. Also, tasting tables set up for our 2008 visit to the factory included products of artisanal cheesemakers who had no apparent corporate connection to Roth Käse, including Sugar River Cheese and Kelly's Kitchen Products.

Perhaps the most direct evidence we got of the old and the new trying to connect came out in our interview with a manager of a large mainstream cheesemaking enterprise. He spoke of his lifelong involvement in the cheese business, including experience as an independent cheesemaker. He spoke enthusiastically about the renaissance in American cheese and described ways, primarily in marketing, in which he hoped that he, or someone else, might be able to help remove the barriers that make it difficult for new cheesemakers to get their products to markets. It was obvious to us that he had a strong commitment to the cheesemaking profession and had thought deeply about securing a better future for it.

Some cheesemakers and some customers might not share this person's vision and might prefer artisanal cheeses to remain small, local, and marginal. Indeed, a session at the 2008 American Cheese Society annual conference posed the question "Is selling up selling out?"

How and to what extent the old and new ultimately connect is far from settled but will be fascinating to observe. Surely some small cheesemakers will find compelling reasons to move more into the mainstream, while others will resolutely and cheerfully remain as they are. It is encouraging for cheesemaking as a whole that bridges continue to be built and that a large-tent organization like the American Cheese Society provides a forum in which the old and the new can discuss and consider the merits of bridge building.

We were struck that just as the basic elements of cheesemaking we observed in our visits and practiced in our kitchen were the same, the pursuits of artisanal and mainstream cheesemakers were fundamentally the same. It is certainly plausible that a cheesemaker milking a handful of goats and making cheese in a corner of a converted garage might have something to learn from a cheesemaker receiving milk from hundreds of farms and working in a factory producing hundreds of thousands of pounds of cheese per day. Nor could we ignore the certainty that a major industrial cheesemaker could learn much from a small artisan experimenting in a tiny cheese room. From the time of Jesse Williams's first cheese factory, collaboration and the free sharing of information have characterized much of the history of cheesemaking in America. We hope that tradition will continue far into the future and that knowledge will be freely shared among practitioners of all kinds.

Say cheese. In the spring of 2006 we were touring Eastern Europe, having completed Peg's Fulbright assignment in the Czech Republic. Visiting the famous salt mines of Wieliczka, near Krakow, Poland, we were whisked far underground and ushered through the 900-year old maze of carved-out shafts and vaulted rooms. The caverns were surprisingly crowded, and guides deftly herded individuals and groups to avoid traffic jams. While awaiting our ride back to the surface, we saw nearby about 30 Polish middle-school students posing for a group photo. We paid the scene little attention until we thought we heard the photographer utter a familiar word. Then in unison, the Polish teenagers said, "cheese," as the photographer snapped the picture and captured the moment. We later learned that the Polish word for cheese is "ser," and understood that the facial expression created by its saying is nothing like the smile on the faces of those who say "cheese." We were pleased that the photographer and his subjects chose to borrow one of the happiest and best of our English words.

Epilogue: Back to the Heritage Cheese House

In early 2009 we were conducting an Internet search to look for more information on a fact we had uncovered before including it in this book. We were in for a shock. The third hit in the Google search we were doing was an item from the September 18, 2008, edition of the *Watertown Daily Times* with the heading "Heritage Cheese to Close Sept. 27." The article described the circumstances of the closing in detail, but the running head "*'LOSING MONEY': Equipment upgrade to increase cash flow was unsuccessful*" seemed to tell it all. The closure, which was to be final this time, would idle 15 full- and part-time employees and eliminate the market for milk produced by the 65 remaining Amish dairy farms in the region that had continued to supply the factory.

When we had visited the plant and interviewed three managers on August 14, 2008, scarcely more than a month before this announcement, we had gotten no hint of financial difficulties. Nor in retrospect did we think the people we had interviewed were aware of the dire financial straits in which Heritage Cheese was operating. The newspaper article told of grants and loans totaling nearly $200,000 to acquire equipment to improve productivity, and the failure of these measures to turn around a desperate financial situation. It also reported the levy of a fine by the village of Heuvelton when the factory exceeded sewage discharge regulations—obviously the same old problem of whey disposal experienced by other cheese factories in the Adirondack Crescent, most of which lacked the technology needed to turn whey into a profitable by-product. Other accounts told of losses at Heritage amounting to as much as $3,000 per day.

The closed Heritage Cheese House. *The scene was forlorn when we visited in mid-2009. The parking area was already sprouting weeds, and there was no sign of the activity we had observed when we had visited a year earlier.*

An announcement by the U.S. Department of Agriculture on August 22, 2008, of new pricing regulations that seemed likely to make cheesemaking more profitable had no effect on the decision of the owners, the Heuvelton Community Irrevocable Trust; the decision to close was clearly final. Operating the plant profitably was evidently a hopeless proposition.

After our 2008 visit and interview with managers, we had been curious about how Heritage could afford to compete with corporate giants. One of the managers we interviewed told us that Heritage was selling all the cheese it could produce and then added, incongruously, that it was seeking additional customers. On a whim, we had done a little informal survey. Our data on the competitive position of Heritage Cheese was obtained in the Star Lake IGA store during the same August we had interviewed people at the factory. We had wondered whether Heritage cheeses were commanding higher prices than mass-produced cheeses. As it turned out, the small store we surveyed (the only supermarket within 30 miles) had an unexpected variety of cheddar cheeses—15 in all. Our results looked like this:

Price Per Pound[1] (USD) of Cheddar Cheese – Star Lake IGA Store 8/27-29/2008						
Brand/Variety	Heritage	McCadam	Helluva Good	IGA	Land O' Lakes	Cabot
Mild	4.92					
Medium	5.10		5.00 (on sale)		7.98	
Sharp	5.28	5.58	5.00 (on sale)	6.38	7.98	6.645
Extra Sharp	7.15	5.58	5.00 (on sale)	6.38		6.645

1- Heritage cheeses were in packages of variable sizes and sold by weight; McCadam, Helluva Good, IGA, and Land O' Lakes were sold in 8-ounce packages; Cabot was available in this store only in 2-pound chunks.

As is shown in the table, the Heritage brand included the least expensive cheese in the store (and the only mild cheddar). It also was the least expensive sharp cheese, except for Helluva Good, which claimed to be on sale. It had the most expensive extra sharp, but this was not the most expensive cheese in the store, being significantly less expensive than medium and sharp cheeses sold by Land O' Lakes. The retail pricing scheme for the cheeses seemed to make little sense, but the overall conclusion was crystal clear; customers—in this store at least—were not paying premium prices for Heritage cheese. The Heritage Cheese House was competing head to head with larger producers.

Reviewing what we knew of the history of Heritage Cheese, we saw it straddling the uncomfortable divide between mainstream and artisanal cheesemakers. It was producing cheeses that in most respects were indistinguishable from other factory-made cheeses. Perhaps Heritage cheeses tasted better than some of its competitors' cheeses, but any difference was not great enough to make Heritage products distinctive.

We were surprised to discover that in addition to supplying grocery and convenience stores in northern New York, Heritage was also in the commodity cheese business. We learned this after finding a February 29, 2008, article in the *Cheese Reporter,* which told of the difficulty Heritage had in selling tractor-trailer loads of cheese blocks. This helped us to better understand the puzzling statement we had heard from the manager. Heritage was probably packaging all the name-brand cheese and curds it thought it could sell, and any surplus not sold to retailers under its name was probably going to the commodity (=wholesale) market. Although Heritage clearly was involved in more than the commodity marketplace, its link to the artisanal cheese business was tenuous at best. It did have a story—a provenance not unlike that of some farmstead cheesemakers—that made it special. People who bought Heritage cheeses knew what factory they came from, and they knew, in a general sense, where the milk going into the cheese had come from. That Heritage cheeses were made with Amish milk surely added cachet by suggesting that even though it produced cheeses of a kind found in every supermarket, something about it might be unique. However, this argument proved to be a weak or poorly articulated one, and evidently not one able to translate into an economic advantage.

We kept thinking about the fact that this cheese was

made from milks produced on farms with owners who resisted mechanization and other accoutrements of modern life. Knowing that this might be considered very important by people we know and probably by a significant number of other potential consumers who might be willing to pay premium prices begged a vexing question. Would more vigorous marketing have been able to overcome the company's many disadvantages?

We knew little of cheese marketing but thought that perhaps Heritage was not particularly sophisticated; on our visit to the factory, we had been surprised to learn that managers had toyed with the idea of getting a Web site but had not yet done so. Despite what was done or not done, we still had trouble deciding whether better marketing could have produced a different outcome. Our meager evidence suggested that it might not have. In Star Lake, where Heritage Cheese was well known, prices were competitive with those of mass-produced cheeses from Wisconsin and elsewhere. In this one place at least, knowledge of what Heritage cheeses were and where they came from was not able to insulate them from competition.

Twenty years earlier, the efforts of Heritage's predecessor, Plumbrook Amish Farms, to sell its cheeses in New York City—presumably to sophisticated and well-off clients—likewise failed to save that enterprise. However, things might be different now that many people are conscious of where foods come from and how they are made and make choices based on such knowledge. We think whimsically that one key to success might have been raising the price. Most artisanal cheeses retail for $15 to $20 or more per pound, and it struck us that the price charged for a cheese, as much as anything else on the label, might tell customers it is something special. Many things have changed in the past two decades, and answering the question of whether inspired marketing could have made the difference for the Amish farmers and the cheesemakers who served them remains elusive.

We learned from later newspaper articles that a plan was being put into place to provide a network of milk stations for the region's Amish farmers so they could sell their milk to other mainstream cheesemakers. This appeared to be as close as we would come to a happy ending for the Heritage story.

We visited Heuvelton again in August 2009 and found the factory looking forlorn. The sign still stood near the road, but the parking lot was already sprouting weeds. The cheese factory, the attached cheese and sundries shop, and the adjacent Amish handicrafts shop were all clearly out of business. A little shelter still bore the sign "For horse-drawn vehicles only. Others will be towed." No signs told that the buildings were for sale or rent, and a still-shiny though obviously unused trailer from a milk-hauling rig stood next to the building. We wondered what would become of the little complex. Would someone with a hopeful business plan see it as an opportunity? We hoped so.

Whatever the ultimate fate of the building and equipment, we were saddened by the closing of the Heritage Cheese House. We weren't sure why. Events had made it clear that the market niche in which the business found itself was not capable of sustaining it. One, and perhaps many, mistakes had been made, and we shouldn't expect failure to be rewarded in cheese or any other business. Of course, we will miss enjoying fresh cheese curds and aged cheeses from the place, but that seemed to account for only part of our feeling of regret. After discussing it at length, we decided that we were in the grips of nostalgia. We mourned the loss of Heritage Cheese because it reminded us of the cheese factories of the past — those already well along on the path to extinction when we were small children.

And yet we recognize that things change and that much in change is often for the good. We could not long mourn the passing of this relic from previous centuries when we had before us the panoply of delights offered by the ever-growing, ever-changing world of the new American cheese.

Literature Mentioned in the Text

Anon. 1903. Butter and cheese factories, milk stations and condenseries in the State of New York together with amount of product and a summary by counties and towns for the season of 1902. Bulletin No. 6 in Wieting, Charles A. *Tenth Annual Report of the Commissioner of Agriculture.* Albany, NY, The Argus Company, Printers.

Anon. 2005. *Canadian Dairy Industry Profile.* Ottawa, ON, Canada, Agriculture and Agri-Food Canada.

Brillat-Savarin. 1949. *The Physiology of Taste: Or, Meditations on Transcendental Gastronomy* (Translated by M.F.K Fisher). New York, NY, Counterpoint.

Brown, Lester R. 2008. *Plan B 3.0: Mobilizing to Save Civilization.* New York, NY, W.W. Norton.

Brown, Robert C. 1955. *The Complete Book of Cheese.* New York, NY, Gramercy Publishing Company. (Distributed electronically by Project Gutenberg)

Calvino, Italo. 1983. *Mr. Palomar.* Orlando, FL, Harcourt Inc.

Carroll, Ricki. *Home Cheese Making: Recipes for 75 Homemade Cheeses.* North Adams, MA, Storey Publishing.

De Kruif, Paul. 1926. *Microbe Hunters.* New York, NY, Harcourt, Brace and Company.

Florida, Richard. 2002. *The Rise of the Creative Class: and How It's Transforming Work, Leisure, Community and Everyday Life.* New York, NY, Basic Books.

Jenkins, Steven. 1996. *Cheese Primer.* New York, NY, Workman Publishing.

Kamp, David. 2006. *The United States of Arugula: How We Became a Gourmet Nation.* New York, NY, Broadway Books.

Katzen, Mollie. 1977. *The Moosewood Cookbook.* Berkeley, CA, Ten Speed Press.

Kaufelt, Rob and Thorpe, Liz. 2006. *The Murray's Cheese Handbook.* New York, NY, Broadway Books.

Kindstedt, Paul. 2005. *American Farmstead Cheese: The Complete Guide to Making and Selling Artisan Cheeses.* White River Junction, VT, Chelsea Green Publishing Company.

Kosikowski, Frank V. and Mistry, Vikram V. 1999. *Cheese and Fermented Milk Products, Volume I Origins and Principles*. Great Falls, VA, F. V. Kosikowski, LLC.

Kosikowski, Frank V. and Mistry, Vikram V. 1999. *Cheese and Fermented Milk Products, Volume II Procedures and Analysis*. Great Falls, VA, F. V. Kosikowski, LLC.

Lappé, Frances Moore. 1971. *Diet for a Small Planet*. New York, NY, Ballantine Books.

McGee, Harold. 1984. *On Food and Cooking: The Science and Lore of the Kitchen* (Consumers Union edition). Mount Vernon, NY, Consumers Union.

McMurry, Sally. 1995. *Transforming Rural Life: Dairying Families and Agricultural Change, 1820-1885*. Baltimore, MD, Johns Hopkins University Press.

Morris, Margaret P. 2003. *The Cheesemakers Manual*. Alexandria, Ontario, Canada, Glengarry Cheesemaking and Dairy Supply.

Paxson, Heather. 2006. Artisanal cheese and economies of sentiment in New England. Pages 201-217 In: Richard Wilk, ed. *Fast Food/Slow Food: The Cultural Economy of the Global Food System*. Lanham, MD, Altamira Press.

Paxson, Heather. 2008. Post-pasteurian cultures: the microbiopolitics of raw-milk cheese in the United States. *Cultural Anthropology* 23:15-47.

Pollan, Michael. 2006. *The Omnivore's Dilemma: A Natural History of Four Meals*. New York, NY, Penguin.

Reuben, David R. 1975. *The Save Your Life Diet: High-fiber protection from six of the most serious diseases of civilization*. New York, NY, Random House.

Roberts, Jeffrey P. 2007. *The Atlas of American Artisan Cheese*. White River Junction, VT, Chelsea Green Publishing Company.

Sanders, George P. 1953. *Cheese Varieties and Descriptions*. Washington, DC, U.S. Department of Agriculture, Agriculture Handbook No. 54.

Schmid, Ron. 2009. *The Untold Story of Milk, Revised and Updated*. Washington, DC, New Trends Publishing.

Stamm, Eunice R. 1991. *The History of Cheese Making in New York State*. Endicott, NY, Lewis Group Ltd.

Thorpe, Liz. 2009. *The Cheese Chronicles: A Journey through the Making and Selling of Cheese in America, from Field to Farm to Table*. New York, NY, HarperCollins.

Werlin, Laura. 2000. *The New American Cheese*. New York, NY, Stewart, Tabori & Chang.